A Need to Know
The Role of Air Force Reconnaissance in War Planning, 1945–1953

JOHN THOMAS FARQUHAR
Lieutenant Colonel, USAF, Retired

Air University Press
Maxwell Air Force Base, Alabama

February 2004

Air University Library Cataloging Data

Farquhar, John Thomas, 1958–
    A need to know : the role of Air Force reconnaissance in war planning, 1945–
1953 / John Thomas Farquhar.
      p. ; cm.
Includes bibliographical references and index.

    1. Aerial reconnaissance--United States--History. 2. United States. Air Force--
History. 3. Military reconnaissance--History. 4. Military planning--United States--
History.

    358.45/09/73--dc22

Disclaimer

Air University Press
131 West Shumacher Avenue
Maxwell AFB AL 36112-6615
http://aupress.maxwell.af.mil

In memory of Ana Jonus
1898–1991
A strong, simple, loving woman
who lived her life one day at a time.

Contents

Illustrations

Tables

About the Author

Born in Fort Wayne, Indiana, in 1958, Lt Col John T. Farquhar, USAF, retired, entered active duty in 1980 following graduation from the USAF Academy (USAFA). He was assigned as a navigator in the RC-135 reconnaissance aircraft with the 38th Strategic Reconnaissance Squadron, Strategic Air Command. Farquhar amassed 4,600 flying hours in Cold War operational reconnaissance missions and more recently in operations to monitor Iraq and Bosnia. He served as director, Wing Plans for the 55th Wing at Offutt Air Force Base, Nebraska, where he coordinated worldwide readiness, operational, and contingency planning for the largest flying wing in Air Combat Command. In 1999 Farquhar served as the US European Command Theater Reconnaissance scheduler for Operation Allied Force.

With a master's degree in US diplomatic history from Creighton University and a PhD in American military history from Ohio State, Columbus, Ohio, Dr. Farquhar specializes in airpower history. As the deputy head for Military History, USAFA, before his retirement, Dr. Farquhar taught courses on sea power, World War II, unconventional warfare, general military history, and the history of airpower. He is currently an associate professor, Military Strategic Studies, 34th Education Group, USAFA. He and his wife Millie are raising three children: Johnny, Kirsten, and Luke.

Acknowledgments

For an active duty Air Force officer, the opportunity to fly operationally, to study military history at graduate school, and to teach at the Air Force Academy represents a rare mix of military and academic service and fun. I appreciate Brig Gen Carl W. Reddel, Col Philip S. Meilinger, and Col Mark K. Wells for their guidance and leadership in making my unique career possible. Professor Allan R. Millett deserves special thanks for serving as primary advisor for my PhD dissertation and providing sage counsel. He understood my time constraints and showed a rare ability to cut through extraneous ideas as I searched for a theme. Professors John F. Guilmartin, Williamson Murray, and Michael J. Hogan also provided astute suggestions for improvement. As former Air Force officers who advanced to the first rank of scholarly achievement, Joe Guilmartin and Phil Meilinger also served as my role models and inspiration. Lt Col Mark Clodfelter played a major role with his penetrating insight into doctrinal issues and his editing of my early chapters. Col Steve Chiabotti and Maj Michael Terry are two of my USAFA colleagues who honed my conceptual thinking in linking strategy, doctrine, and plans. My thanks also go to Dr. Kelly McFall who served as my "sounding board" for ideas during our days as graduate students at Ohio State.

Exploring a topic that borders upon still-classified material poses a problem for researchers. In the decade since my original research, President Clinton's Executive Order 12958, issued in 1995, and the efforts of Task Force Russia (the Joint US-Russian Commission on POW/MIAs) have contributed to declassifying significant amounts of material. I appreciate the administrative and financial support of Brig Gen David A. Wagie and Lt Col Alice Chen for approving Air Force Academy Dean of Faculty research funds that allowed me to search recently opened archival material.

As an Air Force officer and navigator in reconnaissance aircraft, I understand the rationale for maintaining secrecy for more current aspects of the field. This book is based exclusively upon declassified documents, and passes all appropriate security clearance procedures. On the other hand, more work remains to credit the many unsung heroes of Cold War history. I hope my limited exploration spurs further work in the history of strategic aerial reconnaissance. Dr. Cargill Hall, the current historian of the National Reconnaissance Office, deserves praise for his pioneering efforts to open archives and capture the memories of those participants still alive. He organized a tremendous Cold War Overflight symposium that the Defense Intelligence Agency sponsored in February 2001. In addition, Lt Col Rob Hoover, USAF, retired, should be acknowledged for his tireless efforts to preserve the 55th Strategic Reconnaissance Wing's heritage. In recording and examining strategic aerial reconnaissance, Dr. Robert S. Hopkins deserves recognition for the excellent analysis his outstanding doctoral dissertation provided.

Because of the research complexity of this field, I appreciate those who provided help. Lt Col Daniel Kuehl opened the door to the "Association of Old Crows," where Mr. Gus Slayton provided unlimited support. George Cully of the Air Force Historical Center and Dr. Henry Narducci at the Strategic Air Command's office of history directed me to many Air Force archives. Mr. Wilbert Mahoney of the Modern Military Branch of the National Archives introduced me to Record Group 341, which proved to be a gold mine. At the Naval Historical Center, Mr. Bernard Cavalcante, Mr. Mike Walker, and Ms. Ella Nargele proved most helpful. On the West coast, Ms. Linda Long aided my search in the Stanford University Archives. At the Library of Congress, Mr. Jeff Flannery provided able assistance with the LeMay, Vandenberg, Twining, and Spaatz collections. My thanks also go to Mr. Dennis Bilger and staff at the Harry S. Truman Library, Independence, Missouri. Recently, Maj Gen Foster Lee Smith shared his memories of highly classified overflight missions from the late 1940s that opened a new area of inquiry. I would be remiss in not acknowledging my friends Capt Steve Maffeo, US Navy Reserve, and Mr. Duane Reed for their professional assistance at the USAFA's Cadet Library.

As an active participant in Cold War reconnaissance missions of the 1980s, I must acknowledge the professionalism, camaraderie, and spirit of the men and women of the 55th Strategic

Reconnaissance Wing, the 38th Strategic Reconnaissance Squadron, and the 343d Strategic Reconnaissance Squadron. The efforts of these fine units upheld the excellent example of our forebears mentioned in this book. Although my comrades are too numerous to mention, I must thank Lt Col Rich Trentman and Maj Kevin Hurd as special navigator teammates, Capt Dave Webster as a superb Raven, and Col George "Barney" Ballinger and Col Collin Flynn as truly outstanding squadron and group commanders, respectively. In tribute to them, I hope this book fills a gap in the heritage of Air Force reconnaissance.

This work represents a family effort. I owe my parents thanks, not only for emotional support but also for professional advice. My mother, Mrs. Pauline Hunsberger, read each draft of my doctoral dissertation and joined her husband Ted in offering expert bibliographical advice. My father, Dr. John S. Farquhar, inspired my love for military history, taught me to strive for excellence, and backed my dreams for a military career. My in-laws, Joan and Joe Beeber, helped me maintain an even perspective and balance the demands of family life. My late grandfather, Mr. John Micu, always supported my efforts and shared his wisdom. Thanks also go to my children, Johnny, Kirsten, and Luke, whose joy and laughter kept this work in its proper place. My beloved wife Millie provided me the love and understanding each day that made this effort worthwhile. She supported my research efforts and time away from family. She also spurred me to take up the challenge of revising a 10-year-old project. I cannot express in words the depth of my thanks to her.

The photographs in this book are courtesy of the National Archives, Washington, D.C.

Introduction

On 1 April 2001, a US Navy EP-3 Aries II surveillance aircraft collided with a People's Liberation Army Air Force J-8 fighter plane that resulted in the loss of the Chinese pilot and an emergency landing on Hainan Island by the Navy plane. The Chinese government's 11-day internment of the Navy flight crew shocked and amazed the American public. The ensuing diplomatic crisis and war of words reminded many of similar incidents from the supposedly defunct Cold War. Depending on the age of the individual, the EP-3 crisis evoked memories of the 1983 Soviet shootdown of Korean Air Lines (KAL) flight 007 or Francis Gary Powers's ill-fated U-2 mission of 1 May 1960. Avid readers might remember a 1993 *U.S. News & World Report* issue devoted to "America's Top-Secret Spy War" that chronicled many of the 35 US Air Force and US Navy reconnaissance aircraft shot down from 1946 to 1961 with the loss of over 100 American airmen.[1] The April 2001 collision focused world attention upon a still little known but highly significant aspect of the Cold War—strategic aerial reconnaissance.

The vehement charges and countercharges surrounding the EP-3 incident evoked similar periods of international tension involving US reconnaissance aircraft during the early years of the Cold War. For example, the KAL 007 shootdown plunged Soviet-American relations into an icy phase of the latter Cold War, and the infamous U-2 incident aborted a promising 1960 US President Eisenhower–Soviet Premier Khrushchev summit. In the short term, the EP-3 incident resurrected a sense of hostility associated with a series of international incidents occurring in the early 1950s. To assess the apparent impact of aerial reconnaissance upon the early Cold War, many questions must be answered: How and when did reconnaissance flights originate? What factors prompted US reconnaissance operations? Who authorized them? At what point did the president and senior policy makers know about the activities? What information did US policy makers seek that could be provided by aerial reconnaissance? Why did leaders risk international incidents, political turmoil, and potential hostilities to gather information?

At first glance, strategic aerial reconnaissance appears to be a mere technical tool. The term refers to the use of aircraft to collect strategic intelligence using photographic or electronic means. According to the Joint Chiefs of Staff (JCS), strategic intelligence refers to "intelligence that is required for the formation of policy and military plans at national and international levels."[2] Strategic intelligence includes information provided by sources other than aircraft, including naval vessels, ground communications intercept sites, satellites, published literature, defectors, and spies. Because Air Force aircraft provided the bulk of information used by American war plans from 1945 to 1953, this book focuses on the origins of the USAF strategic aerial reconnaissance.[3] Although official JCS publications did not specifically list *strategic aerial reconnaissance,* the term may be defined as the use of aircraft to gather information necessary to conduct strategic air war, also called *strategic air bombardment.* At the core of the topic, recently declassified JCS emergency war plans indicate that a strategic air bombardment campaign formed the heart of American military strategy from the end of World War II to the Korean conflict. A study of strategic aerial reconnaissance illuminates the link between intelligence and strategy and between military capability and doctrine. Finally, a focus upon strategic aerial reconnaissance raises questions of ends and means: did reconnaissance aircraft merely serve as a tool of war planners or did strategic reconnaissance actually shape military strategy?

Traditionally, aerial reconnaissance played a secondary role in the minds of military planners and the public. Although the airplane's ability to provide commanders "eyes in the air" led to the first military use of the new technology, the exploits of pursuit aircraft and fighter aces seized public attention. In addition, despite unique and vital information provided by reconnaissance aircraft during World War I, interwar airpower theorists concentrated upon the use of aircraft in combat.

Following World War I, the long-range bomber became the primary strategic weapon and focus of airpower thinking. Drawing upon the well-publicized theories of Giulio Douhet, Hugh Trenchard, and William "Billy" Mitchell, airpower advocates within the United States advanced theories of strategic air warfare as the justification for Air Force independence. According to the theorists, air attacks upon enemy armed forces in the immediate vicinity of the battlefield constituted *tactical* airpower; *strategic* airpower attacked instead the industrial and economic sources of the enemy's armed strength. In bureaucratic battles for limited defense budgets, air leaders argued that strategic bombing represented a new way of war. Long-range strategic bombardment would destroy the *vital centers* of an enemy's political and economic structure. The combined effect of high explosives, incendiary bombs, and poison gas would destroy the enemy's capability to wage war and break his will to fight. Furthermore, the airplane's ability to bypass armies and navies rendered traditional services obsolete. Since future wars would commence with the clash of air armies, the Air Force represented the nation's new first line of defense.[4]

By the late 1930s, the US Army Air Corps (USAAC) further refined strategic bombing theories to produce a doctrine based upon high-altitude, daylight, precision bombardment. The concept called for the destruction of the enemy's industrial base by the pinpoint bombing of a few carefully selected industrial choke points. Stressing economy of force and the destruction of the enemy's *capacity* to fight, precision bombardment doctrine downplayed attacks upon civilians and the enemy's *will* to wage war. By 1937 the USAAC assembled the means to implement its version of strategic air war—the Boeing B-17 Flying Fortress and the Norden Mark XV bombsight.[5]

To airpower advocates, World War II represented the test of strategic air warfare. Despite prewar theories, the Battle of Britain proved the effectiveness of air defense made possible by the introduction of radar. Similarly, Germany's defense of the fatherland showed that although the bomber may always get through, the cost could be prohibitive. The relative effectiveness of air defenses threatened the strategic bombing theory. To protect its heavy bombers, Britain's Royal Air Force (RAF) abandoned daylight bombing in favor of night attack. Because of problems associated with navigation and target identification, the RAF gradually adopted a doctrine based upon area bombing of German cities aimed at destroying the enemy's morale, as well as physical capacity to wage war.[6]

The US Army Air Forces (USAAF) disagreed with the RAF concept. The USAAF pursued precision daylight bombing doctrine despite heavy losses. Fortunately, relief was provided with the introduction of the North American P-51 Mustang long-range escort fighter in early 1944, along with superior numbers of the rugged Republic P-47 Thunderbolt fighter. With air superiority gained by the spring of 1944 and the increased numbers of heavy bombers, air leaders pointed to devastated German cities as proof of strategic bombing's effectiveness. At the end of the war, the *United States Strategic Bombing Survey (USSBS)* assessed the impact of the air campaign. In the summary volume of the European experience, the survey concluded, "Allied air power was decisive in the war in Western Europe."[7] Meanwhile, the assessment of the bombing campaign against Japan reinforced the view: ". . . no nation can long survive the free exploitation of air weapons over its homeland."[8]

The debate over strategic airpower's effectiveness overshadowed advances in aerial reconnaissance during World War II. For the most part, the glamorous image of the fighter pilots or intrepid bomber crews captured public attention, not their counterparts flying equally dangerous reconnaissance sorties. Nevertheless, military planners appreciated the tremendous advances in aerial intelligence that occurred during the war. By the war's end, aerial reconnaissance aircraft provided prompt battlefield intelligence for commanders (tactical intelligence) and information concerning the enemy's capacity to wage war (strategic intelligence). More than simply providing army commanders with information on enemy troop locations, aerial reconnaissance formed the cornerstone for the strategic air campaign. In particular, photographic reconnaissance surveyed potential targets allowing analysts to identify vital industries, to plot attack routes, and to assemble target folders for aircrews. In addition, poststrike sorties provided bomb damage assessment necessary for evaluating success.[9]

Adding to advances in photographic intelligence, World War II spawned a new form of warfare linked to science and the use of radio waves for communication and detection. Electronic warfare (EW) involves military action to protect friendly use of electromagnetic energy and to deny its use to the enemy. At a basic level, EW consists of electronic countermeasures (ECM), which includes jamming enemy transmissions and electronic counter-countermeasures designed to protect one's own transmissions from enemy jamming. Electronic intelligence (ELINT) seeks to collect information concerning the technical details of enemy radar and communications systems to either exploit their use or design ECM to jam the systems. Normally ELINT refers to efforts to learn about enemy radar systems, but communications intelligence (COMINT) focuses upon the interception and exploitation of enemy radio communications. The famed Ultra secret of World War II (which broke Germany's intelligence code) served as the premier example of a successful COMINT program.[10]

On the other hand, the Allies modified aircraft to collect ELINT, known as "Ferrets." These electronic reconnaissance aircraft carried special equipment to detect and analyze enemy radar signals (radar is explained in app. A). The primary purpose of electronic reconnaissance centers on locating enemy radar stations and analyzing the performance characteristics of their radar sets.[11]

Overshadowing electronic warfare, the advent of atomic weapons in 1945 transformed war. In the mind of some airpower theorists, the atomic bomb fulfilled the terrible promise of strategic bombardment. For many others, the prospect of atomic Armageddon raised fundamental moral questions. As a result, the atomic age focused debate on nuclear strategy, deterrence, and the ethics of war.[12] In contrast, despite the emergence of national security affairs as a field of study, few historians have examined the capability of the United States to wage strategic air warfare with atomic weapons during the early years of the Cold War. Harry R. Borowski provides a notable exception in *A Hollow Threat: Strategic Air Power and Containment Before Korea*, where he argued that the Strategic Air Command (SAC), America's primary instrument for waging atomic warfare, was incapable of implementing strategic bombing doctrine. Inadequate manpower, equipment, and training rendered SAC a hollow threat. Moreover, in "The Origins of Overkill," "American Atomic Strategy and the Hydrogen Bomb Decision," and other articles, David Alan Rosenberg revealed the limited size and capabilities of America's nuclear stockpile in the immediate postwar period.[13] Although it would expand exponentially, America's atomic arsenal proved inadequate for fulfilling the initial war plans of the JCS. Nevertheless, even if SAC possessed adequate planes, well-trained crews, and sufficient atomic bombs, could the United States wage strategic air war based on precision bombardment doctrine? Did US war planners know the locations of enemy targets and the capabilities of Soviet defenses?

A closer look at American war plans in the late 1940s and early 1950s reveals a lack of intelligence data that jeopardized US strategic air war doctrine. Without target information, air planners could not determine the enemy's vital centers. In addition, without knowledge of Soviet radars, jet fighters, and anti-aircraft artillery, unescorted bombers faced perils potentially worse than those faced by the USAAF's Eighth Air Force against Germany. Given the technological limitations of strategic bombers of the immediate postwar period (1945–53) and the limited US nuclear stockpile, strategic aerial reconnaissance became a key to the success of strategic air warfare. And, given the Air Force's reluctance to admit such a dilemma, "a need to know" dominated war planning in the initial years of the Cold War. Therefore, while most scholars concentrate upon the theoretical and moral issues raised by atomic warfare in the postwar period, this book focuses on the impact of aerial reconnaissance upon America's capability for strategic air war.

American experiences in the Korean War revealed the limits of US reconnaissance capabilities and demonstrated the impact of intelligence flaws upon war planning. As the prelude to a general war, the invasion of Korea spurred the development of Air Force strategic aerial reconnaissance. The war strained the technological and manpower resources of the Air Force and revealed significant flaws in aircraft performance, organizational structure, and analytical ability. During the conflict, Air Force electronic reconnaissance capabilities increased exponentially with the creation of a worldwide strategic reconnaissance program. Despite efforts to collect ELINT along the periphery of Communist nations and occasional photographic overflights, the United States still lacked the technology to gather needed intelligence from the Soviet heartland. The Air Force lacked aircraft capable of conducting strategic photographic reconnaissance deep over heavily defended Soviet territory. Without sufficient aerial reconnaissance, American planners could not confirm Soviet atomic capability, assess new technology, or complete target planning.

A lack of strategic intelligence caused by the limits of aerial reconnaissance shaped US war plans between 1945 and 1953. By failing to provide sufficient information for a precision bombardment campaign, war planners resorted to urban-area bombing using atomic weapons. Unable to target specific enemy war-making industries, JCS war plans called for bombing Soviet cities in an effort to destroy the enemy's capacity and will to wage war. Therefore, aerial reconnaissance was more than a tool of the war planners; the limits of strategic aerial reconnaissance shaped doctrine.

Notes

1. Douglas Stanglin, Susan Headden, and Peter Cary, "Secrets of the Cold War," *U.S. News & World Report* 114, no. 10 (15 March 1993): 30–56. Author contributed 1991 PhD dissertation, 1986 Master's thesis, primary documents, and two telephone interviews to Stanglin's research. The aircraft loss figures are from Robert Smith Hopkins, "U.S. Strategic Aerial Reconnaissance and the Cold War, 1945–1961" (PhD diss., University of Virginia, May 1998), 2. Hopkins assembled several different primary sources for his totals and may be considered authoritative.

2. Joint Chiefs of Staff Publication (JCS Pub) 1, *Department of Defense Dictionary of Military and Associated Terms,* 1984, 350.

3. A number of widely read books explore other aspects of strategic intelligence, including William E. Burrows, *Deep Black: Space Espionage and National Security* (New York: Random House, 1986); James Bamford, *The Puzzle Palace: A Report on NSA, America's Most Secret Agency* (Boston: Houghton Mifflin, 1982); Jeffrey Richelson, *American Espionage and the Soviet Target* (New York: William Morrow & Co., 1987); and Bradley F. Smith, *The Shadow Warriors: O.S.S. and the Origins of the C.I.A.* (New York: Basic Books, 1983).

4. For additional explanations of American theories of strategic air warfare, see Robert F. Futrell, *Ideas, Concepts, Doctrine: Basic Thinking in the United States Air Force,* rev. ed. (Maxwell AFB, Ala.: Air University Press, 1989); David MacIsaac, *Strategic Bombing in World War Two: The Story of the*

Strategic Bombing Survey (New York: Garland Publishing, 1976); Alfred F. Hurley, *Billy Mitchell: Crusader for Air Power* (Bloomington: Indiana University Press, 1964, 1975); or Wesley F. Craven and James L. Cate, eds., *The Army Air Forces in World War II*, vol. 1, *Plans and Early Operations* (Chicago: University of Chicago Press, 1948–58), 17–71.

5. Craven and Cate, vol. 1, 597–99; and MacIsaac, 6–10.

6. Sir Charles Webster and Noble Frankland, *The Strategic Air Offensive against Germany 1939–45*, vol. 1, preparation pts. 1, 2, and 3 (London: Her Majesty's Stationery Office, 1961), 167–87.

7. *United States Strategic Bombing Survey (USSBS), Summary Report (European War)*, 30 September 1945, in MacIsaac, vol. 1; Harry R. Borowski, *A Hollow Threat: Strategic Air Power and Containment Before Korea* (Westport, Conn.: Greenwood Press, 1982), 20.

8. *USSBS, Summary Report (Pacific War)*, 1 July 1949, 28, in MacIsaac. For additional studies of the impact of strategic bombing in World War II, see MacIsaac; Haywood S. Hansell Jr., *The Strategic Air War against Germany and Japan* (Washington, D.C.: Office of Air Force History, 1986); David R. Mets, *Master of Air Power: General Carl A. Spaatz* (Novato, Calif.: Presidio Press, 1988); and Phillip S. Meilinger, *Hoyt S. Vandenberg: The Life of A General* (Bloomington: Indiana University Press, 1989). On the other hand, Michael S. Sherry, *The Rise of American Air Power: The Creation of Armageddon* (New Haven, Conn.: Yale University Press, 1987) critiques the morality and rationale behind the bombing campaigns.

9. For a detailed look at photoreconnaissance, read C. Babbington Smith, *Evidence in Camera: The Story of Photographic Intelligence in World War II* (London: Chatto and Windus, 1958); Peter Mead, *The Eye in the Air: History of Air Observation and Reconnaissance for the Army, 1785–1945* (London: Her Majesty's Stationery Office, 1983); Roy Conyers Nesbit, *Eyes of the RAF: A History of Photo-Reconnaissance* (Phoenix Mill, United Kingdom: Alan Sutton Publishers, 1996); and Roy M. Stanley, *World War II Photo Intelligence* (New York: Scribner, 1981); and idem, *To Fool A Glass Eye: Camouflage versus Photoreconnaissance in World War II* (Washington, D.C.: Smithsonian Institution Press, 1998).

10. Perhaps the best surveys of electronic warfare may be found in Alfred Price, *Instruments of Darkness* (Los Altos, Calif.: Peninsula Publishing, 1987); and idem, *The History of US Electronic Warfare*, 2 vols. (Arlington, Va.: 1989). On the other hand, F. W. Winterbotham, *The Ultra Secret* (New York: Harper & Row, 1974); Ronald Lewin, *Ultra Goes to War* (New York: McGraw-Hill, 1978); and David Kahn, *The Codebreakers* (New York: Macmillan, 1974) represent the many books on COMINT during World War II. In addition, F. H. Hinsley, *British Intelligence in the Second World War*, 4 vols. (London: Her Majesty's Stationery Office, 1979–1988) provides a marvelous synthesis of the impact of various intelligence operations, and R. V. Jones, *Most Secret War* (London: Hamish Hamilton, 1978) offers a personal account of the role of the scientist in intelligence and electronic warfare.

11. For further explanation of radar performance characteristics and ferret operations, see appendix A.

12. For a survey of the issues and significant theories, see Lawrence Freedman, *The Evolution of Nuclear Strategy*, 2d ed. (New York: St. Martin's Press, 1989), while Gregg Herken, *The Winning Weapon: The Atomic Bomb in the Cold War 1945–1950* (New York: Alfred A. Knopf, 1980) critiques American reliance on nuclear weapons in the immediate postwar era.

13. David Alan Rosenberg, "The Origins of Overkill: Nuclear Weapons and American Strategy, 1945–1960," in *Strategy and Nuclear Deterrence*, Steven E. Miller, ed. (Princeton, N.J.: Princeton University Press, 1984), 113–81; and idem, "American Atomic Strategy and the Hydrogen Bomb Decision," *Journal of American History* 66 (June 1979): 62–87.

Chapter 1

The Origins of
Strategic Aerial Reconnaissance

Now in those days the tribe of Dan was in search of a territory to live in, because up till then no territory had fallen to them among the tribes of Israel. From their clan the Danites sent five brave men from Zorah and Esthaol to reconnoitre the country and explore it.

—Judges 18:2

The quest for military information predates recorded history. From before biblical times, men conducted reconnaissance whether as hunters, explorers, or as warriors. The concept of reconnaissance, "an exploratory or preliminary survey, inspection, or examination to gain information," offered advantages in gaining surprise or exploiting terrain that seems obvious today.[1] In fact, reconnaissance appears so basic that studies of military history often ignore the subject. Although poor reconnaissance may lead to military disaster, successful reconnaissance seldom assures victory. Most often, good reconnaissance provides the commander an edge that may combine with other important advantages in numbers, equipment, training, or doctrine to defeat an enemy.[2] Yet, good reconnaissance may lead to strategic or tactical surprise. In Western warfare, some military thinkers rank surprise next to numerical superiority as an essential condition of battlefield success. According to the nineteenth-century Prussian theorist Carl von Clausewitz, the desire to achieve surprise is basic to all operations, for without it, superiority at the decisive point is hardly conceivable.[3] Moreover, Eastern traditions of war emphasize surprise to an even greater extent as shown by the writings of Sun Tzu: "Attack where he is unprepared; sally out when he does not expect you. Appear at places to which he must hasten; move swiftly where he does not expect you."[4] Therefore, although relatively unstudied as a separate entity, reconnaissance serves as a means of gaining surprise and of guarding against enemy surprise.

The advent of manned flight offered revolutionary potential for reconnaissance. Two days after Joseph-Michel and Étienne-Jacques de Montgolfier introduced the first practical hot air balloon in September 1783, André-Giroud de Villette ascended in the craft. He recognized the enormous military potential of aviation: "From that moment I was convinced that this apparatus, at little cost, could be made very useful to an army for discovering the position of its enemy, its movements, its advances, its dispositions, and that this information could be conveyed by a system of signals, to the troops looking after the apparatus."[5]

Despite de Villette's foresight, the balloon did not immediately transform warfare. By the time of the American Civil War, although both Union and Confederate armies employed a small number of observation balloons, the invention achieved mixed results. The Federal army planned to use the balloon as early as the First Battle of Bull Run; however, strong winds slammed the balloon against a telegraph pole and ripped it. On 18 June 1861, Thaddeus SC Lowe sent an observation report to President Abraham Lincoln from his balloon *Enterprise.* During the Peninsula campaign of 1862, the Union army developed techniques for artillery spotting and actually linked air-to-ground telegraph lines. Despite aviation's promise, the US Army considered the device expensive, unwieldy, and unreliable. The balloon corps was disbanded in June 1863.[6] By the Franco-Prussian War of 1870–71, the French had deployed balloons in a desperate attempt to overcome the siege of Paris. During the struggle, balloons conveyed 164 persons, 381 carrier pigeons, five dogs, and 3 million letters past the Prussian lines surrounding the city.[7] During the Battle of San Juan Hill in the Spanish-American War, the limitations posed by weather, frail construction, and primitive communications equipment relegated aviation to a novelty status despite discovery of a crucial trail found by American troops using a reconnaissance balloon.

The airplane provided the speed, range, and freedom of maneuver needed to transform aviation from a toy into a tool of war. In 1911 the Italians first used aircraft for military reconnaissance when they observed Turkish positions in Libya. In this brief campaign, Italian aeronauts furthered the military potential of aviation by taking aerial photographs, experimenting with wireless communications, and dropping bombs.[8] Likewise, the French, Mexicans, Bulgarians, and Turks used aircraft in various wars between 1912 and 1913. The United States first flew visual reconnaissance missions in 1913 in the Philippines and along the Mexican border, and Brig Gen John J. Pershing's celebrated pursuit of Pancho Villa in the spring of 1916 introduced the potential of air observation to the American public.[9] Despite these accomplishments, the dynamic events of the First World War acted as the primary catalyst for all fields of military aviation.

During the epic struggle along the western front, aerial reconnaissance provided the most important use of the new weapon. For example, Britain's Royal Flying Corps (RFC) tracked German armies across Belgium and France in August 1914, discovering a critical gap in the enemy's advancing columns. As a result, the Allies successfully counterattacked and saved Paris in the renowned Battle of the Marne.[10] In his dispatch following the battle, British Expeditionary Force commander, Gen Sir John French, lauded the exploits of the airmen: "Their skill, energy and perseverance have been beyond all praise. They have furnished me with the most complete and accurate information, which has been of incalculable value in the conduct of operations."[11] Although not technically reconnaissance in current terminology, the airplane also proved its value by spotting the fire of artillery.

As early as September 1914, British artillery observers sent their reports by wireless.[12] When the German and Allied armies ground to a halt in the morass of trench warfare, the airplane offered the best means to gather tactical intelligence. With cavalry unable to penetrate enemy troops living underground in vast trench and bunker complexes, aircraft scanned the roads and railways behind the trenches for evidence of enemy buildups or troop withdrawals. The introduction of air photography in January 1915 allowed photographic interpreters to analyze long-term trends and subtle changes in enemy dispositions. By the Battle of Neuve Chapelle in March 1915, the Allies had photographed the German trench system and transformed the information into detailed maps.[13] Thus, the airplane proved useful for all aspects of tactical reconnaissance.[14] According to Sir Walter Raleigh, the official British historian of the air war, "Reconnaissance or observation can never be superseded; knowledge comes before power; and the air is first of all a place to see from."[15]

Efforts of the combatants to deny aerial reconnaissance to the enemy reinforced the importance of air observation. Tradition celebrates the evolution of fighter planes from individual airmen firing pistols and rifles to hazardous experiments where pilots fired machine guns and risked cutting their own propeller. Although the real beginning of aerial combat is difficult to define, the introduction in 1915 of the Fokker *Eindecker* E1, a monoplane designed specifically for fighting, increased the lethality of air war. With a synchronization mechanism that permitted a machine gun to fire through the propeller arc, the Fokker drove French and British reconnaissance planes from the skies.[16] From this point, the combatants devoted considerable energy and resources to gaining air superiority. Despite the notoriety achieved by fighter aces and the potential for air-to-ground combat demonstrated in bombing and strafing runs, aerial reconnaissance remained the dominant mission.[17] Air forces sought to provide their armies all-important artillery spotting and intelligence information and to deny these benefits to the enemy.

Although the Battle of the Somme represented trench warfare's futility and slaughter, the campaign served as a milestone in aerial combat. In this battle, control of the air played a direct role in the outcome of the land battle. Beginning in late 1915, the German air force and the RFC battled for air supremacy over the fields of Flanders. At stake were the abilities to adjust artillery fire and to observe infantry in the battle zone. With an initial technological edge provided by the Fokker, German reconnaissance crews spotted British preparations for the summer offensive of July 1916.[18] Later, as the armies locked in horrific struggle, the air forces introduced new aircraft and tactics in the skies over the battlefield. Although air supremacy proved a vital prerequisite and the jousts of air aces gained public attention, aerial reconnaissance remained the critical mission. When the Germans held air superiority, British artillery lagged in its effectiveness. Similarly, when the RFC eroded the German air arm with new aircraft and tactics, British guns pounded enemy trenches. During the course of the battle, British reconnaissance planes registered 8,612 artillery targets and processed 19,000 aerial photographs used to mark terrain features of critical importance in trench warfare.[19] Although air historians emphasize the Somme air campaign for developments in air-to-air combat, the link of air superiority, reconnaissance, and artillery effectiveness remained the most significant relationship.

By the end of World War I, aerial combat emerged as a legitimate instrument of war. Technological advances transformed airplanes from rickety contraptions to serious weapons. The battles for air supremacy played a vital role in developing the technology of air warfare and introduced the "intrepid airman" as a new breed of hero. However, the Great War played an equally important, although less heralded, role in developing the art of aerial reconnaissance. By 1918 reconnaissance planes and observer balloons provided commanders with vertical and oblique aerial photographs, which enabled staffs to map terrain, mark enemy troop positions, spot artillery, and anticipate attack.[20] Advances in wireless communications enabled air observers to adjust artillery fire to counter enemy guns. Moreover, the volume of aerial reconnaissance increased prodigiously. By the end of 1917, German reconnaissance planes produced nearly 4,000 photographs per day, covering the entire western front every two weeks.[21] By the Meuse-Argonne Offensive of September 1918, even the new American Air Service produced 56,000 prints of aerial photographs in just four days. At war's end, the US Army Air Service listed 740 aircraft in 45 squadrons with 767 pilots, 481 observers, and 23 aerial gunners devoted to observation and reconnaissance.[22] As a result of technological and organizational innovations during the First World War, aerial reconnaissance emerged as an indispensable means of gaining tactical intelligence.

The success of military aviation during the First World War launched a bitter debate over its future. In the spring of 1919, two manuals summarized the official US Army view, ". . . in the future, as in the past, the final decision in war must be made by men on the ground, willing to come hand-to-hand with the enemy. When the Infantry loses the Army loses. It is therefore the role of the Air Service, as well as that of other arms, to aid the chief combatant, the Infantry." In addition, the traditional view enhanced the position of aerial reconnaissance. "The greatest value of the Air Service to date has been in gathering information of the enemy and of our own troops."[23] Pursuit, or fighter, aircraft served primarily to protect friendly observation aircraft and to prevent enemy reconnaissance. Aircraft designed for long-range bombing of enemy industrial centers remained a "luxury."[24]

In contrast to this limited vision of aviation, an international band of airpower theorists emphasized strategic bombardment that had been introduced during the Great War. Led by Britain's Hugh Trenchard, Italy's Giulio Douhet, and America's William "Billy" Mitchell, these air enthusiasts considered airpower to be a new, war-winning weapon that rendered armies and navies obsolete. Popularized by numerous speeches, articles, and books, including Douhet's *Command of the Air* (1921) and Mitchell's *Winged Defense* (1925), airpower prophets proclaimed the airplane's dominance of war. The airplane could strike directly the enemy's capacity and will to wage war. By destroying the enemy's "vital centers," airpower would bypass traditional armies and navies. This vision of airpower became known as "strategic bombardment." Moreover, the unique offensive characteristics of the airplane made air defense nearly impossible. Theorists believed the best defense against an enemy air force was to destroy it on the ground.[25] Consequently, because airpower represented a unique new weapon, airmen sought organizational independence from ground and naval forces.

In their polemical writings, Douhet, Mitchell, and others failed to grasp a fundamental flaw of strategic bombardment theory. During the interwar years, air theorists assumed complete knowledge of the enemy's vital centers. Mitchell and Douhet understood the need for reconnaissance, but airpower proponents underestimated the difficulties involved in obtaining air intelligence. For example, Giulio Douhet proposed an ideal reconnaissance plane featuring superior speed and long range even at the cost of defensive armor and armament.[26] Although he showed prescience regarding reconnaissance aircraft, Douhet failed to recognize the need for maps, cameras, specialized equipment for photo analysis, and sophisticated organizations to process and assess information. Along similar lines, although the US Army Air Corps Tactical School refined the concept of precision daylight bombardment during the 1920s and 1930s, it failed to think through the problems associated with strategic aerial reconnaissance. Instead, the Air Corps thinkers stressed bomber development and theoretical analyses of industrial choke points. They failed to study sufficiently the need for pre-strike surveillance and poststrike damage assessment. Further-more, to many airmen, reconnaissance symbolized the shackles of ground-force control. As a result, air reconnaissance occupied a position of secondary importance within the Air Corps. Inter-war reconnaissance training still stressed artillery spotting and First World War observation techniques. By the eve of World War II, American aerial reconnaissance remained little advanced from the techniques and concepts of World War I.[27]

Capt George W. Goddard photographed over 30,000 square miles of uncharted Alaskan territory from US Army Air Corps Martin B-10 bombers during his landmark demonstration of aerial photography in July 1934.

Close-up view of the Martin B-10 bomber

Although the conceptual thinking behind aerial reconnaissance lagged, technological improvements occurred during the interwar years. Head of Army Air Corps photographic research in the 1920s, Capt George W. Goddard introduced new cameras for photoreconnaissance and mapping, plans for specialized reconnaissance aircraft, portable film processing laboratories, and ideas for infrared and long-range photography.[28] Recognizing that a lack of adequate maps and charts not only hindered the development of civilian airlines but also suggested problems for long-range bombers, Goddard stressed peacetime aerial mapping. He introduced a trimetrogon camera utilizing three lenses to take vertical and oblique pictures to either side of an aircraft simultaneously. These lenses broadened the camera's field of view to near horizon-to-horizon coverage.[29] Goddard demonstrated the value of his developments when the Army Air Corps staged a flight of 10 Martin B-10 bombers from Washington, D.C., to Fairbanks, Alaska, in July 1934. Although the mission was designed primarily to showcase the potential of long-range airpower, the planes also mapped 30,000 square miles of Alaskan territory with Goddard's new cameras.[30] By the eve of

World War II, technological advances increased the effectiveness of aerial photography, even though ideas for operational employment remained stagnant.

Alarmed by the rise of Adolf Hitler and the advent of the Luftwaffe, the Royal Air Force pioneered covert, peacetime aerial reconnaissance in the late 1930s. British Squadron Leader Fred W. Winterbotham of the Air Ministry successfully convinced British and French officials of the need to reconnoiter German military installations. Eventually, Winterbotham contacted Frederick Sydney Cotton, an Australian pilot with extensive aerial photography and World War I experience. They procured a Lockheed L12A, a twin-engine plane similar to one made famous by Amelia Earhart's ill-fated last flight. Beginning in March 1939, Cotton flew 15 overflight missions over targets in Germany, Italy, and the Mediterranean, including a flight to photograph German naval vessels in Wilhelmshaven on 1 September 1939. Winterbotham captured Cotton's experiences in an August 1939 memorandum titled "Photographic Reconnaissance of Enemy Territory in War." Summarizing the lessons, Cotton maintained, "The best method appears to be the use of a single small machine, relying on its speed, climb, and ceiling to avoid destruction. A machine such as a single-seat fighter could fly high enough to be well above Ack-Ack fire and could rely upon sheer speed and height to get away from the enemy fighters. It would have no use for armament or radio and these could be removed to provide room for extra fuel, in order to get the necessary range. It would be a very small machine painted so as to reduce its visibility against the sky."[31]

World War II provided a test for airpower theory as well as technology. Early British efforts at strategic bombing revealed that the bomber would not always get through. From the initial RAF sorties against Wilhelmshaven in 1939 to the fall of France in 1940, British bomber raids suffered unacceptable losses to German fighter defenses. Well-armed, high-performance fighters refuted the assumption of bomber omnipotence. In response, the RAF developed a doctrine of night area bombardment that recognized operational limits. Because existing technology could not provide accuracy suitable for precision bombing at night, the RAF Bomber Command emphasized attacks on German cities—

crushing morale and destroying the homes of the enemy's industrial workforce. Area bombing as practiced by Air Marshal Sir Arthur T. Harris, commander of the RAF Bomber Command, resisted the appeal of selective, or "panacea," targets. Incapable of pinpoint bombing, RAF area strikes also required less precise intelligence.[32]

The European air war also demonstrated the difficulty of conducting aerial reconnaissance. At the beginning of the war, confidence in existing reconnaissance procedures vanished when photoreconnaissance Bristol Blenheim aircraft were shot down at alarming rates. Additionally, the valiant efforts of surviving pilots were thwarted by frozen cameras, fogged lenses, and cracked film.[33] These dismal results forced the British Air Ministry to revamp reconnaissance methods.

Despite initial failures, the RAF created the concepts, equipment, and tactics of modern strategic photographic intelligence. Now an RAF officer, Frederick Sidney Cotton added to his civilian photographic expertise. During the first two years of the war, Cotton's exploits with a stripped-down polished Supermarine Spitfire assumed legendary proportions as he gained information unobtainable by other sources. Moreover, technicians at the RAF's Photographic Reconnaissance Unit developed high-altitude cameras—one with a 36-inch focal length that produced high-quality photographs with clear resolution. Equally important, the British Air Ministry recruited talented, highly motivated individuals from a broad range of civilian occupations to serve as photographic interpreters. By refining the equipment, techniques, and methodology of this seemingly mundane field, the RAF furthered the processing and analyzing of data gathered by reconnaissance crews.[34] Finally, the British understood the importance of centralization and coordination of intelligence data. Efforts to streamline the processing of intelligence information furthered the proper analysis of data and the use of information by field commanders.[35]

The entry of the United States Army Air Force (USAAF) into the European air war proved the inadequacy of prewar reconnaissance concepts and training. After a poor showing in the initial phase of North African operations, the Army Air Forces (AAF) reorganized observation units along the lines of RAF tactical reconnaissance.[36] Like their British counterparts, Americans learned from bitter experience the value of aircraft with altitude, speed, and range characteristics superior to enemy interceptors. The lack of aircraft specifically designed for aerial reconnaissance plagued American reconnaissance efforts. Eventually, the AAF paralleled British efforts when American pilots flew modified Lockheed P-38 Lightnings and North American P-51 Mustangs to support the AAF's daylight strategic bombardment campaign. The German introduction of Messerschmitt Me-262 jet fighters during the latter stages of the war menaced Allied photoreconnaissance aircraft. Fortunately, the Allies possessed an overwhelming numerical advantage that allowed the Combined Bomber Offensive to continue. Although American reconnaissance groups performed valiantly, they added little to RAF photoreconnaissance concepts.[37]

Apart from British advances in strategic photographic intelligence, RAF performance in the Battle of Britain demonstrated the capability of aerial defense. Combining communications intelligence with new radar technology, by 1940 the RAF had developed a practical network of early warning and ground-controlled intercept (GCI) stations. These stations notified fighter bases of the approach of enemy aircraft and directed fighters to intercept the enemy. Although many factors contributed to the defeat of the Luftwaffe in the Battle of Britain, British technology played a vital role.[38] Using radar, the British were able to refute earlier assumptions that bombers could attack without warning. By the summer of 1940, the Germans introduced a radio-aided navigational device, known as *Knickebein,* to improve night bombing accuracy. British efforts to counter it resulted in the "Battle of the Beams."[39] By the winter of 1943, electronic warfare played a critical role in RAF night bombing. In support of their night area bombing campaign, the British developed navigational aids (including Gee and Oboe), H2S airborne radar, and radar countermeasures (WINDOW, or chaff, and various electronic devices). The Germans countered with night fighters, SN2 airborne intercept (AI) radar, and a variety of passive radar detection devices. The combination of a German technological breakthrough and innovative night-fighter tactics caused major RAF losses in the Battle of Berlin (November 1943–March 1944) and almost defeated the RAF night bombing campaign.[40] These events emphasized the growing importance of electronic warfare during World War II. Combatants now needed information about the enemy's electronic defenses in order to plan successful strikes.

Although Germany and Britain played the leading role in developing electronic warfare, the United States contributed in the specialized field of airborne electronic intelligence (ELINT). While the RAF introduced ELINT-equipped Wellington bombers in 1942, the United States assumed the lead in electronic reconnaissance with the introduction of specialized electronic reconnaissance aircraft (nicknamed "Ferret") in 1943. To accomplish this feat, the United States mobilized scientific talent and harnessed the production capacity of its vast electronics industry. The Office of Scientific Research and Development, the heart of the American electronic warfare effort, selected Dr. Frederick E. Terman from Stanford University to head the Radio Research Laboratory (RRL), which was responsible for radio and radar countermeasures (RCM). In a shrewd organizational move, the National Defense Research Committee kept Terman's Division 15 independent from Division 14, which was created to advance radar.[41] Hence, there was no bureaucratic pressure from radar proponents to retard the development of radar countermeasures. Therefore, the RRL moved quickly to develop the components necessary for electronic reconnaissance and radar jamming. In early 1942, Terman directed the adaptation of SCR 587 radar intercept receivers for airborne use.[42] This equipment allowed aircraft to identify enemy radar sites and to determine their operating characteristics.[43] In addition to its role in developing electronic countermeasures, the United States offered tremendous production capability to the Allied electronic warfare effort. Dr. George Rappaport observed:

> Once there was an operational requirement for it [the APR-2 Carpet jamming transmitter] the Army Air Force wanted 15,000 and I was sent to Delco at Kokomo, Indiana, to discuss the contract to mass produce [sic] it. Bert Schwarz, their brilliant chief production engineer, showed me around the plant. . . . As we walked around Bert looked rather unhappy and he kept scratching his head. In the end I said to him, "What's wrong, can't you build the 15,000 for us?" He paused for

a while, then answered, "Well, 15,000 a week, that's an awfully tough rate." I looked at him in amazement and told him I did not want 15,000 Carpets per week, 15,000 in a year would do fine. Bert broke out into a smile. "Oh," he said, "I'll have to reduce my production capacity to do that!"[44]

Before the United States could design and build jammers, the AAF needed to understand the performance characteristics of enemy radar.[45] In early 1942, the USAAF established a radar school at Morrison Field, Florida, which moved to Boca Raton, Florida, in June 1942. The radar school developed an RCM course and trained specialists in radar detection (nicknamed "Ravens") for air operations. Initially, training in antiquated Lockheed B-34 bombers, the Ravens operated radar search receivers and pulse analyzers to find radar transmissions and display them on oscilloscopes for analysis.[46] In addition, the RCM school taught the rudiments of electronic jamming and the use of WINDOWS (also called chaff)—small strips of aluminum foil scattered from an aircraft that masked the aircraft's image on a radarscope. Unfortunately, shortages of equipment and experience limited the school's effectiveness.[47] In the words of one participant, "The RCM course was a riot—nobody was sure how anything (equipment) worked, if it worked nobody really knew why, and if it did what it was supposed to accomplish."[48] Since the AAF acknowledged British expertise in the European theater, the first American Ravens headed for the Pacific.[49]

On 6 March 1943, Lts Bill Praun and Ed Tietz flew the first American electronic reconnaissance flight against a Japanese radar on Kiska Island in the Aleutian Islands chain (fig. 1). Spotted by aerial photography, the Kiska radar afforded a unique opportunity to learn about Japanese equipment. Knowing few details, American electronic analysts assumed Japanese radar technology to be inferior. Consequently, "Ferret I," a modified B-24D, conducted a series of flights with varied success. Praun and Tietz received signals in the 100-megacycle (mc) range that suggested a Japanese Mark I Model 1's early warning radar, but the new APR-4 search receivers provided only crude data.[50] Nevertheless, Ferret I blazed the trail for American electronic reconnaissance.

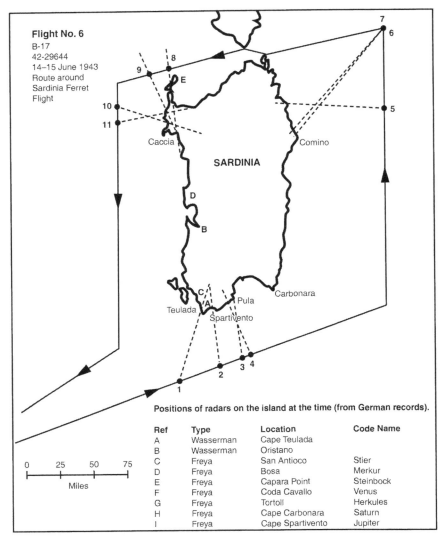

Figure 1. Flight No. 6 of Ferret III, 14–15 June 1943

With the Allied invasion of North Africa, the AAF broadened the scope of Ferret activity. In May 1943 Ferret III entered service with the 16th Reconnaissance Squadron.[51] Later joined by Ferrets IV, V, and VI, the modified B-17s flew night, low-level missions into Axis radar coverage. Initially concentrating on Sicily, the aircraft eventually flew electronic reconnaissance missions over Sardinia, Corsica, Italy, and southern France. Between May 1943 and September 1944, the Mediterranean Ferrets flew 184 sorties and discovered 450 enemy radar sites. As a result of Ferret data, analysts learned the range and operating frequencies of German *Freya* early warning radar, *Gema* coastal surveillance radar, and *Würzburg* GCI radar.[52] This information aided operational planning for amphibious assaults Husky, Avalanche, Shingle, and Dragoon, as well as the strategic bombing missions conducted by the 15th Air Force. In addition, the 16th Reconnaissance Squadron determined that the new American RC-156 Carpet electronic jammer offered protection for bombers against gun-laying radar (now called fire-control radar).[53] Finally, the ELINT B-17s improved new Ferret tactics. American electronic reconnaissance aircraft accompanied RAF Wellington night bombers and established collection orbits during raids. On other occasions, crews braved night missions flying 200–500 feet over mountains—a most "unhealthy" practice—to surprise German radar operators.[54] The daring, often improvised, tactics of the 16th uncovered valuable information about enemy defensive systems. Thus, by fall 1944, AAF Ferrets added a new dimension to strategic aerial reconnaissance.

In the Pacific theater, perhaps to an even greater extent than Europe, US forces relied upon aerial reconnaissance to plan the strategic bombing offensive. Lacking the benefit of an established British intelligence organization, the US strategic air campaign faced a dearth of strategic intelligence. To build target folders, the USAAF relied on strategic photo intelligence to determine basic economic and industrial data and aerial ELINT to form the Japanese electronic order of battle (EOB).[55] Unlike Europe, the Allies lacked a pool of prewar information, a network of spies, and other sources of economic information. The vast distances, long supply lines, and relatively primitive conditions complicated operations, demanding a knack for ingenuity and improvisation.[56]

The air war against Japan introduced the USAAF to night area bombing, but did not refute its belief in precision bombing.

Desires to end the war quickly, avoid a costly ground invasion, and demonstrate airpower's decisiveness influenced the planning.[57] The initial bombing campaign called for the destruction of the Japanese aircraft industry through precision bombardment. From November 1944 to March 1945, Boeing B-29 Superfortresses conducted daylight, high-altitude precision strikes, using tactics similar to the European air war. Unfortunately, chronic bad weather, extreme long-range maintenance problems, and inexperienced crews combined for disappointing results. Impatient with low bomb tonnages and the lack of measurable success, the USAAF switched to low-level, night area attacks.[58] Although the firebombing of Japanese cities resulted in impressive, horrific destruction, AAF leaders viewed the Pacific strategic bombing campaign as a unique expedient. Air planners recognized the unusual vulnerability of Japanese cities to incendiary attack, and many air leaders considered Japan a defeated nation in conventional terms. Night area bombing represented a move to break Japan's will to resist and to force surrender. Because of these unique conditions, the Pacific experience did not alter most airmen's convictions for the concept of precision bombing.[59]

Although the need for ELINT remained significant, air leaders viewed strategic electronic reconnaissance operations in the Pacific as a secondary concern. The ad hoc, freewheeling nature of ELINT operations staged out of China reinforced this view. Apparently, Brig Gen Claire L. Chennault initiated the USAAF's demand for ELINT when Japanese Zeros began intercepting his fighter sweeps in mid-1944.[60] An early graduate of the RCM school, Lt Robert Perry volunteered to lead the Ferret effort. With the aid of an officer assistant and two maintenance men, Perry outfitted a B-24 with ELINT gear and planned the first sortie. What we needed to know was: are there any Jap radars over there? And if so, what kind are they and what kind of threat are they. So I planned the missions on that basis. . . . To start, I planned to go where there was the biggest chance of finding a radar, to prove there were radars in the area. My pilot and I figured that the Hong Kong–Canton area was probably the most likely place. . . . We planned the first mission to go down to the Linchow Peninsular [sic], then to Canton and then home; a run of about 8 hours over enemy territory in darkness. We got over the Kowloon docks about 10 pm local time—not a peep from our receivers. We were very disappointed. Lt Uthe (the pilot) felt that the Japs in Canton were fighting in a very civilized manner, and had probably gone to bed. So, he made a couple of low level passes over the Kowloon docks. Sure enough, by the time he leveled off from the second pass, we began to pick up radar signals loud and clear. We flew a couple of plotting runs and returned to Kunming.[61]

Eventually, the Ferret B-24 flew missions to Formosa, the Pescadores, Hainan Island, and over most of Japanese-occupied China. By the time the B-29 campaign began in earnest, B-29s were being modified to serve in an RCM role at Wright Field, Dayton, Ohio. Each squadron received a B-29 equipped with receivers, a pulse analyzer, and preset jammers. Unfortunately, since the B-29 lacked a crew seat, the RCM operator sat on the airplane's toilet (a move considered painfully symbolic by later Air Force electronic warfare officers).[62]

Although operational analysis proved the value of electronic reconnaissance and radar countermeasures, electronic warfare fought an uphill battle for acceptance. Unlike photographic intelligence, commanders and crews could not "see" the results of electronic countermeasures.[63] Electronic warfare represented a form of mysterious, technical wizardry understood by few. Most pilots objected to the weight and drag induced by electronic gear; they "didn't want any of that crap" on their airplanes.[64] About the time ELINT data enabled scientists and engineers to design and build new jamming devices, other developments made electronic warfare less necessary. For example, large numbers of long-range North American P-51 Mustang fighters gained Allied air-superiority in spring 1944. In addition, the Allied land offensive following the Normandy invasion reduced Luftwaffe radar sites and advanced fighter bases. Instead of jamming enemy early warning and GCI frequencies, Allied fighters wanted the Germans to launch planes so they could be shot down. As Allied numerical superiority mounted, the quantity of existing electronic jammers and WINDOW overwhelmed German radars.[65] Therefore, airborne electronic intelligence decreased in significance even as Ferret effectiveness increased. As a result, in November 1944, the 16th Reconnaissance Squadron became one of the first units to be decommissioned.[66]

In conceptual terms, World War II experience created the foundation for strategic aerial reconnaissance during the Cold War. By May 1945, the term *strategic reconnaissance* or *strategic aerial reconnaissance* was defined by the USAAF as "the program of acquiring aerial intelligence as a basis for carrying on strategic air warfare against the enemy."[67] USAAF staff officers clearly distinguished this concept from *tactical reconnaissance* concerned with "large scale [sic] daily cover of the enemy forward areas, damage assessment photographs for fighter bomber attacks, and enemy defenses, airfields, and other special targets up to 150 miles from the front."[68] For Allied planners, strategic aerial reconnaissance included reconnaissance of naval and antishipping operations, industrial facilities, enemy air forces, longrange weapon sites, communications (rail, road, and waterways), and military installations. In a separate category, weather reconnaissance emerged as a significant component of strategic air warfare since favorable weather directly influenced bombing precision. With 125,600 aerial reconnaissance sorties flown between 1 January 1944 and 8 May 1945, the vast scale of Allied aerial reconnaissance served as one indicator of its importance. Even more dramatic, a study titled, "The Contribution of Air Power to the Defeat of Germany" concluded, "Mastery of the air over the scene of the European conflict gave to Allied arms a singular advantage. No army ever entered a field of battle with more accurate and detailed intelligence of its adversary. The intelligence supplied by aerial reconnaissance remains one of air power's leading contributions to the victory. The information gained thereby was not only to the immediate advantage of air force commanders—both strategic and tactical—but was of unestimable [sic] value to the Allied armies and navies and to strategists responsible for coordinating the plans of all branches."[69]

Despite the accolades for reconnaissance, electronic warfare and electronic reconnaissance failed to establish a permanent foothold in the AAF organization. As a hybrid of operational, research, and intelligence functions, airborne electronic reconnaissance failed to fit neatly into existing staff organizations. AAF balked at creating a separate RCM organization at headquarters level.[70] No single agency centralized and coordinated ELINT activity for the air staff in Washington, although Headquarters US Strategic Air Forces in Europe created an Electronics Intelligence subsection within the Directorate of Intelligence. Charged with the "collection, evaluation, interpretation, and distribution of enemy electronics devices," it focused upon enemy communications, radar, and radio navigation devices associated with controlling antiaircraft fire, fighter control, raid reporting, and counterelectronic devices.[71] Unfortunately, this theater-level organization lacked a counterpart in Washington. In addition, although Division 15 and the RRL attempted to promote electronic warfare and headed research and development, civilians ran these organizations and had little impact on the USAAF hierarchy. When the war ended, the proponents of electronic warfare returned to civilian life.[72] Thus, electronic reconnaissance lacked a "champion" to defend its organizational interests.

By the end of World War II, strategic aerial reconnaissance demonstrated its value in both the conduct of land battles and air campaigns. From the early days of flight, aviation promised advantages in gaining surprise. During the First World War, aerial photography proved vital in assessing enemy battlefield strength, planning operations, and adjusting artillery fire. By the end of the Combined Bomber Offensive in the Second World War, photographic intelligence from high-flying reconnaissance aircraft provided the foundation for strategic air warfare. Unfortunately, although electronic reconnaissance proved important for defeating enemy defensive systems, Ferret aircraft failed to earn the respect of commanders as an essential intelligence gathering system. With abundant forms of ground communications intelligence, photographs, and spy networks, ELINT remained a peripheral "nice to have" source of information. Consequently, strategic aerial reconnaissance emerged from World War II with a mixed legacy. Commanders recognized the need for strategic intelligence and valued aerial photography as the indispensable foundation of campaign planning, but electronic reconnaissance failed to convince leaders of its necessity.

Notes

1. Philip Babcock, ed. in chief, *Webster's Third International Dictionary of the English Language Unabridged* (Springfield, Mass.: G. & C. Merriam Co., 1981), 1897.

2. Peter Mead, *The Eye in the Air: History of Air Observation and Reconnaissance for the Army* (London: Her Majesty's Stationery Office, 1983), 5.

3. Carl von Clausewitz, *On War*, ed. and trans. by Michael Howard and Peter Paret (Princeton, N.J.: Princeton University Press, 1976), 198.

4. Sun Tzu, *The Art of War,* trans. and introduction by Samuel B. Griffith (London: Oxford University Press, 1971), 69, 96.

5. Quoted in Mead, 11. See also Walter Raleigh, *The War in the Air,* vol. 1 (Oxford: Clarendon Press, 1922), 31–32; and Edwin L. Marsh, "The History of Tactical Reconnaissance: 1783 to 7 December 1941," Air University thesis (Maxwell AFB, Ala.: Air University, 1967), 6.

6. Glenn B. Infield, *Unarmed and Unafraid* (New York: Macmillan, 1970), 22–24; Mead, 16–17; and Marsh, 15–43.

7. Mead, 18. See also, Alistair Horne, "The Balloons of Paris," *MHQ: The Quarterly Journal of Military History* 13, no. 4 (summer 2001): 80–87.

8. Lee Kennett, *The First Air War, 1914–1918* (New York: Free Press, 1991), 18; and John Morrow, *The Great War in the Air* (Washington, D.C.: Smithsonian Institution Press, 1993), 25.

9. William E. Burrows, *Deep Black: Space Espionage and National Security* (New York: Random House, 1986), 32; and Infield, 31–32.

10. Morrow, 63; and Raleigh, 329.

11. Mead, 56–57.

12. Ibid., 66–67.

13. Roy Conyers Nesbit, *Eyes of the RAF: A History of Photo-Reconnaissance* (Phoenix Mill, United Kingdom: Alan Sutton Publishers, 1996), 26.

14. Strategic reconnaissance refers to gathering information required for the formation of policy and military plans at national and international levels, whereas tactical air reconnaissance seeks information concerning terrain, weather, the disposition and movement of enemy forces, and artillery adjustment. In other words, strategic and tactical intelligence differ primarily in levels of application, scope, and detail. Department of Defense, Joint Chiefs of Staff Publication 1, *Dictionary of Military and Associated Terms,* 1984, 350, 361.

15. Raleigh, 329; and Mead, 69.

16. See Kennett and Morrow for good surveys of aviation developments during the early years of the war.

17. [Edgar S. Gorrell], "Final Report of the Chief of the Air Service," in *The United States Air Service in World War I,* vol. 1, ed. Mauer Mauer (Maxwell AFB, Ala.: US Air Force Historical Research Center, 1978), 104–5.

18. Kennett, 36; and Morrow, 151–52.

19. Mead, 82.

20. Vertical photographs referred to those taken from directly overhead, while oblique photos used a camera inclined to the earth's surface to produce a panoramic view. Infield, 35–36; and Kennett, 37.

21. Burrows, 33–34.

22. Gorrell, 17.

23. Robert F. Futrell, *Ideas, Concepts, Doctrine: Basic Thinking in the United States Air Force,* vol. 1, *1907–1960* (Maxwell AFB, Ala.: Air University Press, 1989), 29.

24. Ibid., 28.

25. For summaries of airpower theory following World War I, see Futrell, 22–39; and *The United States Strategic Bombing Survey Summary Report (Pacific War)*, 1 July 1946 in David MacIsaac, ed. (hereafter MacIsaac *USSBS*), 4–10. Also for reprints of early airpower theorists see William Mitchell, *Winged Defense: The Development and Possibilities of Modern Air Power—Economic and Military* (Port Washington, N.Y.: Kennikat Press, 1971); and Giulio Douhet, *The Command of the Air*, trans. Dino Ferrare, reprint ed. (Washington, D.C.: Office of Air Force History, 1983).

26. Giulio Douhet, *The Command of the Air*, trans. Dino Ferrari (New York: Coward-McCann, 1942), 120–21.

27. Department of Ground Instruction, Air Corps Primary Flying School, "Reconnaissance," 2d ed. (Brooks Field, Tex.: Department of Ground Instruction, Air Corps Primary Flying School, 1928), 1–8; Air Corps Advanced Flying School, "Observation," Kelly Field, Tex., 34–55; and Wesley F. Craven and James L. Cate, eds., *The Army Air Forces in World War II*, vol. 6, *Men and Planes* (Chicago: University of Chicago Press, 1948–1958), 615–16.

28. Assigned to aerial photographic work in 1918 as a second lieutenant, Goddard worked on aerial photography during most of the interwar period. During the interwar years, he advanced in rank from lieutenant to major in various positions. Before World War II, he served as head of the Air Corps Photographic Section. George W. Goddard, *Overview: A Life-Long Adventure in Aerial Photography* (Garden City, N.Y.: Doubleday, 1969), 155–230; and Infield, 53.

29. Burrows, 38.

30. The Alaskan project also demonstrated the problems of cold-weather photography. Goddard, 224–228; and Infield, 58.

31. Notice the similarity to Douhet's ideal reconnaissance aircraft. Constance Babbington Smith, *Evidence in Camera: The Story of Photographic Intelligence in World War II* (London: Chatto and Windus, 1958), 32.

32. Sir Charles Webster and Noble Frankland, *The Strategic Air Offensive Against Germany 1939–1945*, vol. 1 (London: Her Majesty's Stationery Office, 1961), 349–50.

33. Nesbit, 80; and Robert Jackson, *High Cold War: Strategic Air Reconnaissance and the Electronic Intelligence War* (Yeovil, Somerset, United Kingdom: Patrick Stephens, 1998), 14–15.

34. In her book, *Evidence in Camera*, Constance Babbington Smith showed that a sexist assumption paid great dividends for British intelligence. Reasoning that photointerpretation required long hours of effort, tremendous patience, and attention to detail—the same attributes of sewing—the RAF recruited women to serve as photointerpreters. Judging from Babbington Smith's firsthand tales of inspired deduction that resulted from painstaking effort, successful results justified the RAF decision. Smith, 66.

35. In *British Intelligence in the Second World* War, Sir Francis H. Hinsley emphasizes the organizational efforts to create a comprehensive, rational method for the entire intelligence process. By analyzing the spectrum of ac-

tivities associated with the intelligence cycle, the British enhanced the quality and timeliness of intelligence information. In other words, they not only improved intelligence collection, but the processing of data, analysis, coordination, and dissemination of information. F. H. Hinsley, *British Intelligence in the Second World War,* 4 vols. (London: Her Majesty's Stationery Office, 1979–1988).

36. Craven and Cate, 617.

37. Ibid., 221–23; and Infield, 80–99.

38. Operational errors, poor target selection, and the misuse of an air force designed primarily for tactical air support to wage a strategic bombing campaign also contributed to the German loss in the Battle of Britain. For further details, see R. J. Overy, *The Air War 1939–1945* (New York: Stein and Day, 1985), 98–108; and Williamson Murray, *Luftwaffe* (Baltimore: Nautical & Aviation Publishing Co., 1985), 43–61.

39. R. V. Jones, *Most Secret War* (London: Hamish Hamilton, 1978), 92–100; and Jackson, 20–25.

40. Webster and Frankland, vol. 2, E1, pt. 4, 190–211.

41. Col Hugh Winter, USAF, retired, interviewed by Frank Voltaggio and Alfred Price, 29 August 1980, 1, file 47, Col H. Winter, Association of Old Crows, Association of Old Crows Building, Alexandria, Va. (hereafter AOC Archive); and Alfred Price, *The History of US Electronic Warfare,* vol. 1, *The Years of Innovation—Beginnings to 1946* (Westford, Maine: Murray Publishing Co., AOC Archive, 1984), 21–22.

42. Dr. George Rappaport interviewed by Alfred Price and Armand J. Morin, fall 1981, file 14, AOC Archive.

43. Eventually, the RRL introduced 150 new types of electronic warfare equipment. F. E. Terman, Administrative History of the Radio Research Laboratory, Office of Scientific Research and Development, National Defense Research Committee, Division of Radio Coordination (15), 26 March 1946, folder 1, box 9, SC 160 series 1, Frederick Emmons Terman Papers (hereafter Terman Papers), Stanford University Library Archives, Stanford, Calif.

44. Ibid., 3.

45. With radar, *performance characteristics* refer to measurements of radiated electromagnetic energy used to determine the radar's function, range, and relative accuracy. For further details, see Appendix A, Radar Principles, in this book.

46. The nickname "Raven" derived from the code word used for radar countermeasures at the time. By 1948, the abbreviation RCM was replaced by electronic countermeasures and most electronic warfare officers were referred to as "Crows" (an American Raven). Winter, AOC Archive, file 47, 2–3, 8.

47. Winter, AOC Archive, file 47, 5.

48. Col Robert R. Perry, USAF, retired, to Alfred Price, 2 June 1982, letter, AOC Archive, file 31, Col R. Perry.

49. Winter, AOC Archive, file 47, 5.

50. Ibid., 6; Lt Col Ingwald Haugen, USAF, retired, interviewed by Alfred Price and Frank Voltaggio, 1–2, file 25, Col I. Haugen, AOC Archive; and Price, 52–53.

51. Evidently, Ferret II was a prototype and never deployed overseas. Ferrets III and IV were B-17s modified at Wright Field, near Dayton, Ohio. Winter, AOC Archive, file 47, 7.

52. Maj Charles Eaton, "The Ferrets," (1947), AOC Archive, 1–2, file (North) Africa Ferrets, AOC Archive; and Winter, AOC Archive, file 47, 10.

53. Originally, the Carpet noise jammer was intended solely for use in amphibious assaults. Eaton, 3–5.

54. Ibid., 2.

55. In the spring of 1944, the USAAF's 21st Bomber Command lacked sufficient photographic reconnaissance to target its primary objective—the Japanese aircraft industry. On 1 November 1944, an F-13A (a photoreconnaissance version of the B-29) provided enough photographs for the first series of missions. Haywood S. Hansell, *The Strategic Air War Against Germany and Japan* (Washington, D.C.: Office of Air Force History, 1986), 169, 179.

56. Although this study focuses upon strategic aerial reconnaissance and its impact upon strategic air warfare, interested readers should consult Alfred Price's *The History of US Electronic Warfare* for the extensive US Navy ELINT programs conducted in the Pacific.

57. Hansell, 159, 166, 177, 213; and Curtis E. LeMay with MacKinlay Kantor, *Mission with LeMay: My Story* (Garden City, N.Y.: Doubleday, 1965), 323–52.

58. MacIsaac *USSBS*, 16, reprinted as *The United States Strategic Bombing Surveys: (European War) (Pacific War)* (Maxwell AFB, Ala.: Air University Press, 1987); and Hansell, 212.

59. Hansell, 217–57.

60. Price, letter, AOC Archive, file 31, 8.

61. Ibid., 6–7.

62. Ibid., 5, 7. Since bomber squadrons possessed few personnel trained for electronic warfare, a few specialists set the frequencies for aircraft jamming equipment before flight.

63. For this study, the terms *electronic countermeasures* and *radio countermeasures* are interchangeable. Contemporary documents followed this practice for the most part, although the official designation remained "Radio Countermeasures" until 1948.

64. Perry letter, AOC Archive, file 31, 4. On more than one occasion, local commanders reconverted their specially modified ELINT aircraft back into standard bombers. They did not want "a lot of signals junk" loading down their planes. Haugen interview, AOC Archive, file 25, 2.

65. Winter interview, AOC Archive, file 47, 13.

66. Frank Voltaggio, "Out in the Cold. . . . Early ELINT Activities of the Strategic Air Command" (unpublished, n.d.), AOC Archive, file Voltaggio.

67. Assistant chief of staff, A-2, Headquarters United States Air Forces in Europe, "The Contribution of Air Power to the Defeat of Germany," app. M,

Miscellaneous Aspects of Air Power, 1, n.d., Carl A. Spaatz Papers, National Archives, Washington D.C., box 274, Library of Congress.

68. Ibid.

69. Ibid.

70. O. G. Villard Jr., Office of Scientific Research and Development, to A. Earl Cullum Jr., RRL, letter, subject: London Mission, 9 July 1944, AOC Archive, 2, file: Dr. O. Villard.

71. Memorandum, subject: Electronics Intelligence Sub-Section, Directorate of Intelligence, 3 September 1944, file: USSTAF, D/Intel, Organization, box 297, Terman Papers.

72. From a wartime peak of 923 scientists, engineers, technicians, and administrative personnel, the RRL declined to 401 employees by December 1945 and to less than 25 by April 1946. All official research projects were closed by January 1945. Personnel Distribution Weekly Lists, folder 2, box 3, SC 160 series 1, Terman Papers.

Chapter 2

Groping in the Dark: Reconnaissance before Containment, 1945–1946

Who controls the reconnaissance watches the enemy;
Who watches the enemy perceives the threat;
Who perceives the threat shapes the alternatives;
Who shapes the alternative determines the response;

—William Burrows
Deep Black: Space
Espionage and National
Security, 25

Aerial reconnaissance failed to rank as a priority of American political and military leaders following World War II. Faced by broad challenges inherent in creating a new world, leaders concentrated their efforts on major domestic, international, and military issues of greater magnitude rather than establishing a capability for aerial surveillance. Demobilization and the economy were of prime importance to the American public and government officials. Although strained US-Soviet relations caused distress, a bewildering array of international events called for attention. In addition, military professionals grappled with structuring national defense for a postwar world. From the end of World War II until President Harry Truman's declaration of containment in 1947, intelligence gathering received little attention; yet, the inability to provide accurate and perceptive threat assessment plagued decision makers. In other words, because the American public and its leadership failed to perceive an impending threat, they ignored the need to establish a mechanism to gather information. When US-Soviet tensions mounted, military leaders lacked the intelligence base for proper strategic planning. Consequently, the intelligence shortcomings of the first Joint Chiefs of Staff (JCS) war plan (called Pincher) provided the impetus for America's initial postwar aerial reconnaissance.

In the euphoria following victory in World War II, domestic issues dominated American politics. To most Americans, victory signified the end of war and the beginning of normal life. Returning soldiers to civilian life and demobilizing the huge wartime military establishment received top priority. Of more than 12 million men under arms at the end of the war, only 3 million remained by July 1946, and fewer than 1.6 million served a year later.[1] Likewise, combat capability declined dramatically. The Army dropped from 91 combat-ready divisions to 10 under-strength divisions; the Navy retained only 343 combat ships from 1,166 vessels; and the AAF shrank from 68,400 aircraft in 213 combat groups to 20,800 planes organized in 63 groups (of which only 11 groups were fully operational).[2] Nevertheless, despite the decline in capability, Americans felt secure from outside threat. After all, the United States had just defeated the most powerful military powers in history and alone possessed an awesome new weapon.

Of more immediate concern than external problems, government officials worried about renewed economic depression. The reentry of 10 million men into the workforce and the conversion of factories from military to civilian goods posed significant challenges. The release of pent-up demand for consumer goods fueled inflation. In an effort to maintain balanced budgets, the Truman administration slashed government spending. As a result, defense spending dropped from $42.7 billion and 39.1 percent of gross national product (GNP) in 1945 to $12.8 billion and 5.7 percent of GNP by 1947.[3] Consequently, military leaders pared units to the bone and cut all nonessential programs.

Despite the surrender of the Axis powers in 1945, peace did not bring tranquility. Although the United States backed the United Nations (UN) with enthusiasm, the creation of the new organization failed to establish international harmony. Throughout the globe, nationalism appealed to peoples under European colonial rule. Moreover, Japan, the Soviet Union, and most European nations struggled to rebuild devastated areas and resettle millions of displaced persons. Perhaps most disturbing from an American perspective, the wartime alliance of the United States and the Soviet Union crumbled over German surrender terms, termination of the Lend-Lease Act, the future of Eastern

Europe, and other issues. Although the Cold War had not begun in earnest, fundamental differences hardened attitudes and fore-shadowed outright hostility.[4]

By February 1946, George F. Kennan's "Long Telegram" indicated a fundamental shift in the perception of the Soviet threat by leading policy makers. According to Kennan, the Soviet Union represented a long-term economic and political threat ruled by an opportunistic, brutal regime. Despite wartime cooperation, Soviet Communism remained ideologically opposed to the world's capitalist nations. A traditional and instinctive Russian sense of insecurity formed the basis for a worldview that centered upon conflict rather than cooperation. As a result, the Soviet state maintained a large, well-equipped army that demanded Western world vigilance. Although the Soviets suffered enormous damage from the German invasion and did not seek war in the near future, the Soviet Union represented a fanatical political force sworn to oppose the United States. With dedicated leadership, vast raw materials, and a resourceful population, the Soviet Union emerged as a dangerous foe. According to Kennan, the problem of dealing with Soviet hostility "is undoubtedly [the] greatest task our diplomacy has ever faced and probably the greatest it will ever have to face."[5]

Faced with an exodus of personnel, severe funding cuts, and growing international tension, American military leaders grappled with restructuring national defense for the postwar world. Questions of the size, composition, and organization of the armed forces arose, as well as bitter arguments over the roles and missions of the services. In addressing the issue of future manpower needs, Gen George C. Marshall and President Truman backed the concept of *universal military training* providing peacetime basic military training for male citizens and reducing future mobilization problems. Furthermore, the Army and the AAF supported a proposal to unify the services into a single department of defense with three coequal branches—Army, Navy, and Air Force. Worried that such a proposal would result in the loss of the naval air arm and the Marines, the Navy countered with the Eberstadt plan that proposed less centralization.[6] For airpower proponents, an independent Air Force remained the key issue.[7] Worried that a return to peacetime concerns would jeopardize its wartime gains in status, the AAF redoubled efforts to achieve autonomy. Convinced of the dominant role of aviation during World War II, Henry H. "Hap" Arnold, USAAF command-ing general, commissioned studies to assess the impact of new technology upon airpower doctrine. In the first series, *The United States Strategic Bombing Survey (USSBS)*, utilized a team of his-torians, economists, and operations analysts to assess the effec-tiveness of strategic air warfare during the past war. For the most part, the *USSBS* affirmed the precision bombardment doctrine practiced in the Combined Bomber Offensive. In the overall re-port for Europe, the survey concluded, "Allied air power was de-cisive in the war in Western Europe."[8] Additionally, the *USSBS* summary report of the Pacific war stated, "It seems clear that, even without the atomic bomb attacks, air supremacy over Japan could have exerted sufficient pressure to bring about un-conditional surrender and obviate the need for invasion."[9] Never-theless, the specter of Hiroshima and Nagasaki forced the USAAF to study the impact of atomic weapons on strategic air war.

In two reports issued in October and November 1945, Gen Carl A. Spaatz headed a panel to assess the role of the Air Force in the atomic age.[10] Joined by Gens Hoyt S. Vandenberg and Lauris Norstad, Spaatz produced relatively cautious documents that paralleled the findings of the *USSBS*. In the first report, the Spaatz board concluded that the Air Force now served as the na-tion's first line of defense since aircraft would be the first units to engage the enemy. Furthermore, because of the destructive-ness of atomic weapons, the United States could not afford a surprise attack. Hence, the United States must maintain a strategic bomber force *in being* capable of "smashing an enemy air offensive, or launching a formidable strike force."[11] In the sec-ond report, the generals predicted future atomic weapons ca-pable of devastating a 10-mile-square area and that other na-tions would develop atomic bombs and delivery systems.[12] They recognized the atomic bomb's usefulness in strategic air war, but argued that the weapon did not dictate a change in basic strate-gic doctrine.

1. The atomic bomb does not at this time warrant a material change in our present conception of the employment, size, organization, and composition of the postwar Air Force.

2. The atomic bomb has not altered our basic concept of the strategic air offensive but has given us an additional weapon.

3. Forces using non-atomic bombs will be required for use against targets which cannot be effectively or economically attacked with the atomic bomb.[13]

In addition, because of the range limitations of existing bombers, the Spaatz board urged the creation of a network of overseas air bases.

When viewed from a later perspective, the Spaatz board missed the revolutionary impact of atomic weapons on strategy. Its conservative assessment merely reinforced existing doctrine by presenting the atomic bomb as a weapon to augment, but not replace, existing bombers. Although the generals advocated the funding of a large scientific research and development program, they failed to anticipate technological breakthroughs that resulted in smaller atomic weapons easily assembled and transported. However, such criticisms overlooked the extreme secrecy surrounding the bomb. For example, even these distinguished AAF generals lacked access to details of bomb yields and existing stockpile numbers. The generals assumed the atomic bomb would be a scarce, specialized weapon: "The bomb is enormously expensive and definitely limited in availability."[14] In fact, although they lacked access to the specific numbers, Spaatz, Vandenberg, and Norstad proved right about the scarcity of American atomic bombs. Before technological breakthroughs in atomic weapons design in the Sandstone tests of 1948, the United States possessed a minuscule number of atomic weapons. The US atomic stockpile only numbered two weapons at the end of 1945, nine by July 1946, 13 by July 1947, and 50 by July 1948.[15] Thus, although the Spaatz board presented an overly cautious assessment of the impact of atomic weapons, actual American capability reinforced the board's findings.

In another perceptive assessment, the Spaatz board's criticism of US intelligence systems reflected the American experience with British intelligence during World War II. Despite its occasional lapses, the British intelligence system represented a successful fusion of data collection, collation, analysis, and dissemination of intelligence information. For much of the war, except for a few Americans involved in breaking the Enigma signals and the distribution of the resultant intelligence (ULTRA) and wireless intercept (Y-service), the British controlled the Allied intelligence organization in Europe.[16] Because of the close wartime association of Spaatz, Vandenberg, and Norstad with the British, the Americans appreciated their counterparts' attributes. Nevertheless, they believed that although the United Kingdom remained a close ally, the United States could not afford to be dependent on British intelligence.[17] As a result, the Spaatz board considered the establishment of a worldwide intelligence service of "paramount importance" and recommended an organization capable of knowing the strategic vulnerability, capabilities, and intentions of any potential enemy.[18]

Moreover, General Vandenberg served on a separate subcommittee to evaluate the Army's Intelligence Division (G-2). Headed by Robert A. Lovett, assistant secretary of War for Air, the committee's report chided the Army for a lack of cooperation between producers and users of intelligence information and the poor quality of Army intelligence personnel.[19] Therefore, in its various assessment efforts, the AAF recognized problems with its intelligence organization. Unfortunately, intelligence weaknesses remained only one of the major shortcomings facing the Air Force on the verge of its independence.

In an effort to prepare the AAF for its postwar defense roles and to enhance its transition to autonomy, General Arnold reorganized the air arm on functional lines. Effective 21 March 1946, the War Department authorized three combat commands for the AAF: Air Defense Command (ADC), Strategic Air Command (SAC), and Tactical Air Command (TAC).[20] Although theoretically coequal, SAC received priority because of the air leaders' conviction that strategic bombardment represented the future of war. Accordingly, SAC's initial mission statement of 12 March 1946 carried the doctrinal torch passed by Douhet, Mitchell, and the Air Corps Tactical School, "The Strategic Air Command will be prepared to conduct long-range offensive operations in any part of the world either independently or in cooperation with Naval forces; to provide combat units capable of intense and sustained combat operations employing the latest and most advanced weapons; to train units and personnel for the maintenance of the Strategic Forces in all parts of the world; to perform such special missions as the Commanding General, Army Air Forces may direct."[21]

Initially under the command of Gen George C. Kenney, SAC served as the focus of the AAF's attempt to organize a strategic strike force. SAC received responsibility for most of the AAF's heavy bombers. In addition, AAF regulations charged SAC with the responsibility of preparing plans for strategic aerial reconnaissance on a global scale and training "very long-range" reconnaissance, photographic, and mapping crews. In October 1946, SAC modified its mission statement to acknowledge the reconnaissance mission, "The Strategic Air Command will provide and operate that portion of the AAF which is maintained in the United States, and in such other areas as may be designated from time to time, for employment against objectives of air attack in any location on the globe and will conduct long-range reconnaissance over land or sea, either independently or in cooperation with other components of the armed forces."[22]

Despite its prominence in AAF doctrine and organization, SAC suffered from demobilization and budget cuts that drained it of genuine capability. In overall terms, the AAF had released 734,715 officers and men by February 1946. This exodus of personnel reduced the overall number and experience of those assigned to SAC. In May 1946, the AAF authorized SAC 43,729 men, but the command actually possessed only 37,426 (86 percent). Throughout the year, numbers continued to decline—by December 1946, America's strategic strike force numbered 32,190 personnel (74 percent).[23] To make matters worse, nearly 25 percent of this meager force consisted of first-term airmen with six months experience or less.[24] Moreover, aircraft strength proved inadequate; in March 1946, SAC possessed 221 very heavy bombers (VHB), 90 heavy bombers, and 191 reconnaissance and liaison aircraft.[25] By the end of the year, SAC's bomber force declined to 148 VHBs, eight heavy bombers, and numbered only 53 reconnaissance planes, including only two F-13 long-range photoreconnaissance aircraft.[26] Adding to SAC's woes, poor training and inadequate leadership exacerbated personnel shortages and equipment. With the end of the war, the average soldier or airman lost interest in training. Attempts to reinstitute training programs failed as experienced personnel left the service.[27]

General Kenney headed SAC on paper; in reality, he spent most of his time on duties associated with his position as special advisor on military affairs to the US delegation at the UN. Instead, his deputy, Maj Gen St. Clair Streett ran SAC operations.[28] Lacking guidance from General Kenney, General Streett and his replacement, Maj Gen Clements McMullen, drifted from SAC's primary purpose. They viewed basic flying proficiency, mobilization, and deployment as SAC's principal mission (as opposed to combat readiness). In other words, SAC stressed activities necessary for generating a combat force rather than training to conduct combat operations.[29] Thus, in 1946 SAC lacked the capability to wage strategic air war.

Ironically, even as SAC struggled, the JCS produced war plans based upon the strategic bombing doctrine seemingly vindicated by World War II. Although the JCS had produced previous assessments of Soviet intentions and capabilities, the series of war plans known as Pincher established the basic outline for America's military response to the Soviet Union in the event of an all-out conflict.[30] In other words, Pincher addressed the questions of how and when a war would begin, the initial course of operations, and the strategic framework for US operations. Like the World War II's Rainbow plans, Pincher formed the basis for conceptual thinking about the next war. The plan showed the JCS's perception of the Soviet threat and its acceptance of AAF strategic bombing doctrine.[31] Indeed, an analysis of Pincher revealed glaring limits in American intelligence capability.

Although the JCS realized tensions between the United States and the Soviet Union were growing, American strategists considered the outbreak of war unlikely. In Joint Planning Staff (JPS) 789, *Concept of Operations for "PINCHER,"* the Joint Staff planners estimated that Soviet economic potential remained undeveloped and "at least for the next ten or fifteen years, the gains to be derived internally during peace outweigh the advantages of any external objective that might be attained at the risk of war."[32] However, planners believed that the Soviets would apply maximum political pressure to attain

Soviet domination of bordering countries. Therefore, they created a scenario in which World War III started because of a Soviet miscalculation—leading to a Soviet invasion of Turkey. The loss of Turkey threatened the Suez Canal, and Great Britain intervened in defense of the empire's lifeline.[33] For planning purposes, the staff officers assumed M day (mobilization day) as 1 July 1947, and the United States would enter the war on 1 January 1948. Conveniently, the Joint Staff planners assigned Britain its time-honored role of battling the enemy until the United States mobilized. Pincher even debated whether the United States would declare war without an overt act similar to Pearl Harbor.[34]

In contrast to War Department thinking during World War II, Pincher adopted wholeheartedly the assumptions of the strategic AAF's bombing doctrine. Because US, British, and French forces could not resist the Soviet invasion of Europe that followed its thrust into Turkey, the JCS relied on strategic airpower to stem the tide.[35] Moreover, because allied military capabilities paled in comparison to World War II (with a low ebb predicted for mid-1946), the United States lacked the strength to pursue other strategies.[36] Planners concluded, "The cost of liquidating her [the Soviet Union] massive ground forces in a war of attrition by the direct application of our ground armies would be prohibitive. It thus becomes necessary to select operations which are more in consonance with our military capabilities and in which we can exploit our superiority in modern scientific warfare methods."[37] Thus, Pincher's war plans stressed the destruction of the Soviet *will to resist* by crushing her war-making capacity through air bombardment. Echoing the air prophets of the preceding generation, the Joint Staff planners stated confidently, "There are a number of factors which could lead to the capitulation of the U.S.S.R. prior to the defeat of her armed forces, such as: the collapse of her totalitarian government; destruction of her industry or the complete disruption of her communication system."[38] Accordingly, the Pincher Plan proposed destroying "definite areas which contain a substantial portion of vital resources, without which the Soviet war effort would be seriously curtailed (if not prevented)." These "vital areas" (reminiscent of Mitchell's vital centers) included in order of precedence: (1) Moscow, (2)

Caucasus, (3) Ploesti, (4) Ural, (5) Stalingrad, (6) Kharkov, (7) Lake Baikal, and (8) Leningrad.[39]

The JCS relied on the theory of strategic aerial bombardment as the primary American response to war with the Soviet Union. This reliance was due to the perceived American weakness shown by demobilization and severe budget limits.

At the heart of JCS planning, the Joint Intelligence Committee (JIC) presented a Soviet military machine of awesome potential. Like the United States, the Soviet armed forces had reduced their strength from World War II levels. According to the Joint War Plans Committee (JWPC) 432/3 (later, adopted as the Pincher estimate), Soviet armed forces consisted of 6.4 million men (347 divisions) in March 1946. By September 1946, Soviet land strength would drop to 4.8 million, and further cuts reduced it to 3.11 million (113 divisions) by the projected date of Pincher in 1947.[40] Nevertheless, the still-massive Soviet army possessed up-to-date armor and capable tactical air forces. Although not rated as highly as the German Luftwaffe, the Soviet air force deserved respect for its overall size, roughly 20,000 aircraft in tactical units, 50,000 overall, and proficiency in ground attack.[41] On the other hand, the JCS considered Soviet naval forces, amphibious lift, and strategic air forces "ineffective."[42] In addition, JCS planners believed the Soviets incapable of fielding atomic weapons by the outbreak of the war.[43] As a result, Soviet offensive military capabilities rested upon land operations. In overall terms, the JCS considered the Soviets capable of a blitzkrieg more impressive than the famed German drive across France in 1940. The Pincher Plan envisioned the following Soviet offensives:

a. to consolidate her positions in western Europe, Italy, Greece, Turkey, Persian Gulf area, Manchuria and Korea.

b. to overrun and occupy Spain.

c. to overrun and occupy the Scandinavian countries. . . .

d. to advance into Afghanistan.

e. to conduct air operations against the British Isles, Spain, North Africa, Middle East, North China, Japan, the Aleutians and Alaska.

f. to conduct limited raids against Iceland, Greenland, the Azores, and Philippines.

g. to conduct naval operations in the Black, Baltic, and Okhotsk Seas, limited raids in the Atlantic and Pacific, and submarine operations in both these latter areas.[44]

In sum, Pincher's estimate of Soviet capabilities matched a land juggernaut against a strategic air force armed with a limited number of atomic weapons. Since the JCS plan covered only the initial stages of the war, Pincher neither made definite predictions of the war's outcome nor included plans for the reconquest of Europe.

Besides its importance for presenting the JCS perception of the Soviet threat and acceptance of strategic air war doctrine, Pincher's plans revealed significant gaps in US intelligence capabilities. Although designed as a conceptual outline for a later *basic war plan*, Pincher acknowledged the JCS's inability to plan a strategic air campaign due to a lack of intelligence data.

> The scarcity of reliable and detailed intelligence on the U.S.S.R. precludes the determination at this time of specific target systems for air attack. Any strategic bombing program established at this time would be provisional even for purposes of current planning; it is certain to be altered radically when additional information becomes available. The current lack of intelligence on the U.S.S.R. is due not only to the rigid security maintained by that country, but also to the fact that such information as is available has not yet been properly assembled. It will be possible to improve this appreciation by incorporating in it new intelligence as the information now available to the various intelligence agencies is correlated.[45]

To conduct an air war, strategic planners needed information concerning all aspects of the Soviet economy and war potential. For a start, a precision air campaign along the lines of the USAAF bombing of Germany required information on the Soviet transportation network, electric power grid, key plant locations, and raw material supply.[46] Planners needed this information to prioritize missions and determine specific targets. In order to hit their targets, bombers must find them. Aircrews required detailed maps, charts, weather information, and supplemental data that comprised the target folders of World War II. To circumvent this lack of information, Pincher resorted to naming urban areas as targets. Thus, 30 cities became the *vital centers* of the projected strategic air campaign.[47]

The Pincher Plan's intelligence shortcomings focused attention on target selection in strategic air warfare. According to *USSBS*, "The importance of careful selection of targets of air attack is emphasized by the German experience. . . . In the field of strategic intelligence there was an important need for further and more accurate information, especially before and during the early phases of the war."[48] Furthermore, the *USSBS* criticized the inadequate strategic intelligence in the Pacific that made prewar plans "unreliable." The survey concluded that a comparable situation in a future war might prove disastrous. The only remedy appeared in a peacetime program designed to gather adequate information.[49]

Unfortunately, the Soviet Union posed an unprecedented intelligence challenge. Imperial Russia, as well as its communist successor, possessed a historical tradition influenced by xenophobia, secrecy, and limited contact with the outside world. Moreover, the Soviet Union presented vast distances, uncharted resources, and a formidable secret police network. In many ways, the United States knew less about the Soviet Union than prewar Japan.

In order to conduct a precision bombing campaign, the United States needed a vast amount of accurate information. Dr. James T. Lowe, an analyst for Air Intelligence, offered the *four foundation stones* of target analysis:

1. An exact knowledge of the 70,000 or more potential bombing objectives.

2. An exact knowledge of the mission of the attacking air force.

3. Reasonable approximation of the capabilities of the attacking air force.

4. Some professional "know how" with respect to analyzing these 70,000 or more targets, sifting them down to a very fine mesh, until we finally arrive at the minimum number of targets within the capabilities of the attacking air forces, the destruction of which would make the maximum contribution to an accomplishment of the mission of the attacking air forces.[50]

In addition, planners sought to look at the enemy's entire industry, identifying the segment supporting his offensive capability. Ideally, initial air strikes could disarm the enemy and prevent retaliatory strikes upon the United States.[51] Dr. Lowe agreed with the *USSBS* that target intelligence files required information gathered in peacetime. No time interval existed in modern warfare to gather information, select targets, and collect operational data needed for weapons delivery.[52] In sum, both Pincher's flaws and air intelligence requirements pointed to the need for peacetime aerial reconnaissance.

Given the limitations of US intelligence capability, what types of information could the United States collect in the immediate postwar period? Before the establishment of the Central Intelligence Agency (CIA) in 1947, a centralized agency did not exist for the coordination of American intelligence efforts; however, various projects sought to plug intelligence gaps. Perhaps the most noteworthy involved the interrogation of former Soviet internees and prisoners of war. Eventually called Project Wringer by the Air Force, the program was started in December 1946 by the joint service Far East Command (FEC). Wringer employed 1,800 specially trained military and civilian personnel in Germany, Austria, and Japan, questioning thousands of prisoners repatriated by the Soviet Union. By 1951 Wringer provided a vital source of strategic intelligence for the Air Force.[53] In addition, various allied intelligence agencies sifted through German intelligence archives from World War II.[54]

During the turmoil of demobilization, aerial reconnaissance efforts centered on long-range photomapping and ad hoc Ferret missions. SAC's 311th Reconnaissance Wing controlled AAF reconnaissance assets from its headquarters at MacDill Field, Florida. With less than 5 percent of the earth's surface mapped in detail, including only half of the continental United States, the 311th Reconnaissance Wing concentrated on long-range photomapping as its primary mission.[55] Of the areas already mapped, a major problem existed: each country in the past established a point within its boundaries as a reference position and determined latitude and longitude in relation to that point. Before the age of air travel, the lack of map cohesion made little difference, but long-range bombers required pinpoint accuracy. The navigational problems posed for an aircraft flying from one geographic reference area to another dictated a need for expanded and improved aerial mapping.[56] Therefore, the 311th Reconnaissance Wing mapped areas of occupied Europe, occupied Asia, selected Pacific areas, South America, and the continental United States according to a priority established by the Joint Mapping board.[57] Although the wing's mission statement included providing intelligence for SAC's long-range mission, most postwar flying fulfilled mapping requirements.[58]

A series of agreements between the United States and Britain established the initial tasking for postwar photographic reconnaissance and mapping. On 10 May 1945, Headquarters AAF directed the United States Air Forces in Europe (USAFE) to map occupied Europe.[59] Within a month, SAC and the RAF reached an agreement to cooperate in the task. The parties split central Europe at 50° 20' north latitude, with the British covering the northern portion and the United States mapping the southern section. According to the agreement, each plane would simultaneously operate two cameras and deliver one negative to each party.[60] By November 1945, the JCS accepted a British proposal to extend the photographic exchange worldwide.[61] Thus, the British-American agreements established procedures for high-priority photoreconnaissance and continued the intelligence sharing of the war years.

Like other AAF units, the 311th Reconnaissance Wing struggled to accomplish its mission in the period of postwar ferment. Personnel shortages and inexperienced crew members plagued the wing, forcing it to rely on technical schools and on-the-job training to relieve critical deficiencies.[62] The AAF also detached photographic squadrons from 311th Wing control, placing them under overseas theater commanders. This practice scattered experienced crews, creating rifts between operational units and their parent training and support organizations. As a result, photographic effectiveness and organizational efficiency declined.[63] Attempts to restore organizational control and the accomplishment of assigned missions with existing resources diverted SAC reconnaissance from important long-range problems.

The introduction of jet aircraft threatened World War II-vintage photoreconnaissance aircraft with obsolescence. During the war modified Spitfires, Mosquitoes, and P-38 Lightnings relied on speed and altitude for protection. When the Germans introduced jet fighters, this margin of safety vanished, but the overwhelming number of Allied aircraft assured continued air superiority. Unfortunately, US photographic reconnaissance in the immediate postwar period faced a dilemma. Existing jet aircraft lacked the range and reliability for penetration missions into the Soviet Union and photoreconnaissance aircraft based on bomber airframes lacked the speed and altitude for safety. Until technological advances solved the dilemma (in the form of the RB-57 and U-2), the Soviet Union remained largely impervious to American photographic reconnaissance, whether for target information, mapping, scientific/technical intelligence, or attack warning.

On the other hand, electronic intelligence represented an area open to US aerial reconnaissance in the early years of the Cold War. With American war plans relying on strategic bombardment, electronic reconnaissance missions offered a means to assess enemy defenses. By flying along the periphery of the Soviet Union, Ferret aircraft identified radar sites and analyzed their signals. Even though the combination of radar and jet fighters threatened the founding assumptions of strategic bombardment doctrine, initially the AAF showed little interest in ELINT or Ferret flights.

The ad hoc origins and shoestring budgets of postwar ELINT reflected a general apathy for electronic warfare. According to Dr. George W. Rappaport, a pioneer of US military electronics, electronic countermeasures faced opposition on three fronts: the radio industry, radar scientists, and the military hierarchy. With the end of World War II, major companies in the radio industry ceased to be concerned with defense contracts. Instead, Zenith, RCA, and Motorola wished to build radios and televisions for the domestic market. Moreover, scientists involved in developing advanced microwave radar argued that their innovations made radar immune to jamming. Finally, Rappaport summed up the attitude of high-ranking officers with the phrase, "Forget about countermeasures—it was a wartime weapon and there's no need for it in peacetime."[64] Consequently, postwar demobilization and budget cuts eliminated the US electronic reconnaissance program developed during World War II.

The postwar resurrection of electronic reconnaissance emanated from two separate sources. With growing tensions in

US-Soviet relations, SAC explored the possibility of attacking Soviet targets via great circle routes flown over the North Pole. The Nanook Project directed 311th Reconnaissance Wing aircraft to map the northern section of Greenland, while a separate Ferret aircraft searched for Soviet radar sites in this uninhabited area.[65] The second project began when Yugoslavia downed an American C-47 transport in August 1946. The incident sparked USAFE's interest in a Ferret program to determine whether the Yugoslavian antiaircraft guns were radar guided.[66] Although the projects reflected relatively uncoordinated, improvised efforts, they formed the basis for postwar aerial reconnaissance.

The first SAC postwar ELINT operation reflected concern for Soviet radar employment along potential Arctic approach routes for bombers. Capt Lester E. Manbeck served as the SAC action officer for electronic reconnaissance. He started his planning of the Greenland operation from scratch, recruiting 1st Lts John E. Filios and Henry C. Monjar on 27 August 1946 to serve as Ravens for a B-17G Ferret.[67] In addition, Manbeck arranged for Mr. Jim Scott, electronic specialist from Wright Field, Ohio, to *jury-rig* the plane with the necessary equipment to detect Soviet radar.[68] After installation, the B-17G Ferret deployed to Bluie West 8 (later Sondestrom Air Base), Greenland. From 2 to 20 September 1946, the crew searched for signals over Greenland and the adjacent Arctic regions with no success. Although the first SAC Ferret failed to detect any Soviet radar units, it served as the foundation for further ELINT efforts.[69]

In an unrelated episode, USAFE inaugurated an electronics reconnaissance program in response to the Yugoslavian downing of an American C-47 transport.[70] USAFE staff officers suspected that the Yugoslavs used radar-directed antiaircraft guns for the shootdown. As a result, Headquarters USAFE outfitted two B-17s with two AN/APR-4 search receivers and AN/APA-17 and AN/APA-24 direction-finding (D/F) antennas to investigate the incident. A former RCM observer, 1st Lt Ingwald Haugen, operated the equipment.[71] Using British GEE radar navigation equipment to prevent infringement of Yugoslav airspace, the B-17 Ferrets discovered the distinctive 570 MHz signals of a World War II German *Würzburg* radar.

The D/F bearings crossed at the site of a former German radar school. Evidently, Yugoslav air defense forces restored one of the German *Würzburg* fire control systems.[72]

Having solved the Yugoslav mystery, USAFE utilized the B-17 Ferrets as the nucleus of an ongoing ELINT program. Designated the 7499th Squadron, the Ferrets flew roughly three missions a week along the borders of Soviet-occupied Germany and Austria and over the Baltic Sea. These initial electronic reconnaissance sorties proved useful in assessing Soviet radar capabilities along the East-West frontier. They determined that the Soviets employed a small number of 70 MHz early warning radars of Russian manufacture, nicknamed "Dumbo," with a range limited to 100 miles. Only operating between six and 12 sets at a time, the Soviets periodically shifted locations to mask their limited capability. With the exception of the Yugoslav *Würzburg*, the Ferrets detected no antiaircraft fire control radar.[73] Unfortunately, the USAFE Ferrets could not confirm the reasons for this lack of coverage. Perhaps, the Soviets established more extensive radar coverage near vital areas of the Soviet Union. Nevertheless, the USAFE Ferret program provided the first hard evidence of Soviet defense capability against air attack.

The creation of a postwar aerial reconnaissance program illustrated the dichotomy between American intelligence collection capabilities and its need for information. With the initial Ferret program, the United States collected data on Soviet radar systems useful for planning bomber penetration and designing jamming equipment; however, the AAF required basic economic information to determine target priorities. Furthermore, SAC needed photographic reconnaissance for chart preparation and target folders. On a larger scale, the United States lacked the information necessary for proper threat assessment. As Pincher showed, the JCS grappled with producing a war plan without knowing the actual threat. Without empirical evidence, American political leaders struggled to understand Soviet capabilities and intentions during a period of rapid change. Although preoccupied by domestic concerns, demobilization, and reduced budgets, the Truman administration remained confident in America's atomic arsenal. Air chiefs also focused on the atomic bomb with hopes its unique capability would lead to service independence.

Without understanding the capabilities and limits of US power, from 1945 to 1946 the United States failed to assess the threat or appreciate the need to gather information systematically.

Notes

1. John Lewis Gaddis, *Strategies of Containment: A Critical Appraisal of Postwar American National Security Policy* (New York: Oxford University Press, 1982), 23.

2. Steven L. Rearden, *History of the Office of the Secretary of Defense*, vol. 1, *The Formative Years 1947–1950*, Alfred Goldberg, gen. ed. (Washington, D.C.: Historical Office of the Secretary of Defense, 1984), 12; and Steven T. Ross, *American War Plans, 1945–1950* (New York: Garland Publishing, 1988), 12.

3. Executive Office of the President, Office of Management and Budget, *Historical Tables Budget of the United States Government, Fiscal Year 1989* (Washington, D.C.: Government Printing Office [GPO], 1988), 39–40, 46–47.

4. For a more comprehensive interpretation of the origins of the Cold War, consult John Lewis Gaddis, *The United States and the Origins of the Cold War, 1941–1947* (New York: Columbia University Press, 1972); Idem, *Strategies of Containment*; Idem, *We Now Know: Rethinking Cold War History* (Oxford: Clarendon Press, 1997); George F. Kennan, *Memoirs 1925–1950* (Boston: Little, Brown & Co., 1967); Adam B. Ulam, *The Rivals: America and Russia Since World War II* (New York: Viking Press, 1971); and Walter LaFeber, *America, Russia, and the Cold War, 1945–1966* (New York: John Wiley & Sons, 1967).

5. Kennan, 557. The text of Kennan's "Long Telegram" is between pages 547–59.

6. Under the leadership of Ferdinand Eberstadt, the Navy plan emphasized governmentwide coordination of defense policy through a national security council and an independent intelligence agency. The military departments would remain separate entities, but would work together through the JCS, the World War II theater command system, and an array of interservice boards and committees. Rearden, 19–20, 142; Allan R. Millett and Peter Maslowski, *For the Common Defense: A Military History of the United States of America* (New York: Free Press, 1984), 479–80; and Idem, revised 1994, 503–5.

7. Rearden, 11–23.

8. *United States Strategic Bombing Survey (USSBS), Over-all Report (European War)* (hereafter *USSBS European War*), 30 September 1945, 107, in David MacIsaac, ed, *The United States Strategic Bombing Survey*, vol. 1 (New York: Garland Publishing, 1976; and *The United States Strategic Bombing Surveys*, reprinted (hereafter *USSBS* reprint) (Maxwell AFB, Ala.: Air University Press, 1987), 40.

9. *USSBS European War*, vol. 7, 26; and *USSBS* reprint, 106–7.

10. In September 1945, Gen Carl A. Spaatz had just returned from the Pacific where he commanded the strategic air campaign in the latter stage of the war. Slated to replace Arnold as the next commanding general of the AAF, Spaatz possessed unique qualifications to head this special assignment. During World War II, Spaatz commanded forces involved in joint, combined, strategic, and tactical operations in North Africa, Europe, Italy, and the Pacific. John T. Greenwood, "The Atomic Bomb—Early Air Force Thinking and the Strategic Air Force, August 1945–March 1946," *Aerospace Historian* 34 (fall/September 1987): 159.

11. Gen Carl A. Spaatz, "Spaatz Board Report," 23 October 1945, 1, file 5: AEC (Atomic Energy Commission) & Atomic Weapons, box 3, series 3, MS 39, Harry R. Borowski Papers (hereafter Borowski Papers), Special Collections, US Air Force Academy Cadet Library; quoted in Phillip S. Meilinger, *Hoyt S. Vandenberg: The Life of a General* (Bloomington: Indiana University Press, 1989), 63.

12. Borowski Papers.

13. Ibid., 8; and Greenwood, 161.

14. Borowski Papers, 8.

15. David Alan Rosenberg, "The Origins of Overkill: Nuclear Weapons and American Strategy, 1945–1960," in *Strategy and Nuclear Deterrence*, ed. Steven E. Miller (Princeton, N.J.: Princeton University Press, 1984), 129; and Rearden, 439.

16. American intelligence personnel assisted the British effort to break codes produced by the German Enigma cipher machine; others distributed the product, known as ULTRA intelligence; and another group analyzed Axis radio traffic, called the "Y-service" by the British. Although the official American term was *radio intelligence*, USAAF documents from World War II frequently adopted the British terminology. "Y-service" or "Y-intelligence" refers to low-grade encoded or plain-text radio communications. Sixty-eight Americans worked at Bletchley Park, the center of British code-breaking and communications intelligence activity. Alexander S. Cochran Jr., Robert C. Ehrhart, and John F. Kreis, "The Tools of Air Intelligence: ULTRA, MAGIC, Photographic Assessment, and the Y-Service," in *Piercing the Fog: Intelligence and Army Air Forces Operations in World War II,* gen. ed. John F. Kreis (Washington, D.C.: Air Force History and Museums Program, 1996), 94–95; and Meilinger, 68.

17. From September 1944 until the end of the war, the US Strategic Air Forces in Europe made a considerable effort to create a viable, stand-alone intelligence organization. The Directorate of Intelligence studied British organization and techniques in preparation for independent operations with some success, but American intelligence officers in Europe acknowledged the relative immaturity of the US organization. Maj Gen F. L. Anderson, deputy commander, operations to Maj Gen Barney M. Giles, chief of air staff, letter, 8 November 1944, file: USSTAF, D/Intel (Directorate of Intelligence), Organization, Carl A. Spaatz Papers (hereafter Spaatz Papers), Library of Congress, box 297; memorandum, subject: Conference Held in the Office of

Deputy Commander, Operations, USSTAF, 9 October 1944, file: USSTAF, D/Intel, Organization, Spaatz Papers; and memorandum, subject: Functions of the Office of the Director of Intelligence, n.d., file: USSTAF, D/Intel, Organization, Spaatz Papers.

18. Spaatz Papers, 4, 8; and Greenwood, 161.

19. Meilinger, 66.

20. Harry R. Borowski, *A Hollow Threat: Strategic Air Power and Containment before Korea* (Westport, Conn.: Greenwood Press, 1982), 32.

21. Headquarters SAC, Strategic Air Command Statistical Summary, vol. 1, no. 1, June 1946, 1, file no. 416.01, 21 March–31 December 1946, vol. 4, United States Air Force Historical Research Center (hereafter USAFHRC), Maxwell AFB, Ala. (hereafter SAC Statistical Summary).

22. Headquarters AAF, AAF Regulation no. 20-20, *Organization: Strategic Air Command*, 10 October 1946, quoted in SAC Statistical Summary, vol. 1, no. 4, 1 November 1946, file no. 416.01, 21 March–31 December 1946, vol. 4.

23. SAC Statistical Summary, vol. 1, no. 6, 1 January 1947; and Borowski, *Hollow Threat*, 30.

24. Borowski, *Hollow Threat*, 45.

25. In March 1946, the AAF considered B-29s very heavy bombers (VHB) and B-17s and B-24s heavy bombers. With the introduction of new aircraft in 1947–1948, the categories changed. The massive B-36 was considered a VHB, B-50s and B-29s became heavy bombers, and the few remaining B-24s and B-17s were classified medium bombers. SAC Statistical Summary, 2, 1 January 1947.

26. Ibid. The F-13 consisted of a B-29 airframe modified during assembly to accommodate cameras. In 1948 the Air Force redesignated the aircraft as an RB-29. The decline in reconnaissance capability is shown below.

SAC Reconnaissance and Liaison Aircraft, 1946

Mar	Apr	May	Jun	Jul	Aug	Sep	Oct	Nov	Dec
191	116	96	80	67	65	65	62	58	53

27. Historian Strategic Air Command (hereafter Historian SAC), Strategic Air Command 1946: Organization, Mission, Training and Personnel, vol. 1, Text (n.p., April 1948), 66, file no. 416.01, vol. 1, 21 March–31 December 1946, USAFHRC, Maxwell AFB, Ala.

28. Borowski, *Hollow Threat*, 39.

29. In essence, during this period SAC trained and operated under peacetime conditions and lacked the capability to fly arduous combat sorties. The official SAC history attributes the shortcoming to "the floodgates of demobilization," but historian Harry R. Borowski blames misguided leadership. Historian SAC, 66; and Borowski, *Hollow Threat*, 36–48.

30. For a description of JCS thinking about the Soviet Union in the latter stages of World War II, see Ross, 4–6. In addition, the *Pincher* plans consisted of a number of documents, including; Joint Planning Staff (JPS) 789, *Concept of Operations for "PINCHER,"* 2 March 1946; JPS 789/1, *Staff Studies of Certain Military Problems Deriving from "Concept of Operations for 'PINCHER,'"* 13 April 1946; Joint War Planning Committee (JWPC) 432/3, *Joint Basic Outline War Plan* (short title *Pincher*), 27 April 1946; JWPC 432/7, *Tentative Over-all Strategic Concept and Estimate of Initial Operations* (short title *Pincher*), 18 June 1946; and JWPC 458/1, *Preparation of Joint Plan "Broadview,"* 5 August 1946. For a reproduction of these documents in facsimile form, see Steven T. Ross and David Alan Rosenberg, eds., *America's Plans for War Against the Soviet Union, 1945–1950,* vol. 2, *The Pincher Plans* (New York: Garland Publishing, 1989).

31. Ross and Rosenberg, 25–49.

32. JPS 789, encl. B, 4, in Ross and Rosenberg, vol. 2.

33. The Joint Staff planners' reasoning shows more wishful thinking than analysis. In 1947 would Britain really declare war on the Soviet Union over Turkey and a threat to the Suez Canal? Did the British have the resources or the will to fight following the destruction of World War II? Perhaps the initial scenario paid homage to America's traditional reluctance to enter *foreign wars.* Regardless, the plans reflect the lack of political guidance received by the military from the Truman administration. JPS 789, encl. B, 6, Ross and Rosenberg, vol. 2.

34. Ibid.; and JWPC 432/3, encl. B, 3, in Ross and Rosenberg, vol. 2. (All other citations of Pincher documents cited are found in the Ross and Rosenberg facsimile collection, *America's Plans for War,* vol. 2.)

35. JPS 789, encl. B, 8.

36. Ibid., 14.

37. Ibid., 15–16.

38. Ibid., 3.

39. Ibid., 16.

40. JPS 789, annex A to encl. B, 23; JWPC 432/3, app. to encl. B, 17. The estimated breakdown of Soviet army forces follows.

Estimated Breakdown of Soviet Army Forces

70 rifle divisions	840,000
5 mountain divisions	60,000
5 airborne divisions	50,000
20 tank and mechanized corps	240,000
5 cavalry corps	75,000
8 artillery divisions	96,000
independent units, garrisons	200,000
113 combat divisions	1,561,000
overhead, services, schools, and training	1,250,000
NKVD (border guards and troops)	500,000
Total	3,311,000

41. JPS 789, annex A to encl. B, 25. Pincher listed Soviet air force strength as follows.

Soviet Air Force Strength

Source	Fighters	Bombers	Ground Attack	Total
Obsolescent	400	1,000		
New Soviet Types	15,000	7,000		
Lend-Lease	1,600	1,500		
Total Combat Aircraft	17,000	9,500	9,000	35,500
Trainers				12,000
Transports				2,500
*Total Aircraft				50,000

*Of this total, only 20,000 were in tactical units; 15,500 were in training units and stored reserves. The total included 3,800 naval aircraft.

42. JWPC 432/3, app. to encl. B, 17.

43. In JPS 789 planners estimated the Soviets could complete the abstract research for atomic energy within two years. Three additional years would be required to design and construct the mining, power, transportation, and manufacturing facilities needed for weapons production. By JWPC 432/7, the JCS considered it unlikely that the Soviets would be able to develop an atomic device before 1948, and it might take until 1956. In turn, the planners predicted that the Soviets would not be able to produce atomic energy by June 1949 although they might be capable of producing weapons based upon radioactive dust or gas. JPS 789, annex A to encl. B, 28; JWPC 432/7, annex A to app. A to encl. B, 29.

44. JWPC 432/3, app. to encl. B, 18.

45. The Pincher documents do not specify the information to be collated. In all probability, they refer to captured German intelligence archives, including aerial photographs and interviews with former prisoners of war. JPS 789/1, app. B, 19.

46. Ibid.

47. Annex A to app. B lists the urban industrial concentrations: Moscow, Gorki (Gorky), Kuibyshev (Samara), Sverdlovsk, Novosibirsk (Novo Sibirsk), Omsk, Saratov, Kazan, Leningrad, Baku, Tashkent, Chelyabinsk, Nizhni Tagil, Magnitogorsk, Molotov, Tbilisi (Tiffis), Stalinsk, Grozny, Irkutsk, Yaroslavl, Dnepropetrovsk, Stalino (Stalin), Khabarovsk, Vladivostok, Ufa,

Chkalov (Orenburg), Kirov, Kemerovo, Komsomolsk, and Zlatoust. JPS 789/1, app. B, 20 and 31–33.

48. Ibid., 39; MacIsaac, *USBBS Over-all Report (European War)*, vol. 1; and Dr. James Lowe, "Intelligence Basis for Selecting Strategic Target Systems," address to Air War College, 13 December 1946, 1–2, file no. K239.716246-22, 13 December 1946, USAFHRC.

49. MacIsaac *USSBS*, vol. 7; *USSBS* reprint, 117; and Lowe, 1–2.

50. Hired in November 1940, Dr. James T. Lowe was one of the most respected and experienced civilian air intelligence analysts. He worked in the Strategic Vulnerability Branch of the Air Staff's Intelligence Directorate. Lowe, 15; and Kreis, 41.

51. This concept evolved into the *blunting* strikes called for by later war plans. Lowe, 6.

52. Ibid., 3.

53. "Japanese-American Friction over 'Wringer' Program," in Far East Air Force Historical Report, Development of Far East Air Force's Intelligence Collection Plan, November 1953, 44, file no. K-720.02, box 4, USAFHRC.

54. Rosenberg, 125. For an early attempt to gather information on the Soviet army, see Harry A. Jacobs, "Operation Strakonice: In Pursuit of the Soviet Order of Battle," *Journal of Military History* 65 (April 2001): 391–400.

55. Harold A. Schwandt, "Camera Equipment for Reconnaissance over Unmapped Areas," Research Paper (Maxwell AFB, Ala.: Air Command and Staff College, May 1949), 2, file no. 239.04349A-385, USAFHRC.

56. History, 55th Strategic Reconnaissance Wing (hereafter 55th SRW) (M), Forbes AFB, Topeka, Kans., March 1953, iii, file no. KG-WG-55-HI, February 1953, USAFHRC.

57. Commanding general, SAC, to commanding general, AAF, letter, subject: Operational and Administrative Control of the 311th Reconnaissance Wing and Its Assigned Units, 15 August 1946, file no. 416.01, vol. 2, 21 March–31 December 1946, USAFHRC.

58. Ibid.

59. Maj Gen I. H. Edwards, US Army Headquarters, USAFE, office of the commanding general to the commanding general, AAF, letter, subject: British Cooperation on Post Hostilities Mapping Program, Europe, 25 April 1946, Top Secret (TS) control no. ABI-294, file no. ABI-201-400, box 37, entry 214, Records Group 341, Modern Military Branch, National Archives, Washington, D.C. (hereafter RG 341, NA). Document is now declassified.

60. Ibid.

61. The series of documents outlining the program did not mention aerial photography of the Soviet Union. Because of the potential political ramifications, even at this early date, I believe this omission indicates that photomapping of the Soviet Union did not occur. Col E. P. Mussett, chief, Plans and Policy Branch, Executive Division, AC/AS-2, memorandum for record, subject: Daily Activity Report, n.d., ABI-150, file no. ABI 1-200, box 37, entry 214, RG 341, NA.

62. Historian SAC, vol. 1, *Text* (n.p.: April 1948), 153–54, file no. 416.01, vol. 1, 21 March 1946–31 December 1946.

63. In June 1946, the 311th Wing consisted of the First, Third, 12th, 16th, and 91st Reconnaissance Squadrons and the 7th Geodetic Control Squadron. By September 1946, the AAF detached the First, Third, 12th, and 91st squadrons. Commanding general SAC to commanding general, AAF, letter, subject: Operational and Administrative Control of the 311th Wing, 15 August 1946, file no. 416.01, vol. 2, 21 March 1946–31 December 1946, US-AFHRC.

64. Dr. George Rappaport, interviewed by Alfred Price and Armand J. Morin, fall 1981, file 14, Association of Old Crows Archive (hereafter AOC).

65. Historian SAC, 154; and Col Hugh Winter, USAF, retired, interviewed by Frank Voltaggio and Alfred Price, AOC Archive, 29 August 1980, 15, file 47.

66. Ingwald Haugen, Lt Col, USAF, retired, interviewed by Alfred Price, n.d., 4–5, file no. 25, Col I. Haugen, AOC Archive.

67. Both Filios and Monjar were trained as RCM Radar Observers, military occupational specialty 7888 or commonly referred to as MOS, during World War II. H. C. Monjar to Frank Voltaggio, letter, 10 June 1982, 4, file no. 59, Lt Col H. Monjar, AOC Archive.

68. This equipment included AN/APR-4 and AN/APR-5 search receivers, AN/APA-10 and AN/APA-11 pulse analyzers, a Hewlett-Packard audio oscillator, an associated pulse repetition frequency (PRF) analyzer, and an ink-on-tape recorder. Frank Voltaggio, "Out in the Cold . . . Early ELINT Activities of the Strategic Air Command," 6, file no. Voltaggio, AOC Archive.

69. Ibid., 4–5.

70. Against the background of a Yugoslav-Italian dispute over Trieste, Anglo-American occupation forces faced Yugoslav troops. On 19 August 1946, Yugoslav forces shot down another C-47, which created an international incident. Dean Acheson, *Present at the Creation: My Years at the State Department* (New York: W. W. Norton & Co., 1969), 194–96.

71. Haugen interview, 4–5.

72. Ibid., 5.

73. Ibid., 5–6.

Chapter 3

From Containment to Berlin: Organizational Steps to Fill Intelligence Gaps, 1947–1948

It is sufficient to estimate the enemy situation correctly and to concentrate your strength to capture him. There is no more to it than this. He who lacks foresight and underestimates his enemy will surely be captured by him.

—General Ts'ao Ts'ao
The Art of War

During the time between the president's announcement of the Truman Doctrine in March 1947 and the Berlin crisis in the summer of 1948, international events contributed to a growing awareness of the Soviet threat and American military weakness. From an American perspective, increased Soviet intransigence with regard to Eastern Europe, Soviet encroachment in Turkey, and civil wars in Greece and China signified the spread of communism. In terms of military preparedness, the United States suffered from the constraints imposed by reduced budgets and a public unwilling to sacrifice for defense. The context of domestic politics remained the same while international political crises were growing in intensity; the future would bring the full specter of the Cold War. Strategic reconnaissance evolved during this time frame from relative neglect to a regularized bureaucratic organization of vital interest to policy makers. Despite major advances, reconnaissance proved unable to overcome technological hurdles and provide the target information necessary for strategic planning. Consequently, strategic war plans reflected a profound change in doctrine. In Joint Emergency War Plan Broiler, the JCS continued their reliance on strategic air war, but the doctrinal basis for the plans shifted from precision bombardment to an atomic area bombing campaign. A lack of specific target information played an important role in this doctrinal transformation, although the perception of American military weakness played an even greater role. By the outbreak of the

Berlin crisis, the United States faced a lack of strategic intelligence that compounded its shortages of men and equipment. Moreover, the Berlin crisis awakened policy makers to the genuine possibility of war with the Soviet Union.

Even though the United States lacked the means to assess the specific Soviet military threat, many Americans grasped the growing political menace of communism. By July 1947, US foreign policy adopted the tenets of George F. Kennan's concept of containment. Calling for a "long-term, patient but firm and vigilant containment of Russian expansive tendencies," Kennan's policy considered the Soviet Union as primarily a political threat, not a military one.[1] Confronted by an immense rebuilding effort to repair war damage, the Soviet economy and the Russian people were in no condition to start another war in the near future.[2] However, Soviet involvement in the communist takeover of governments of Eastern Europe; communist agitation in France, Italy, and other governments in Western Europe; and communist leadership in nationalist movements active in European colonial empires presented alarming challenges. Therefore, the Truman administration concentrated upon the economic challenge of a devastated Europe.[3] The assumptions of containment presented American military leaders with a double-edged sword. On one edge was the need to rebuild European economies while preserving American economic health dictating a reduced national defense budget. The other edge faced the huge armed forces maintained by the Soviet Union.

Airmen backed strategic air warfare and the atomic bomb as the solution to the problem. Simultaneously, airpower advocates in the military, Congress, and the media pushed for the creation of an independent air force as the organizational vehicle to best implement the new *air-atomic* strategy. On 26 July 1947, the National Defense Act of 1947 created the United States Air Force (USAF). Despite years of propaganda and lobbying, the Air Force struggled to adapt to its newfound status. In practical terms, independence meant administrative overload, lost specialists (many remained in the Army), and personnel turnover as the new organizational structure formed.[4] Thus, a mountain of administrative details absorbed the new organization at the same time international hostility increased.

Influenced by growing political turmoil, Air Intelligence focused on the Soviet military threat related to strategic bombing. Although intelligence reports considered the outbreak of war unlikely, they acknowledged the risk of miscalculation. Of greater concern, a Headquarters AAF Air Intelligence report from June 1947 identified two significant trends: (1) indications of indigenous production of advanced electronic equipment and (2) the appearance of significant numbers of new jet fighters of native design.[5] Air Intelligence warned against underestimating the enemy based upon perceptions of Russian backwardness.[6] By November 1947, Air Force Intelligence passed reports of possible Soviet atomic energy facilities near the Lake Baikal area of Siberia and the Uzbek-Kazakh area of Central Asia.[7] In addition, intelligence briefs from September 1948 warned of increased Soviet testing of guided missiles in the Arctic, the sighting of Soviet B-29-type bombers, and Soviet exploitation of German technology to produce jet engines.[8] In sum, preliminary Air Intelligence reports pointed to an enemy with significant technological potential.

In the case of Strategic Air Command, the creation of an independent Air Force solved few problems. During 1947 the command continued to rebuild by reorganizing units, training individuals to form efficient combat crews and competent support teams, and filling personnel shortages.[9] In an effort to economize, General McMullen established reduced officer manning levels for SAC. He reasoned that using rated officers for both flying duty and administrative positions would develop career officers with broad experience.[10] Although McMullen's plan appeared sound on paper, assigning significant administrative duties to inexperienced flyers resulted in disaster. Overburdened, demoralized flight crews failed to achieve the desired proficiency levels in either area. Despite these personnel problems, SAC viewed the arrival of new B-50 and B-36 bombers in 1948 as a sign of hope. Although SAC's bomber force reached 530 aircraft by the end of 1948, personnel shortages and managerial errors sapped the command of combat effectiveness.[11] The creation of an independent Air Force did not prove a panacea for SAC's problems.

Considered a second-priority mission by the SAC bomber force, strategic aerial reconnaissance reached a nadir during the transition to Air Force independence. SAC's aircraft inventory reflected a continued decline in SAC reconnaissance aircraft—below the low level of 1946. The 55 SAC reconnaissance planes of January 1947 declined to 24 by September 1947.[12] Additionally, General McMullen's manning policies capped reconnaissance personnel strength at minimal levels.[13] Although aircraft strength improved in 1948, aerial reconnaissance continued as a peripheral concern for SAC and the independent Air Force.

During 1948, commanders at SAC and Headquarters Air Force raised the questions eventually leading to the formal establishment of a peacetime aerial reconnaissance program. Upon his return from Operation Sandstone nuclear tests in June 1948, Brig Gen Paul T. Cullen, commander of SAC's 311th Air Division, recommended a study of reconnaissance by SAC Headquarters.[14] With the rapid development of atomic and biological weapons, Cullen believed the reconnaissance techniques of World War II no longer sufficed in the *atomic age*. Modern warfare did not permit the development of tactics and equipment during a war's early stages. According to General Cullen, operations analysts and other experts must study the "tactics, techniques, operations, and tools of reconnaissance."[15] He also suggested the study of motion picture, high-speed recording equipment, atomic photography, and other technologies to produce systems capable of fulfilling wartime demands.[16]

When no action appeared by September 1948, General Cullen backed his position emphatically by stating, "I am enclosing a copy of my original letter and once more would like to recommend that a vigorous program be initiated immediately. I think our reconnaissance techniques are antiquated, I think our equipment is inadequate and insufficient, but I hesitate to make positive recommendations regarding new equipment without analysis of the entire field."[17] Furthermore, Cullen proposed the use of ultraviolet and infrared rays to gather information either as independent methods or in conjunction with conventional photography. He also speculated that television might enhance night photography. Regardless of the validity of these ideas, Cullen argued for SAC's guidance

Maj Gen Earle E. "Pat" Partridge, director of training and requirements, Air Staff, urged a fundamental rethinking of strategic aerial reconnaissance in January 1948.

Maj Gen George C. McDonald served as director of Intelligence, Headquarters USAF, until May 1948 and is responsible for having organized strategic aerial reconnaissance.

in analyzing reconnaissance: "This, I believe, is recognized by the various agencies of your [*McMullen's SAC*] Headquarters but very little specific action or thought seems to be taking place. Frankly this disturbs me a great deal."[18]

Joining Cullen's critique of SAC's reconnaissance concepts, General Partridge, director of training and requirements, urged a fundamental rethinking of strategic aerial reconnaissance. In a memorandum to Maj Gen George C. McDonald, director of Air Force Intelligence, Partridge observed, "The scope of the reconnaissance needed to carry out atomic bomb attacks in Russia staggers my imagination. Some means must be devised to narrow this field to the point where a reasonable number of missions can accomplish the objectives." Partridge disputed the Air Force decision to extend World War II methods by gradual technical improvements. Instead, he suggested that long-range daylight photographic missions in good weather might prove impossible. Enemy fighter opposition and the present inability to forecast weather threatened existing reconnaissance methods. Moreover, he raised three penetrating questions:

1. Are we right in sticking to a plan for photographing our targets in daytime? As you know, the Russian winter provides little useable [*sic*] photographic weather.

2. Should we go entirely to radar scope photography and to radar mapping for location of targets? Our experts agree that visual bombing at high altitudes at high speed is practically out. Maybe we should concentrate on improvement of our radar so that accurate mapping can be done by that method alone.

3. Should we change our bombardment doctrine so that every atomic bomb mission will be a search attack?[19]

Partridge observed that the Air Force was spending hundreds of millions of dollars on individual items of equipment without a comprehensive plan to employ them. In response to General Partridge's questions and comments, the Air Staff surveyed Air Force reconnaissance.

As a first step in developing an Air Force strategic reconnaissance plan, the Air Staff assessed the current state of strategic intelligence. The study concluded that target photography from World War II German sources existed for areas south and west of the line marked by Leningrad-Kazan-Astrakhan-Baku. Unfortunately, coverage of the remainder of the Soviet Union remained sparse. At current levels of technology, radar mapping did not provide sufficient image definition for targeting, and the survey did not anticipate radar's use for basic intelligence collection in the near future.[20] Although the survey offered no solutions, it joined Cullen and Partridge in defining the reconnaissance problem.

Air Force aerial reconnaissance lacked direction until mid-1948. Concerned with acquiring desperately needed information, theater commanders adopted ad hoc collection efforts.[21] Although the Directorate of Intelligence Headquarters Air Force was in charge theoretically, in practice intelligence collection remained decentralized. Therefore, Cullen's appeal for a reconnaissance study and Partridge's critique of existing reconnaissance concepts sparked an effort to organize Air Force reconnaissance.

Prompted by Cullen and Partridge, a series of policy letters established formal requirements for Air Force strategic intelligence.[22] On 28 January 1948, General McDonald presented a brief on strategic reconnaissance operations, "which must be executed before the Air Force can undertake successful air operations against the enemy."[23] Titled *Requirements for Strategic Reconnaissance of the U.S.S.R. and Satellite States*, the brief outlined requirements for photographic and electronic intelligence and identified the priority targets for photographic coverage. The document stressed photographic intelligence for selecting and evaluating strategic target systems and for preparing strategic target material for operational units.[24] In addition, the plan called for electronic reconnaissance to "determine the exact location, density, and effectiveness of early warning nets of radar or other electromagnetic character" and to investigate radio transmissions that might be used to control guided missiles or pilotless aircraft.[25] Air Intelligence established the following list of areas for photoreconnaissance (in priority order):

a. Industrial area of the Urals (no cover at present) [original annotations in report].

b. Industrial area of Kuznetsk Basin (no cover at present).

c. Industrial areas of Dnepr and Don Basins (1941–43 cover now available).

d. Central industrial region (centered about Moskva 1941–45 cover now available).

e. Stalingrad-Kuybyshev [*sic*] Industrial Area (1941–43 cover now available).

f. Leningrad industrial area (1941–43 cover now available).

g. Industrial Area of Fergana Valley in Uzbek [Autonomous Soviet Socialist Republic] A.S.S.R. and Kirgis [Soviet Socialist Republic] S.S.R. (no cover at present).

h. Petroleum areas of Caucasus and Caspian (1941–45 cover now available).

i. Khabarovsk-Vladivostok area (no cover at present).

j. Uncovered strips of the Trans Siberian Railway.

k. Industrial areas of Karaganda (no cover at present).

l. Industrial area of Alma Ata, Kazakhstan (no cover at present).

m. Industrial areas of Western White Russian S.S.R. (1941–45 cover now available).

n. Northern regions, including Arkhangelsk, Kola Peninsula, and Pechora Valley (spotty 1941–43 cover at present).

o. Industrial area of Magadan in eastern Siberia (no cover at present).[26]

Ideally, photographic reconnaissance would provide coverage at a minimum scale of 1:10,000 for principal industrial cities and 1:20,000 for major rail lines.[27] The brief also directed electronic reconnaissance around the perimeter of the Union of Soviet Socialist Republics (USSR), satellite states, and in the vicinity of strategic industrial and population centers. The report cited the Russo-European landmass and the maritime areas of the Far East between Korea and the Bering Strait as areas of greatest interest.[28] By establishing formal intelligence requirements, Headquarters USAF provided missing guidance and direction from previous intelligence efforts. In addition, the articulation of intelligence requirements focused Air Force thinking on the capabilities and needs for reconnaissance. By addressing these issues, the Air Force established the vital first link in the intelligence cycle.[29]

The Soviet Union's emergence as a potential military threat prompted SAC's interest in potential surprise attack. General Kenney, SAC commander, worried about the Soviet atomic potential. Disagreeing with earlier AAF assessments, he viewed the atomic bomb as the decisive weapon.

> When we consider that 100 atom bombs will release more foot pounds of energy than all the TNT bombs released by all the belligerents of World War II combined . . . and that that effort could be put down in a single attack, it is evident that the long drawn out war is out of date. When it is further considered that probably 80 percent of World War II's bombs were wasted, 100 atomic bombs would cause at least four times the destruction. No nation, including our own, could survive such a blow.[30]

Kenney's strategic concept emphasized a *short destructive war* that would be over in a few days. He considered the bombing of targets that would affect enemy production in a few months to be "meaningless." Kenney's SAC regarded the advantage gained by a surprise attack as "so great that it can almost be considered decisive. I believe this should be studied, analyzed, and discussed far more than we are doing today."[31] As a result, SAC focused on the vast, uninhabited expanse of the Arctic as offering the greatest potential for surprise attack. Whether as a route for SAC bombers or as an avenue for a Soviet atomic strike upon the United States, the potential for surprise directed SAC's attention to transpolar operations.

Aerial reconnaissance played a vital role in transforming polar operations from theory to reality. Before SAC bombers could use Arctic routes, reconnaissance aircraft had to overcome formidable challenges. First, navigators faced tremendous obstacles in the combination of vast uncharted areas, featureless terrain, magnetic disturbances, and celestial anomalies.[32] As a result, the 46th Reconnaissance Squadron deployed to Ladd Field, near Fairbanks, Alaska, to explore and map the Arctic.

From August 1946 until September 1948, SAC reconnaissance aircraft tested the feasibility of transpolar operations. Before the deployment, little was known about Arctic flying except for the perils of a small band of early aviators who braved the elements in open-cockpit planes. Following World War II, the research and development branch of the War Department general staff initiated Project No. 5 to explore the frozen North. Approved by both General Spaatz, chief of Air Staff, and Gen Dwight D. Eisenhower, Army chief of staff, instructions were given by the Air Staff to SAC to accomplish the photomapping and electronic reconnaissance required.[33]

Under the auspices of Project No. 5, the 46th Reconnaissance Squadron solved many of the navigational problems involved with Arctic flying. Originally composed of aircraft and crews assigned to SAC, the 46th Reconnaissance Squadron conducted the most ambitious photomapping projects to date.

In Operation Floodlight, reconnaissance crews searched uncharted Arctic waters for new landmasses for possible future bases or weather stations (fig. 2). Sorties from Ladd AFB attempted to map area A (between 160 and 180 degrees east longitude and 73 and 77 degrees north latitude), area B (north and east of area A), area C (the route between Alaska and Iceland), and area D (the area between 85 degrees north latitude and the

From August 1946 until September 1948, crews from the 46th and 72d Reconnaissance Squadrons tested the feasibility of polar flight operations, solved significant Arctic navigational problems, and conducted the most ambitious photomapping operations to date.

Personnel from the 72d Reconnaissance Squadron clad in cold-weather gear. Early reconnaissance crews and maintenance personnel braved temperatures as low as -50° F.

North Pole, except for a portion of northeast Greenland).[34] As a result of Floodlight, the F-9s of the 46th Reconnaissance Squadron discovered "Target X," a floating ice mass roughly 14 by 17 miles in size, which provided considerable oceanographic information about the Arctic.[35] Reconnaissance crews also established scheduled air service between Ladd Field and Iceland in Operation Polaris.[36] By May 1947 SAC had added Operation Eardrum, the trimetrogon photomapping of Greenland, to the tasks of aerial reconnaissance.[37] In each of these projects, reconnaissance crews gathered weather data, searched for potential emergency landing fields, recorded magnetic and electronic phenomenas, and experimented with various navigational techniques.[38] By September 1948, the 46th and 72d Reconnaissance Squadron had flown 103 missions, 1,500 flying hours that included 17 flights over the North Pole, and explored 829,000 square miles of the North Polar ice cap. Although perhaps less

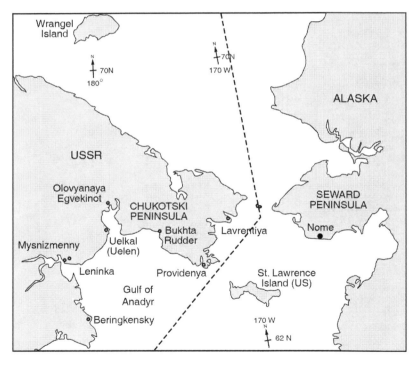

Figure 2. Alaska and the Chukotski Peninsula

heralded, Project No. 5 also involved 12 air aborts, 43 ground aborts, two crashes, and three fatalities.[39]

Of equal importance to Arctic exploration, two additional reconnaissance projects sought photographic information on the Soviet threat. In Project No. 20, aircraft flew surveillance missions twice a month from Point Barrow, Alaska, to the tip of the Aleutian Islands by way of the Bering Strait. During the missions, crews photographed any unusual object or activity for intelligence purposes.[40] Moreover, Project No. 23 combined ELINT and photography, utilizing two aircraft flying each mission along the Siberian coast adjacent to Alaska. One aircraft flew at high altitude "directly over the coastline" while the second plane flew a parallel course several miles out to sea. Although the primary electronic intelligence mission gathered valuable radar information, the oblique photos from K-20 aerial cameras provided poor pictures and little usable information.[41]

Adding to the frustration caused by poor long-range photography, a Project No. 23 sortie caused a Soviet diplomatic protest, illustrating the political limitations of aerial reconnaissance. On 5 January 1948, the Soviets protested the USAF reconnaissance activity in the Arctic with the following note:

> The Embassy of the Union of Soviet Socialist Republics presents its compliments to the Department of State and has the honor to communicate the following: On December 23, 1947 at 14 hours and 15 minutes an American airplane violated the Soviet frontier in the region of Cape Chukotsk, flying for about seven miles along the coast of the Chukotsk Peninsula at a distance two miles from the shore. In communicating the foregoing, the Embassy, upon instructions of the Soviet Government, requests that the case under reference of a violation of the Soviet frontier by an American airplane be investigated and that measures be taken not to permit such violations in the future.[42]

The US Department of State asked the Air Force for an explanation. Project officers at the Air Staff traced the violation to Project No. 23, Mission No. 7 M 263A. In conjunction with the Alaskan Air Command (AAC), the investigation revealed that the aircraft violated a restriction mandated by the Department of State of flights closer than 12 miles to Soviet territory. However, no means existed to determine whether the plane had violated the Soviet frontier as alleged.[43] Nevertheless, the incident revealed the Soviet radar's ability to track peripheral Ferret flights. Although the Soviet protest resulted in political embarrassment for the United States and the Air Force, it also foreshadowed future trouble over strategic aerial reconnaissance.

The early Arctic reconnaissance missions proved valuable both for their significant accomplishments and for revealing limits to aerial activity in northern regions. Throughout the period, aerial reconnaissance missions collected data that added to basic scientific and geographic knowledge of the Arctic. In addition, Air Force personnel pioneered cold-weather operations. Encountering severe obstacles posed by extreme temperatures, nonexistent weather forecasts, long periods of twilight that hindered celestial navigation, and other problems, the crews tackled the most difficult flying conditions imaginable.[44] In addition to the above, psychological stresses taxed the aircrews. In 1947 the flight surgeon of the 28th Bombardment Group (assigned to Ladd AFB) noted marked deterioration in the morale and performance of the aircrews:

> It is not believed that the extreme cold itself increased the mental stress and strain of our flying crews; however, the types of terrain over which they were flying did. The terrain being vast, uncharted, very sparsely populated, with inherent navigational difficulties plus overwater flying and frequent icing conditions increased the stress of flying in Alaska. Survival in some areas would be impossible for long periods of time. The crews had very little confidence in the adequacy of Air-Sea rescue.[45]

Finally, Arctic weather conditions set absolute limits to polar flying. Following a January 1947 crash in a takeoff attempt at minus 50 degrees Fahrenheit, AAC restricted flying operations for temperatures below minus 35 degrees Fahrenheit.[46] SAC valued the vast amount of information gathered by its reconnaissance crews in the Arctic, but the Alaskan experience demonstrated the sobering limits to Air Force capability. One report concluded that "one of the large lessons learned in this winter's operations in Alaska is that AAF knows how to operate aircraft in flight at any temperature, but it does not know how to preserve and maintain aircraft on the ground at extreme temperatures with limited facilities."[47]

If the photomapping sorties sought information basic to the Arctic operations, SAC polar Ferrets explored the unknown capabilities of Soviet Arctic defenses. Following the SAC B-17 Ferret failure over Greenland in August 1946, Capt Lester E. Manbeck coordinated the modification of a B-29 for ELINT purposes. Later in the year, Captain Manbeck arranged for Mr. Jim Scott and Capt Robert R. Perry to prepare a B-29 Ferret for January 1947.

The first B-29 Ferret represented a significant technological advance over the previous *jury-rigged* aircraft. In addition to the increased range of the B-29, the new Ferret included equipment able to span a wider portion of the electronic spectrum. To accommodate the added electronics, technicians removed the B-29's guns and converted the rear pressurized section to an electronic intercept station. The conversion also transformed the bomb bay into additional fuel storage tanks.[48] The ELINT B-29 featured a 13-man crew, two pilots, three navigators, six Ravens, a radio operator, and a flight engineer.[49] The Raven crew consisted of three positions operating search and analysis equipment and three positions dedicated to D/F.[50] Captain Perry worked with Mr. Scott and the Wright Air Development Center team to enhance the human factor layout of the equipment (placing equipment within reach of the operator).[51]

Before deploying to Alaska, the ELINT B-29 crew trained at Wright Field, Dayton, Ohio, for Ferret operations. Under the command of Capt Landon Tanner, command pilot, and Capt Robert R. Perry, senior Raven, the crew flew familiarization sorties over Ohio. The Ravens operated their search receivers to intercept radars and analyze their frequency, pulse repetition frequency (PRF), pulse length, scan rate, and other characteristics. Furthermore, the new Ravens learned to take D/F bearings, plotting them with the assistance of the navigators.[52] By March 1947 the crew had proceeded to Andrews AFB, Maryland, where Maj John A. Guyton of the AAF's Research and Development branch explained that their mission would be to fly long-range Ferret missions north of Siberia.[53] Following this briefing, the ELINT B-29 with full crew proceeded to

Ladd AFB. Captain Perry explained that the vagueness of their assigned task complicated mission planning:

> My orders were explicit enough in giving us first priority on fuel, maintenance and support at all USAAF bases world-wide, but vague enough to allow us to file a clearance and fly anywhere in the world we wanted to go. Now this may seem funny, but I never got a briefing on what they wanted us specifically to do in Alaska. Maybe somebody else did, but I never got one, and I was the project officer. . . . Nobody gave me a briefing on what was where or what they wanted or anything. They just said "Go and see what radars are there."[54]

Officially designated "B-29 No. 812," and nicknamed *Sitting Duck* by its crew, the B-29 Ferret probed the Siberian coast for signs of Soviet radar. From 11 June to 21 August 1947, the *Sitting Duck* flew nine reconnaissance sorties, first along the northern coast of Siberia and then along the southern edge.[55] Before the Ferret flights, the Air Force had no information on Soviet radars in this area. After the B-29 Ferret exploration, the crew uncovered a chain of scattered Soviet RUS-2 early warning radars along the southern periphery of the Soviet Far East and the absence of Soviet radars along the USSR's Arctic coast.[56] In addition, the plane's navigators discovered the existence of three uncharted ice islands. According to Captain Perry, the crew inadvertently drifted into Soviet territory on one sortie as described here:

> On one of those missions we were supposed to make a little dip into Anadyr Bay, which is a big bay maybe 120 miles wide and 120 miles deep . . . we were just supposed to make a little "V" into it. All of a sudden I looked at the radar and I called up Kelly (the radar navigator). I said, "Kelly we're over land!" He says, "I know it." I said, "Why don't we get the hell out of here?" I said, "Flanagan (1st navigator), what the hell are we doing?" Flanagan said, "Well, we've hit a reverse jet stream and we're trying to get out. It's carried us inland about 50 miles and we're making about 20 knots ground speed trying to get out."[57]

Eventually, Headquarters USAF passed instructions to the commanding general of AAC prohibiting flights closer than 15 miles to Soviet territory.[58]

The Alaskan reconnaissance sorties demonstrated the value of the B-29 Ferret. The aircraft's long range allowed coverage of the vast distances encountered in the Arctic and northern Pacific, and the data gained by the ELINT crew established the initial EOB for the Soviet Far East.[59] The flights revealed weaknesses in Soviet radar defenses along the Arctic Circle. As polar flying experience and advances in navigation technology reduced the uncertainty of Arctic operations, Alaskan reconnaissance operations confirmed the validity of polar routing for SAC's new long-range B-50 and B-36 bombers.

Like the Alaskan sorties, European Ferret flights gathered information of interest to Air Force planners. During the first half of 1947, periodic B-17 Ferret flights ranged from the Baltic Sea to the southern tip of Greece in order to expand the radar information collected

Lt Gen Curtis E. LeMay played an important role in early aerial reconnaissance, first as USAFE commander during the Berlin airlift and then as SAC commander.

the previous year. The Ferrets identified nine new radar stations and two guided missile launching sites in Yugoslavia and observed 8,000-foot runways on Gotland Island in the Baltic.[60] Although of intelligence interest, the latter information revealed flaws in the collation and dissemination of Air Force intelligence data. On 23 July 1947, Maj Gen George C. McDonald, assistant chief of Air Staff for Intelligence, dispatched a blistering memorandum that demanded the prompt reporting of Ferret results.[61] Additionally, McDonald instructed that photographic equipment be installed on RCM aircraft if space permitted.[62] A cable from General Spaatz to General LeMay, commanding general of USAFE, suggested that photoreconnaissance aircraft should follow-up Ferret sightings. Both McDonald and Spaatz expressed dismay that no photographs were taken of the Gotland Island runways. Nevertheless, General Spaatz emphasized that the primary mission of the Ferret "should not be curtailed for photos as all material being received from this project is vital. . . . Results so far are considered very good, and continued operations to the fullest extent is urged as dictated by existing flying restrictions, rules and regulations and safety factor[s] for both personnel and equipment."[63]

Whereas flights over the Arctic involved only the United States and the Soviet Union, reconnaissance missions in Europe raised complex diplomatic issues. The potential for international incidents involving Ferret aircraft caused the Air Force to coordinate flights with the State Department. In July 1947, the State Department sanctioned three sorties over the Baltic Sea.[64] Although the Air Force persuaded the State Department to accept future flights, the State Department worried that additional flights would antagonize friendly states in the area. Therefore, General Spaatz advised General LeMay to delay further Baltic missions until the arrival of the prototype B-29 Ferret in September.[65] When the Air Force briefed officials at the State Department on the information being collected, the officials agreed to further missions as long as the aircraft remained over water and approached Soviet-occupied territory no closer than 12 miles.[66] Unfortunately, although the State Department and Air Force discussions appeared satisfactory, the State Department offered no assistance to repatriate aircrews in the event of their force down and capture.[67] The implications of this action contributed to the Air Force decision to curtail B-17 Ferret activity and wait for the ELINT B-29.

Compared to the ad hoc origins of previous Ferret projects, the B-29 Ferret's *European tour* reflected the desires of the Air Staff in Washington. First suggested in late July, General Partridge, assistant chief of Air Staff for Plans, coordinated the B-29's transfer to Europe following its Alaskan missions. He proposed a 30-day deployment that included two flights to the Spitzbergen–Jan Mayen area of the Arctic Ocean and two or three missions in the Baltic. The Air Staff planned for the B-29 Ferret to be equipped with the new AN/APR-9 search receivers, enabling the aircraft to intercept a wider range of radar, navigational aid, and guided missile signals. Because of the Gotland Island experience, the Ferret also conducted visual reconnaissance, limited aerial photography, and radarscope photography as secondary missions.[68] In addition, planners hoped to slip the Ferret into a formation of B-29s scheduled to take part in a World War II victory parade in Czechoslovakia, but the Czech government withdrew the invitation.[69]

According to the crew of the *Sitting Duck*, flights along the Berlin air corridor proved the most eventful during the Ferret's deployment. On 12 September 1947, the ELINT B-29 flew from its base at Giebelstadt, Germany, to Frankfurt, Germany, and then along the southern air corridor to Berlin. Without landing, the plane entered the northern corridor and flew to Hamburg, Germany. At this point, the aircraft reversed course and retraced its original route. At one stage of the flight, the crew encountered Soviet fighters. Capt Robert R. Perry described the scene as follows:

> About halfway up the south corridor, Tanner [the pilot] calls on the intercom and says, "Hey, we've got Yaks on both sides!". . . "Nobody has fired yet, so let's just keep on the way we are going." We didn't have any guns, . . . and they could see it. I just didn't want to make any sudden moves and get them excited. I said, "If we make a sudden move, it's going to trigger something. Just let those guys stay behind and don't tell them anything." [Two armed B-29s flew a few miles behind. The original plan called for the ferret to tuck between the armed aircraft for protection.] The Yaks flew with us for . . . about 10 minutes and then Tanner says they dropped off.[70]

Originally designated the F-13A during World War II, the Boeing RB-29A was a modified B-29 Superfortress with a combat range of 4,075 nautical miles (with a payload of 500 pounds of camera equipment) and a maximum speed of 345 knots. A typical mission profile called for a cruising speed of 200 knots at 25,000 feet.

At the completion of the B-29's deployment, the crew returned to the United States and formed the nucleus for SAC's first permanent electronic reconnaissance organization. The new 324th Radio Countermeasures Squadron consisted originally of the ELINT B-29 and an old B-17, but the unit grew to six RB-29 Ferrets by the summer of 1948. Based at McGuire AFB, New Jersey, the 324th provided crews for sorties flown from Mildenhall, England; Frankfurt, Germany; Yokota, Japan; and Ladd AFB, Alaska. Although the unit suffered greater than usual *teething* problems, the establishment of the 324th RCM Squadron represented an attempt by SAC leadership to address existing intelligence gaps.[71] Nevertheless, even though the expansion of Ferret efforts in 1947 provided valuable information on Soviet radar defenses, USAF still lacked a means of obtaining the strategic photographic intelligence needed for target analysis.

The problem of creating target folders emerged as the leading operational dilemma for strategic bombardment planning. In a sense, strategic target folders represented the bridge from abstract theories of air war to operational reality. The Air Force assigned overall responsibility for target folders to the Strategic Vulnerability Branch of the Air Staff. This organization divided the task into the following three phases:

1. The compilation of a world bombing encyclopedia that located potential targets.

2. The analysis of the data compiled in the bomb encyclopedia to include the plant's name, geographic coordinates, function, output, and transportation routes.

3. The creation of operational target folders for bomber crews that contained the name, identity, location, and profile of the specific objective. In addition, the Strategic Air Command was tasked to provide the necessary maps and charts to reach the target.[72]

Thus, the Strategic Vulnerability Branch received tasking to provide the analysis and target selection for a precision bombing campaign.

The USAAF's World War II experience dramatized the importance of target selection. The *European Summary Report* of the *United States Strategic Bombing Survey (USSBS)* noted that Germany feared attacks on basic industries (oil, chemicals, or steel) more than attacks on their armament industry or cities.[73] The *USSBS* also stressed the need for strategic intelligence, particularly during the early phases of the war.[74] In fact, the Air Staff created the Strategic Vulnerability Branch expressly to avoid the pitfalls of World War II's intelligence flaws. The USAF hoped to avoid the European theater's reliance on a foreign power (Britain) for target intelligence and the two-to-three-year delay in the Pacific for acquiring sufficient information.[75]

Unfortunately, despite its awareness of the importance of target information, the United States lacked operational target folders in 1947. The Strategic Vulnerability Branch gathered sufficient information for target sheets ranging between 8,000 and 10,000 particular installations in the USSR; however, SAC lacked the resources to produce the necessary maps and charts.[76] Consequently, SAC's bomber and reconnaissance crews lacked the target folders needed to wage a precision bombing campaign.

Faced with a shortage of strategic intelligence, the Air Force sought alternate sources of information. In 1947–48 the Air Force explored intelligence arrangements with German, Swedish, and Turkish military intelligence organizations. The greatest effort involved projects to exploit World War II German intelligence efforts. An unsigned Air Staff memorandum listed the following sources of information available:

a. Some specific information on various Russian oil refineries

b. The complete operational plan of the German operation known as "[E]isenhammer" to include maps and annotated photographs

c. Certain military geographical information on Russia (Published by OKW [Oberkommando der Wehrmacht], the World War II German high command)

d. Exact information regarding the bridge near KIEV and the highway between LEMBERG and VORONESCH

e. Meteorological information on Russia

f. Target photographs of various Russian airfields

g. Some aerial photos of certain Caucasian ports

h. Aerial photographs of the Crimea

i. Certain photographs covering Central and South Russia[77]

In addition, the Air Force hired remnants of the German military intelligence organization established by German general Reinhard Gehlen during World War II. The former *Abwehr* system operated a network of agents in the Soviet Union and satellite countries.[78] Although Germany's numerous intelligence failures on the Eastern front cast doubt on the quality of information provided, USAF had few other sources. According to General LeMay, "Certainly what they [the German spy network] provided was far better than what we could have gathered on our own, because at this time we were really babes-in-the-woods as far as intelligence was concerned."[79] The Air Force also interrogated German scientists in an effort to learn more about the V-2 missile and other technological projects. In Project Abstract, Lt Col Malcolm D. Seashore interviewed scientists to ascertain the location of V-2 documents buried in the Bad Sachsa and the Harz mountains. With Peenemünde in Russian hands, not only did the project aim to acquire documents and equipment for the United States but to deny such information to the Soviets.[80]

In another unusual effort to gather target information, the USAF arranged a highly secret reconnaissance agreement with the Swedish general staff. In exchange for USAF cameras and photographic supplies, the Intelligence Service for the Swedish general staff of defense, agreed to provide photographs from Swedish aerial and naval reconnaissance.[81] The Air Force supplied Sweden with four K-22 aerial cameras with 24- and 40-inch lenses and ample photographic supplies, and the US Navy provided two type F-56 cameras for Swedish naval craft. In return, the Swedes furnished two prints and one contact-film base positive for each negative produced with the equipment.[82] Due to the political sensitivity surrounding this act, the Air Force sought absolute secrecy. Air Intelligence even suggested removing the *loaned* cameras from Air Force supply records.[83]

Furthering the search for additional strategic intelligence, the Air Force explored electronic reconnaissance along the border of the USSR and Turkey. The Air Staff Air Communications Group proposed giving the Turkish air force a C-47 transport modified for electronic intelligence. SAC strongly disagreed, worried over comprising US ELINT capabilities if

American electronic reconnaissance equipment were operated by a foreign air force. Instead, SAC suggested the addition of an Air Force Ferret aircraft to a detachment of the 311th Reconnaissance Wing already scheduled for a photomapping project over Turkey. While waiting approval of the Turkish government, the Air Staff apparently tabled the projects.[84]

Despite wide-ranging efforts, the dilemma posed by inadequate strategic intelligence influenced strategic war planning. On 11 February 1948, the Joint Staff Planning Group (JSPG) completed Joint Emergency War Plan Broiler, which resembled Pincher's plans in some respects. The United States assumed an accidental outbreak of war; overwhelming Soviet superiority in land forces; a Russian capability to overrun Europe with little resistance; the need to safeguard North America, the United Kingdom, and a few key air bases; and an American strategic air campaign as the principal response to Soviet aggression. Nevertheless, while Pincher reflected the Spaatz board assessment, Broiler relied heavily on atomic bombs. In other words, instead of a strategic campaign featuring conventional bombardment augmented by a few atomic bombs, Broiler reversed the equation. The atomic bombing of "the vital centers of Soviet war-making capacity" formed the heart of Broiler.[85]

The political assumptions of Broiler paralleled the Truman administration's containment doctrine. According to the JCS planners, the Soviet political objectives sought a Soviet-dominated *Communist World* as a maximum aim and a barrier of communist-dominated countries on Soviet borders as an immediate goal.[86] As a result, the national objectives of the United States consisted of the following:

a. To destroy the war-making capacity of the U.S.S.R. to the extent and in such manner as to permit the accomplishment of b, c, and d below.

b. To compel the withdrawal of Soviet military and political forces from areas under their control or domination at least to within Soviet 1939 boundaries.

c. To create conditions within the U.S.S.R. which will insure abandonment of Soviet political and military aggression.

d. To establish conditions conducive to future international stability.[87]

To achieve these goals, the JCS advocated a strategic concept based on Douhet's view of airpower. The US plan sought "to destroy the will of the U.S.S.R." by launching an air offensive designed "to exploit the destructive and psychological power of atomic weapons against vital elements of the Soviet war-making capacity."[88]

The Broiler Plan's outline for the strategic air campaign reflected a subtle, but important, doctrinal shift. At first glance, Broiler's key target systems resembled the precision bombing campaign of World War II.

a. Key government and control facilities

b. Urban industrial areas

c. Petroleum industry

d. Submarine bases, construction and repair facilities

e. Transportation system

f. Aircraft industry

g. Coke, iron and steel industry

h. Electric power system[89]

Moreover, the planners claimed the campaign would attack the following percentages of Soviet industry: "Airframes 98.8%, Autos and Trucks 88%, Aero Engines 100%, Tanks and Self-propelled guns 94%, Armament 65%, Crude Oil Refineries 63.7%, Coke 67.5%, Steel 65%, Zinc 44%, Aviation Gasoline Refineries 77.8%, Submarine Construction Facilities 89%, Total Shipbuilding Facilities 45%."[90]

Although Broiler contained the language and industrial emphasis of previous precision bombardment doctrine, the plans assumed the destruction of urban areas as inseparable from the destruction of the industry itself. In other words, whereas precision bombing doctrine targeted a specific industry within a city, Broiler targeted a city to destroy a specific industry. Because of American military weakness and a lack of target information, the Air Force abandoned the precision bombing doctrine formed by the Air Corps Tactical School and advocated to the War Department during World War II. The Air Force, frustrated by existing conditions, reverted to area bombing.

With reduced emphasis on conventional bombing, Broiler reflected revised thought about the strategic implications of the atomic bomb. The following three assumptions provided the foundation for American war planning at this time:

a. The United States is the only country now possessing atomic bombs.

b. The United States will possess reasonable stockpiles of atomic bombs at the outset of an emergency, will be in production of atomic bombs during hostilities, and will have the capability of continued and increased production of atomic bombs during hostilities.

c. No agreement exists for the international control of atomic weapons nor will such agreement be reached during this period.[91]

The joint planners realized that the Soviet Union would exert every effort to develop and produce atomic weapons, but America's atomic *monopoly* served as the cornerstone of its defense strategy.[92] Although the United States believed the bomb to be a tremendous strategic advantage, JCS planners did not know the extent of the atomic bomb's psychological impact. Advocates asserted that "the combined physical destruction and psychological effect would be so great as to cause the Soviets to capitulate and accept Allied terms of surrender."[93] On the other hand, Broiler contained provisions for the long-term conventional bombing of 39 petroleum industry targets and 36 submarine bases.[94] Regardless of the war's duration, the early effectiveness of the strategic air campaign would determine the success of Broiler. The United States based its strategy upon the atomic bomb either forcing immediate Soviet surrender or providing time for mobilization.

Although Broiler's reliance on atomic area bombing reduced the need for precise target information, the war plan still required effective aerial reconnaissance for success. Even though an area bombing campaign needed strategic photographic intelligence only to the extent of providing routes to the cities and a general layout of *urban industrial areas*, the bombers still required accurate intelligence for penetration of Soviet air defenses. Unlike the latter stages of the Combined Bomber Offensive, the American bombers of War Plan Broiler faced overwhelming numbers of enemy fighters and antiaircraft guns. In October 1943, the Luftwaffe massed roughly 1,000 fighters

and 14,000 heavy antiaircraft guns to defend Germany, but Soviet air defenses featured 6,000 fighters, including 800 jets, and
at least as many antiaircraft weapons.[95] The JCS estimated that
an attacking force might be intercepted three times: (1) once
passing over the satellite boundary, (2) once at the target area,
and (3) again on withdrawal over the boundary. Furthermore,
Broiler warned of Soviet conventional fighters capable of 35,000-
foot altitudes and speeds up to 366 knots and jet fighters
capable of 40,000-foot ceilings and effective speeds of 465
knots.[96] Despite these numbers, Soviet fighter performance
mattered little if the Soviet radar systems proved inadequate.

Broiler's estimate of Soviet radar defenses reflected the findings of Air Force electronic reconnaissance. According to the
Joint Intelligence Group, the USSR possessed *adequate* early
warning radar for *sufficient* coverage of the entire border. Nevertheless, in the immediate future, available Soviet GCI equipment only permitted the defense of six critical areas with a dia-
meter of 100 miles each.[97] Obviously, SAC bombers sought
additional information to avoid strong air defense zones.

Like the previous Pincher plans, Joint Emergency War Plan
Broiler reflected desired, rather than actual, US capabilities.
For instance, Broiler outlined the following schedule (table 1)
for the required strategic air forces.[98] Furthermore, the air
campaign called for 10,184 air sorties on primary targets, including 2,700 reconnaissance missions.[99]

Closer analysis of War Plan Broiler revealed a number of
flawed operational assumptions. In considering the mobilization
of air forces, the plan overlooked the difficulty of assembling,
equipping, and training crews. The idea of recalling World War II
veterans, retraining them, and sending them into combat within
30 days of mobilization was pure fantasy. The plan's schedule
failed to consider where aircraft could be procured. Regardless of
whether aircraft came from factories or represented refurbished
World War II equipment, it would take longer than a month to
ready them for flight. Ironically, War Plan Broiler's unquestioned
reliance on the atomic bomb represented a major problem. JCS
planners did not understand the limits of the atomic bomb
stockpile, the operational limits to the bomb's deployment, or the
actual capabilities of atomic weapons since the planners were

Table 1

Offtackle Deployment of USAF Aircraft

Continential US	D-day	D+1 (month)	D+2	D+3
Heavy Bomb Groups	1	1	1	1
Medium Bomb Groups	2	-	-	-
Alaska				
Strategic Recon Group	1⅔	⅔	⅔	⅔
Okinawa				
Medium Bomb Group	1	1	1	1
Strategic Recon Group	⅔	⅓	⅓	⅓
Escort Fighter Group	1	1	1	1
United Kingdom				
Medium Bomb Group	2	5	6	7
Strategic Recon Group	-	1⅔	2	2
Escort Fighter Group	-	3	5	5
Iceland				
Medium Bomb Group	(staging facilities only)			
Strategic Recon Group	-	⅓	⅓	⅓

Source: JSPG 1844/46, enclosure, 367, in Steven T. Ross and David Alan Rosenberg, eds., *America's Plans for War against the Soviet Union, 1945–1950* (New York: Garland Publishing, 1990), vol. 2.

denied clearance to these details by the Atomic Energy Commission.[100] In other words, the war planners lacked access to the types of information required by the emergency war plans. In a sense, Joint Emergency War Plans, Pincher and Broiler, operated in an information vacuum with little knowledge of actual Soviet or American capability.

The Berlin crisis of 1948 awakened American policy makers to the danger of inadequate strategic intelligence. Upset with the allied opposition to a new regulation requiring inspection of US personnel entering the Soviet Zone, the Soviets closed highway, railway, and river access to Berlin. The Soviets denied access from 1 April to 1 July 1948 under the guise of "technical difficulties."[101] By July the rationale for the blockade shifted to protecting the Soviet Zone from the currency reform sponsored by the Western powers.[102] Despite the immediate reasons, President Harry Truman viewed the Berlin crisis as significant in greater terms. He believed the blockade represented a Soviet test of Western resolve and patience. At issue was the Western presence in Berlin and the viability of the Marshall Plan. Truman's perception of the crisis saw the Soviets trying to convince the people of Europe that the United States would only support them in economic matters, backing away from any military risk. The question remained: How could the United States remain in Berlin without risking all-out war?[103] Although the Berlin airlift provided a means of facing the challenge without hostilities, President Truman appreciated the gravity of the situation:

> Our position in Berlin was precarious. If we wished to remain there, we would have to make a show of strength. But there was always the risk that the Russian reaction might lead to war. We had to face the possibility that Russia might deliberately choose to make Berlin the pretext for war, but a more immediate danger was the risk that a trigger-happy Russian pilot or hotheaded Communist tank commander might create an incident that could ignite the powder keg.[104]

Thus, the Berlin crisis resembled the political miscalculation that launched the war envisioned by the Joint Emergency War Plans. Rather than planning exercises based on hypothetical scenarios, the Berlin crisis illustrated the distinct possibility of war with the Soviet Union.

On a broad scale, the Berlin airlift demonstrated the patience, resolve, and political acumen of the West. In many ways, the aerial convoy represented an unprecedented achievement by American and British airpower.[105] Less well publicized, the Air Force mobilized units of SAC to signal US military resolve. Following a presidential cabinet meeting on 25 June 1948 and presidential authorization for a maximum-effort airlift the next day, Headquarters Air Force ordered a SAC alert and the transfer of the 301st Bomb Group to Germany. Adding to the B-29s of the 301st, the 307th, and 28th Bomb Groups assumed alert postures in England.[106] Significantly, none of the units involved were nuclear capable. In addition, SAC ordered the 311th Air Division to send six reconnaissance aircraft to Europe.[107] As shown in Broiler, photoreconnaissance aircraft would play an important role in the event of hostilities.

Faced by the prospect of war in the immediate future, USAFE authorized the B-17 Ferret aircraft of the 7499th Squadron to conduct electronic reconnaissance missions along the Berlin air corridor. To avoid Soviet suspicions over the distinctive appearance of the B-17 Ferret, the ELINT aircraft flew only at night, slipping into the stream of C-47s and C-54s. The Ferret never landed in Berlin. Instead, the pilot would radio the tower and report "landing gear trouble," and return to base via the outbound air corridor.[108] Although the Ferret only discovered a few additional Soviet RUS-2 radar sites code-named Dumbo, the action joined other preparations for hostilities.

Combining with the tension of the Berlin crisis, reports of Soviet activities in Alaska raised additional worries over potential Soviet attack. A memorandum for the secretary of the Air Force from General Spaatz listed Soviet jamming of reconnaissance flights, Soviet aerial reconnaissance of the Arctic Ocean and Greenland, and construction of airfields on the Chukotski Peninsula as examples of alarming activities.[109] Considering the impact of America's intelligence failure prior to Pearl Harbor, the prospect of airfields capable of launching long-range bombers prompted US efforts to reconnoiter the areas of Siberia adjacent to Alaska (see fig. 2). W. Stuart Symington, secretary of the Air Force, pushed the program further when he asked General Spaatz why no pictures existed of Soviet airfields on the Chukotski Peninsula.[110]

The effort to photograph the Soviet bases on the Chukotski Peninsula illustrated the technological and political constraints present for strategic photographic intelligence. On one hand, vertical air photographs of Soviet airfields risked the loss of the plane and risked a grave international crisis. Yet, existing aerial cameras proved inadequate for long-range oblique photography.[111] To solve the dilemma, the director of Air Force Intelligence proposed the reduction of the State Department's restriction on aerial operations from 12 miles to three miles and to use 40-inch focal-length cameras. When the Air Staff finally agreed to send this proposal to the Department of State for approval in May 1948, the Berlin crisis had changed the political climate. Not seeking to further inflame international tensions, Lt Gen Lauris Norstad, deputy chief of staff for operations, preempted the request for reduced restrictions. By 13 May 1948, the De-

Col George W. Goddard operates a K-15A camera. He pioneered the development of the 48-, 60-, and 100-inch focal-length cameras in the late 1940s.

partment of State had increased the restriction to 40 miles to avoid provoking the USSR.[112] Although the actions avoided igniting the volatile political situation, the increased buffer zone left unsolved the operational problem of how to photograph the Chukotski Peninsula.

The resolution of the Chukotski Peninsula Airfield dilemma demanded technological innovation. Ironically, Col George W. Goddard, the man who pioneered aerial photography in the interwar period, provided

Brig Gen George W. Goddard

the breakthrough in the form of 48-, 60-, and 100-inch focal-length cameras at the AMC.[113] In addition, by October 1948, lessened tensions caused by the success of the Berlin airlift permitted reduction of the reconnaissance restricted area from 40 miles to 20 miles from the Soviet shore.[114] The reduction of the restricted area and the experimental 100-inch camera mounted for oblique photography allowed an Air Force F-13 (RB-29) to complete needed coverage of the Chukotski Peninsula during October and November. Further analysis of the photos dispelled fears of substantial Soviet bases at the sites capable of long-range missions upon the United States.[115]

Complementing the Chukotski photography campaign, Maj Gen Charles P. Cabell, the new director of Air Force Intelligence, revamped the AAC's RCM mission in a letter to the AAC commanding general dated 26 July 1948. The letter rescinded previous electronic reconnaissance directives, defined ELINT objectives, and established uniform policy, operating procedures, and search areas. Headquarters Air Force directed AAC to concentrate its efforts on discovering radar chains and operating schedules and to determine which signals, if any, belonged to identification friend or foe systems.[116] The policy letter also established a 10-day deadline for complete mission reports to be forwarded to the Directorate of Intelligence. This action reflected the failure of previous AAC reporting to keep higher headquarters informed of current developments.[117] Finally, the director of Intelligence summarized worldwide Ferret accomplishments: In Europe, Ferrets established the locations and characteristics of 39 radar stations, and Far East Air Forces (FEAF) and AAC's Ferrets combined to identify 11 Soviet radar sites.[118] In addition, General Cabell's letter urged special attention towards the identification of Soviet shipborne radar to prevent mistaking ships in port for land-based stations.[119] The net effect of the AAC policy letter resulted in standardized procedures and centralized control for the two RB-29 Ferret aircraft dedicated to the Alaskan RCM program.[120]

In sum, the establishment of a formal Alaskan RCM program represented the steady bureaucratic progress of strategic aerial reconnaissance. From Truman's declaration of containment in July 1947 to the Berlin crisis of 1948, the Air Force's efforts to gather strategic intelligence advanced in direction, standardization, and centralization. Moreover, technological developments in the form of RB-29 Ferret aircraft and advanced 100-inch focal-length cameras enhanced the collection effort. Nevertheless, the need for target intelligence and Soviet radar information increased dramatically as international events intensified fears of Soviet surprise attack. Aware of US weakness in conventional forces, American strategic planners emphasized the atomic bomb as both deterrent and primary war-fighting weapon. Furthermore, significant gaps in US strategic reconnaissance capabilities jeopardized strategic air doctrine based on precision bombing. As shown by Joint Emergency War Plan Broiler, American air doctrine reverted to area bombing concepts reminiscent of Giulio Douhet. Until strategic aerial reconnaissance crossed the technological barriers required for specific target intelligence, American war plans relied on an atomic bludgeon.

Notes

1. [George F. Kennan] "X," "The Sources of Soviet Conduct," *Foreign Affairs*, 25 (July 1947): 575.

2. A Joint Intelligence Committee document prepared in 1945, "Soviet Capabilities," estimated that the Soviet economy would be unable to support a major war for at least five years. JIC 250/6, "Soviet Capabilities," 29 November 1945, folder 12: Intelligence Reports and Briefs, box 4, series 3, Harry R. Borowski Papers (hereafter Borowski Papers).

3. John Lewis Gaddis, *Strategies of Containment: A Critical Appraisal of Postwar American National Security Policy* (New York: Oxford University Press, 1982), 4.

4. Frank Voltaggio, "Out in the Cold . . . Early ELINT Activities of the Strategic Air Command," 2, file: Voltaggio, Association of Old Crows, Association of Old Crows Building, Alexandria, Va. (hereafter AOC Archive).

5. Headquarters AAF Air Intelligence report no. 100-146/4-34, "Operational Capabilities of U.S.S.R. in Certain Areas," Headquarters AAF, assistant chief of staff-2 (Intelligence Division) study no. 146/4, 5 June 1947, 1, file no. 2-200 to 2-299, July–August 1947, box 39, entry 214, Record Group (RG) 341, National Archives (NA).

6. Ibid., 2.

7. Intelligence brief no. 26, "Indications of Atomic Energy Facilities in U.S.S.R.," Andrews AFB, Washington, D.C.: Headquarters SAC, 25 November 1947, file: 416.606-26, US Air Force Historical Research Center (hereafter USAFHRC).

8. Air Intelligence collected sightings of a Soviet version of the B-29 on 54 different occasions from June 1946 to August 1948. Intelligence brief no. 67, "Soviet Long-Range Missiles," Andrews AFB, Washington, D.C.: Headquarters SAC, 15 September 1948, file no. 416.606-67, USAFHRC; "U.S.S.R. Jet Engines," in Col Robert Taylor, chief, Collection Branch, Air Intelligence requirements division, directorate of Intelligence, memorandum to Col Hugh D. Wallace, subject: Distribution of Studies, 8 March 1948, TS control no. 2-8389, file no. 2-8300 to 2-8399, box 45, entry 214, RG 341, NA; and "The Russian B-29," in RG 341, NA. Document is now declassified.

9. Historian SAC, 1947, vol. 1, Narrative (Offutt AFB, Nebr.: 1 June 1949), 1, file no. 416.01, vol. 1, 1947.

10. Ibid., 56. In the Air Force, pilots and navigators possess aeronautical ratings and are referred to as *rated* officers.

11. The SAC bomber force included the following aircraft: 22 B-36s, 17 B-50s, 426 B-29s, three B-17s, 46 B-25s, eight B-26s, and eight others. Historian SAC, SAC Technical Manual 122-1, *Command Summary*, December 1948, 23, file no. 416.01, vol. 8.

12. By October, the reconnaissance inventory increased slightly, but the 311th Reconnaissance Wing's flying squadrons only listed 39 aircraft of the following types:

7th Geodetic Control Squadron, 13 total: one B-29, two F-9s, one F-13, two OA-10s, and seven C-47s;

16th Photo Squadron, nine total: one B-25, one F-2, three F-9s, three F-13s, and one C-54; and

343d Recon Squadron, 17 total: 10 B-17s, one F-2, and six F-9s.

Statistical Control Office, SAC, Statistical Summary Strategic Air Command, 1 October 1947, 31, in Historian SAC, 1947, vol. 7, Statistical Summaries (pt. 2), file no. 416.01, vol. 7, 1947.

13. SAC established the following manning limits for the 311th Reconnaissance Wing found in Historian SAC, SAC Statistical Summary, 1 October 1947, 32:

Unit	Officers	Warrant Officers	Enlisted Men
HQ 311th Recon Wing	20	2	48
HQ 55th Recon Group VLR*	14	0	60
343d Recon Sq VLR	54	1	396
6th Photo Tech Unit	2	1	50
10th Photo Tech Unit	32	1	305
11th Photo Tech Unit	2	1	50
7th Geodetic Control Sq	155	0	540
16th Photo Sq (Special)	(1)	(1)	
36th AAF Base Unit	28	0	100

*VLR stands for very long range.

14. The 311th Reconnaissance Wing was upgraded to an Air Division in early 1948.

15. Brig Gen P. T. Cullen, commander, Headquarters, 311th Air Division, Reconnaissance, to commanding general, SAC, letter, subject: Proposal for Study of Reconnaissance, 4 June 1948, Historian SAC, 1948, vol. 4, Supporting Documents, file no. 416.01, vol. 4, 1948.

16. Ibid.

17. Although General Cullen suggested new ideas, he believed that "those of us who are directly involved in reconnaissance operations are so occupied with the ever present problem of personnel and training, that we have little opportunity to survey the field of industry for new techniques." Brig Gen P. T. Cullen, Headquarters, 311th Air Division to Maj Gen Clement McMullen, Headquarters SAC, letter, no subject, 8 September 1948 in Historian SAC, vol. 4.

18. Ibid.

19. Maj Gen E. E. Partridge to Maj Gen George C. McDonald, memorandum, subject: Strategic Reconnaissance, 31 January 1948, TS control no. 2-848, file no. 2-800 to 2-899, box 40, entry 214, RG 341, NA. Document is now declassified.

20. Enclosure 1, "Strategic Reconnaissance Necessary for Implementing Long Range Bombardment," in General McDonald to director of Training and Requirements, letter, no subject, 19 February 1948, TS control no. 2-848, file no. 2-800 to 2-899 January 1948, box 40, entry 214, RG 341, NA. Document is now declassified.

21. On 14 December 1946, the JCS agreed to continue the World War II practice of organizing operational units stationed outside the continental United States into unified theater commands. The Air Force components of

the three theater commands were Alaskan Air Command, United States Air Forces in Europe, and Far East Air Forces. In practice, each Air Force theater commander retained a considerable amount of autonomy. Robert Frank Futrell, *Ideas, Concepts, and Doctrine: Basic Thinking in the United States Air Force* (Maxwell AFB, Ala.: Air University Press, 1971 [1989]), 195–96.

22. Letters to the SAC and AAC commanders were sent on 29 March and 14 May 1948. Memorandum for record, subject: To present an electronic intelligence requirement, n.d., TS control no. 2-1585, file no. 2-1500 to 2-1599, box 41, entry 214, RG 341, NA. Document is now declassified.

23. Gen George C. McDonald to director of Training and Requirements, letter, subject: Transmittal of Intelligence Requirements, 28 January 1948, TS control no. 2-823/3, file no. 2-800 to 2-899, box 40, entry 214, RG 341, NA. Document is now declassified.

24. Ibid. Enclosure 1, "Requirements for Strategic Reconnaissance of the U.S.S.R. and Satellite States."

25. Ibid.

26. Ibid.

27. Ibid.

28. Ibid.

29. The intelligence cycle refers to the process by which information is converted into intelligence and made available to users. There are five steps in the cycle: planning and direction, collection, processing, production, and dissemination. Joint Chiefs of Staff Publication 1, *Dictionary of Military and Associated Terms*, 1984, 189.

30. Historian SAC, 1947, vol. 1, 138.

31. Ibid., 139.

32. To compensate for the difficulties of using a magnetic compass in polar regions, the Air Force developed gyrostabilizers, electric compasses, and grid navigation techniques. For an in-depth look at the problems of polar navigation, see chap. 17 of Air Force Manual 51-40, *Air Navigation*, Departments of the Air Force and Navy (Washington: Government Printing Office [GPO], 1983), 17-1, 17-12; and Headquarters SAC, Operations Analysis Section, "Report no. 9: Radar in Arctic Regions," 11 March 1947, folder 10, box 3, series 3, in Borowski Papers.

33. Routing and Record (R & R) Sheet, Air Intelligence Requirements Division, Reconnaissance Branch, Directorate of Intelligence (AFOIR-RC) to chief of staff General Intelligence Division (CSGID), subject: Photography of Floodlight (Project no. 5), 18 November 1948, TS control no. 2-5373, file no. 2-5600 to 5699, box 43, entry 214, RG 341, NA. Document is now declassified.

34. Historian SAC, 1948, vol. 1, 248–49.

35. Maj Carl M. Green, Reconnaissance Branch, Air Intelligence Requirements Division, Directorate of Intelligence to Chief, Air Intelligence Requirements Division, memorandum, subject: Coordination of Photo and Photo Intelligence Activities, 11 December 1947, TS control no. 2-682, file no. 2-600 to 2-699, box 40, entry 214, RG 341, NA; and Air Intelligence Division, memorandum for record, subject: Coordination and Dissemination of

Aerial and Radar Scope Photography by the Alaskan Air Command with Headquarters AAF, n.d., n.p., TS control no. 2-450, file no. 2-400 to 2-499, box 39, entry 214, RG 341, NA. Documents are now declassified.

36. Green memo; and Historian SAC, 1948, vol. 1, 248. Document is now declassified.

37. In early 1948, the Air Force redesignated the 46th Reconnaissance Squadron as the 72d Reconnaissance Squadron and transferred the unit to ACC control. Col Kenneth P. Bergquist, deputy assistant chief of Air Staff to commanding general, SAC, letter, subject: Operation Eardrum, 3 March 1947, Historian SAC, 1947, vol. 4, tab 113.

38. 1st Lt Enos L. Cleland, Flight "B" commander to commanding officer, 46th Reconnaissance Squadron (VLR) Photographic, letter, subject: Progress Report for Flight "B," 30 July 1947, Historian SAC, 1947, vol. 4, tab 116: Supporting Data (Operations) (Offutt AFB, Nebr.: 1 June 1949), tab 116, file no. 416.01, vol. 4, 1947.

39. Historian SAC, vol. 1, 249.

40. Green memorandum.

41. Ibid.

42. Soviet note no. 261, Embassy of the Union of Soviet Socialist Republics, 5 January 1948, TS control no. 2934, file no. 2-900 to 2-999, box 40, entry 214, RG 341, NA. Document is now declassified.

43. Existing documents regarding the Project 23 border incident present conflicting information as to the border restriction. Documents that resulted from the investigation of the incident confirm that the pilot violated the Department of State limitation of 12 miles from the Soviet coast as shown in Air Intelligence Requirements Division, Collection Branch (AFOIR-CM) to commander in chief, Alaska, letter, subject: Violations of Soviet Frontier, n.d., TS control no. 2-934, file 2-900 to 2-999, entry 214, RG 341, NA. Yet, a memo explaining Alaskan photographic efforts stated that the AAC had no boundary restrictions when this sortie was flown. See memorandum for record, subject: Photographic Coverage—Chukotski Peninsula, n.d., TS control no. 2-1378, file no. 2-1300 to 2-1399, 1948, box 41, entry 214, RG 341, NA. Documents are now declassified.

44. Cleland letter; and Historian SAC, 1947, vol. 1, 141.

45. Historian SAC, 1947, vol. 1, 145.

46. Ibid.,140.

47. Carroll L. Zimmerman, "Trip to Alaska," Office of Operations Analysis, 10 February 1947, Historian SAC, 1947, vol. 4, tab 112.

48. Although B-29s modified for photographic or Ferret missions were designated RB-29s in 1948, the first B-29 Ferret was simply referred to as an ELINT B-29 or "the prototype B-29 Ferret." Col Joe Wack, electronic warfare officer, interviewed by Alfred Price in AOC Archive, n.d., 10, file no. 11.

49. Ibid., 12.

50. H. C. Monjar to Frank Voltaggio, letter, 10 June 1982, AOC Archive, file no. 59; and Voltaggio, 8–9.

51. Col Robert R. Perry, USAF, retired, interviewed by Alfred Price, in AOC Archive, file 31.

52. In addition to Capt Robert R. Perry, the other Ravens were 1st Lt Joseph H. Wack, 1st Lt Harry A. Lehmann, 1st Lt Walter A. Spindler, 1st Lt Henry C. Monjar, and 2d Lt Walter M. Hudek. Voltaggio, AOC Archive, file 11.

53. Ibid.; and Wack interview.

54. Voltaggio, 11; and Perry interview, 9.

55. This total does not reflect training and ferry missions. See AAF Forms 5A, Individual Flight Record attached to Voltaggio.

56. Although American documents of the time refer to the Soviet RUS-2 early warning radar as a single system with a range of less than 100 miles, contemporary analyst Steven J. Zaloga explains that there were three distinct versions of the system. The initial RUS-2 *Redut* (Redoubt) was accepted for service in July 1940 and consisted of a transmitter and a receiver mounted on two trucks. It had a 95-kilometer (59-mile) maximum range. An improved RUS-2 *Redut-41*, consisting of a single truck-mounted transmitter and receiver unit appeared in 1941. Later in the war, RUS-2 *Pegmatit* incorporated further advances but all three versions lacked the ability to provide the target aircraft's altitude. According to Mr. Zaloga, the Soviets produced 12 *Reduts*, 132 *Redut-41s*, and 43 *Pegmatit* models of the RUS-2 during World War II. Steven J. Zaloga, "Soviet Air Defense Radar in the Second World War," *The Journal of Soviet Military Studies* 2, no. 1 (March 1989): 103–116; and Wack interview.

57. Voltaggio, 12.

58. The documents available do not specifically link the Headquarters Air Force action to the Ferret overflight. Instead, the documentary trail stops at a 16 August 1947 request from the commanding general, AAC, for special instructions regarding boundaries. Deputy AC/AS-2, staff summary sheet, subject: Reissuance of instructions regarding operation of two 46th Recon Sq [aircraft] A/C now being fitted w/RCM [with] Ferret equipment, 20 August 1947, TS control no. 2-296, file no. 2-200 to 2-299, July–August 1947, box 39, entry 214, RG 341, NA. Document is now declassified.

59. The term *electronic order of battle* refers to a list of enemy radars and other electronic equipment that catalogues the location and characteristics of the equipment for intelligence and mission planning purposes.

60. The documents do not elaborate on what type of missile launchers were noted, and they do not explain why the Air Staff wanted pictures of the airfields since Gotland Island is Swedish territory. Maj Gen George C. McDonald, assistant chief of Air Staff-2, to deputy, assistant chief of Air Staff-2, memorandum, subject: Ferret Operations, 23 July 1947, TS control no. 2-196, file 2-100 to 2-199, June–July 1947, box 39, entry 214, RG 341, NA. Document is now declassified.

61. Ibid. Evidently, General McDonald learned of the European Ferret activity second hand. He directed the immediate reporting of Ferret data to the Air Intelligence Requirements Division for "proper evaluation." In addition, he

insisted that all Ferret activities should follow these procedures to include Alaska, FEAF, and "such places in the future where we may operate."

62. Major Langbehn, memorandum for record, subject: "To prepare cable to Headquarters USAFE requesting information as to Photo material and whether photos were being taken of Targets of Opportunity during Ferret operations," 24 July 1947, TS control no. 2-221, file 2-200 to 2-299, July–August 1947, box 39, entry 214, RG 341, NA. Document is now declassified.

63. Gen Carl A. Spaatz, Cable, Collection Branch, Air Intelligence Requirements Division (AFACE) to COMGENUSAFE (commanding general USAFE), Wiesbaden, Germany, 24 July 1947, TS control no. 2-221, file no. 2-200 to 2-299, July–August 1947, box 39, entry 214, RG 341, NA. Document is now declassified.

64. Langbehn memorandum.

65. Memorandum for record, subject: To advise COMGENUSAFE Wiesbaden, Germany, regarding further flights in the Baltic Area, n.d., TS control no. 2-237, file no. 2-200 to 2-299, July–August 1947, box 39, entry 214, RG 341, NA. Document is now declassified.

66. Ibid.

67. Ibid.

68. Maj Gen Earle E. Partridge, assistant chief of Air Staff-3 to AC/AS-5, AC/AS-2 in turn, letter, subject: Northern European Ferret Flights, 20 August 1947, TS control no. 2-311, file no. 2-300 to 2-399, August–September 1947, box 39, entry 214, RG 341, NA. Document is now declassified.

69. Wack interview.

70. Voltaggio, 15.

71. Joseph H. Wack described the unit as extremely unmilitary in appearance and attitude. In addition, as the Air Force eliminated pilots, some were required to become Ravens. Many of these men proved bitter and unmotivated for electronic warfare. Wack interview, 15–16.

72. As early as 1947, the Air Force used IBM punch cards and first-generation computers for this task. Dr. James Lowe, "The Intelligence Basis of Selection of Strategic Target Systems," lecture, Air War College, Maxwell AFB, Ala., 13 November 1947.

73. The USSBS Summary Report (European War), 30 September 1945, 16, in David MacIsaac, ed., (hereafter MacIsaac USSBS) The United States Strategic Bombing Survey, vol. 1 (New York: Garland Press, 1976).

74. Ibid., 17.

75. Ibid., 6; and Dr. James Lowe, "The Intelligence Basis of Selection of Strategic Target Systems," lecture, Air War College, Maxwell AFB, Ala., 13 December 1946.

76. MacIsaac USSBS, vol. 1, 6.

77. Memorandum, unsigned, subject: "Project for Procuring Special Information Pertaining to USSR," 29 September 1947, TS control no. 2-450, file no. 2-400 to 2-499, September–October 1947, box 39, entry 214, RG 341, NA. Document is now declassified.

78. Gen Reinhard Gehlen's network also collaborated with the US Army's Intelligence (G-2). In 1949 Gehlen entered a contract with the Central Intelligence Agency. See Rhodri Jeffreys-Jones, *The CIA and American Democracy* (New Haven, Conn.: Yale University Press, 1989), 104.

79. In 1948 Lt Gen Curtis E. LeMay commanded USAFE. General LeMay, interviewed by John T. Bohn, 9 March 1971, March AFB, Calif., US Air Force Oral History program, file no. K239.0512-736, 9 March 1971, USAFHRC.

80. AC/AS-2 to deputy chief of Air Staff for Research and Development, staff summary sheet, subject: Project Abstract, 29 July 1947, TS control no. 2-224, file no. 2-200 to 2-299, July–August 1947, box 39, entry 214, RG 341, NA. Document is now declassified.

81. Maj Gen George C. McDonald, USAF, director of Intelligence to Military Attaché, US Embassy, Stockholm, Sweden, letter, subject: Loan of Aerial Cameras, 20 November 1947, TS control no. 2-377A, file no. 2-300 to 2-399, August–September 1947, box 39, entry 214, RG 341, NA. Document is now declassified.

82. Ibid.

83. Security was the key goal, but the staff officers involved in the project worried that they might be held "remuneratively liable" for any lost equipment that was loaned. Memorandum for record, subject: To Request that Director of Supply and Services, deputy chief of staff, Materiel (DCS/M) direct Base Accountable Officer, Bolling AFB, Washington, D.C., issue property for urgent use, 4 February 1948, TS control no. 2-963, file no. 2-900 to 2-999, February 1948, box 40, entry 214, RG 341, NA. Document is now declassified.

84. Maj Gen George C. McDonald, USAF, to Air Communications Group, deputy chief of staff, Operations (DCS/O), letter, subject: "Electronic Reconnaissance Project, 24 February 1948," and memorandum for record, subject: "To comment on a proposal by Air Communications Group for Electronic Reconnaissance of USSR from Turkey," n.d., TS control no. 2-951, file no. 2-900 to 2-999, February 1948, box 40, entry 214, RG 341, NA. Document is now declassified.

85. JSPG 496/4, Broiler, 11 February 1948, 2, Steven T. Ross and David Alan Rosenberg, eds., *America's Plans for War against the Soviet Union, 1945–1950* (New York: Garland Publishing, 1990), vol. 6, *Plan Frolic and American Resources.* (This citation also references all the following notes for JSPG 496.)

86. Ibid., annex A to app., 22.

87. Ibid., app., 6.

88. Ibid., app., 7.

89. Ibid., annex C to app., 178.

90. Ibid., annex C to app., 176.

91. Ibid., annex A to app., 14.

92. Ibid.

93. Ibid., annex A to app., 17.

94. Ibid., tab A to annex C, 192.

95. For German fighter strength, see Williamson Murray, *Luftwaffe* (Baltimore: Nautical & Aviation Publishing Co., 1985), 214. The Soviet figures represent the Joint Intelligence Committee estimate for total Soviet fighters. Ross and Rosenberg, JSPG 496/4, 11 February 1948, 3, annex A to app., 27, and tab A to annex A, 71. The antiaircraft figures are found in Headquarters SAC, "Intelligence Brief no. 44: Capabilities of Soviet Anti-Aircraft for Defense Against VHB Operations," 12 April 1948, folder 13: Intelligence Reports & Briefs, box 4, series 3, Borowski Papers.

96. The JIC estimated the Soviet Air Defense Fighter Force (PVO) strength of 1,600 [*sic*] fighters deployed in the following areas:

Far East	200
Black Sea	500
Murmansk-Archangel	300
USSR interior	700

The PVO force did not include other fighters assigned to Soviet tactical aviation units. Ross and Rosenberg, JSPG 496/4, 11 February 1948, annex A to app., 26–27.

97. Ibid., 27–28.

98. Ibid., annex B to app., 126. D refers to D day, the day the plan commenced.

99. Ibid., tab A to annex C, 192.

100. Maj Gen George C. McDonald, USAF, memorandum to Lt Gen Lewis H. Brereton, chairman, Military Liaison committee, Atomic Energy Commission, subject: Denial of Clearances by the Atomic Energy Commission of AAF Key Personnel, 23 July 1947, TS control no. 2-195, file no. 2-100 to 2-199, June–July 1947, box 39, entry 214, RG 341, NA. Document is now declassified.

101. On 31 March 1948, General Dratvin, the deputy military governor of the Soviet Union, announced that the Soviets would check all US personnel passing through their zone for identification and inspect all freight shipments. The allies objected since they had received assurance of free access to Berlin at the end of the war. Harry S. Truman, *Memoirs by Harry S. Truman* (Garden City, N.Y.: Doubleday & Co., 1956) vol. 2, *Years of Trial and Hope*, 122; and Roger G. Miller, "Freedom's Eagles: The Berlin Airlift, 1948–1949," *Air Power History* 45, no. 3 (fall 1998): 8.

102. On 18 June 1948, France, Britain, and the United States announced that the three Western powers would establish a new currency for the Western zones in order to integrate Western Germany into the European economy; and Miller, 8.

103. Truman, 123, 125.

104. Ibid., 124.

105. For details of airlift operations, see Roger D. Launius, "The Berlin Airlift: Constructive Air Power," *Airpower History* 36 (spring 1989): 8–22; and Miller, 4–39.

106. The authorized strength of a bomb group numbered 75 B-29s. Most units possessed fewer aircraft, but the SAC deployment represented a sizable percentage of the Air Force's bombardment force. Maj Raymond B. Holden (for Brig Gen J. B. Montgomery, director of Operations), to Historical Section, Headquarters SAC R & R sheet, 18 August 1949, in Historian SAC, 1948, file no. 416.01, vol. 4, 1948, USAFHRC.

107. Ibid., vol. 1, 245.

108. Lt Col Ingwald Haugen, interview by Alfred Price, n.d., file no. 25, Colonel Haugen, AOC Archive, 8.

109. Directly across the Bering Strait from Alaska, Cape Chukotski was usually addressed as the "Chukotski Peninsula" by the documents. For the sake of simplicity, I have adopted this transliteration. Gen Carl Spaatz, Air Force chief of staff, to secretary of the Air Force, memorandum, subject: Some Reports of Soviet Activities in Alaska and Adjacent Thereto, 25 March 1948, TS control no. 2-1193, file no. 2-1100 to 2-1199, box 40, entry 214, RG 341, NA. Document is now declassified.

110. W. Stuart Symington, secretary of the Air Force, memorandum to Gen Carl Spaatz, 5 April 1948, TS control no. 2-1378, file no. 2-1300 to 2-1399, 1948, box 41, entry 214, RG 341, NA. Document is now declassified.

111. The existing photographs originated from short focal-length coverage made as a secondary function of Mission 7 M 263A, the Project 23 flight that allegedly violated the Soviet frontier. Unfortunately, the photographs produced no information of significant intelligence value. R & R, Air Intelligence Requirements Division, Reconnaissance Branch (AFOIR-RC), subject: Photographic Coverage—Chukotski Peninsula, n.d., TS control no. 2-1378, file no. 2-1300 to 2-1399, 1948, box 41, entry 214, RG 341, NA. Document is now declassified.

112. Director of Intelligence to director of Plans and Operations, R & R sheet, subject: Photographic Coverage—Chukotski Peninsula Airfields, 7 May 1948, TS control no. 2-1560, file no. 2-1500 to 2-1599, box 41; Memorandum for record, subject: To brief background facts on establishment of 40-mile limit for reconnaissance flights in Pacific Area, TS control no. 2-3015, file no. 2-3003 to 2-3099, box 42, entry 214, RG 341, NA. Document is now declassified.

113. Brig Gen Walter R. Agee, chief Air Intelligence Requirements Division, directorate of Intelligence, to commander in chief, ACC, letter, 15 December 1948, TS control no. 2-5676A, file no. 2-5600 to 2-5699, box 43, entry 214, RG 341, NA. Document is now declassified.

114. The existing documents fail to mention the exact date of the shift to a 20-mile buffer. Col H. M. Monroe, Headquarters AAC to chief of staff, USAF, letter, subject: Importance of Long-range Photography to Alaskan Theater, n.d., TS control no. 2-5676A, file no. 2-5600 to 2-5699, box 43, entry 214, RG 341, NA. Document is now declassified.

115. Specifically, the flights photographed Soviet facilities located at Uelen, Lavrentiya, Mys Caplina, and Provideniya areas. Memorandum for record, subject: To present recently established Photo Intelligence to sup-

plement the information contained in the article "Chukotsky Peninsula" appearing in the March issue of the Air Intelligence Digest, n.d., TS control no. 2-6725, file no. 2-6700 to 2-6799, March 1949, box 44, entry 214, RG 341, NA. Document is now declassified.

116. Maj Gen C. P. Cabell, director of Intelligence, Office of Deputy Chief of Staff, Operations, to commanding general, AAC, letter, subject: RCM Ferret Program—AAC, 26 July 1948, TS control no. 2-3037, file no. 2-3003 to 2-3099, July 1948, box 42, entry 214, RG 341, NA. Document is now declassified. Specific objectives of the electronics reconnaissance mission are as follows:

   a. To search and report upon the following frequency spreads:
      (1) 50 Mcs (Megacycles) to 1,500 Mcs
      (2) 1,800 Mcs to 2,000 Mcs
      (3) 2,400 Mcs to 3,100 Mcs
   b. While intense searches should be centered on the above spreads, systematic full-range searches should not be ignored.

117. Ibid.; Maj Gen C. P. Cabell, acting director of Intelligence, to secretary, JIC, memorandum for record, 12 March 1948, TS control no. 2-1136, file no. 2-1100 to 2-1199, March 1948, box 41, entry 214, RG 341, NA. Document is now declassified.

118. Ibid.; Maj Gen C. P. Cabell, letter, subject: RCM Ferret Program, 26 July 1948, tab B. AAC Ferret results as follows:

1948

Location	Frequency	PRF	Pulse Width (Microseconds)
1. Wrangel Island	45	570	3.0
2. Diomede Island	1,100	1,500	-
3. Vel'kal	148	-	1.25
4. Anadyr	148	-	1.25
5. Cape Kronotski	280	low	wide
6. Petropavlovsk	1,445	-	1.0
7. S. of Petropavlovsk	2,866	820	1.6
8. Cape Pervernets [sic]	1,000	2,750 & 450	1.2
9. Valdivostok	215		1.2
10. Wondan, Korea [sic]	1,820	450	1.3
11. Dairen, Manchuria	58.2 & 64	200 & 480	

119. Ibid.

120. On 10 March 1948, the AAC Ferret program was suspended until new aircraft could be procured. When two B-29s equipped for Ferret operations appeared, the program resumed on 10 June 1948. Memorandum for record, subject: To provide the Alaskan Air Command with a directive to cover the electronic reconnaissance activities of the Ferret aircraft under the control of that command, n.d., TS control no. 2-3027, file no. 2-3003 to 2-3099, July 1948, box 42, entry 214, RG 341, NA. Document is now declassified.

Chapter 4

Strategic Bombing Questioned: Intelligence Shortfalls and War Plans, 1949–1950

We consider that strategic air warfare, as practiced in the past and as proposed for the future, is militarily unsound and of limited effect, is morally wrong, and is decidedly harmful to the stability of a postwar world.

—Rear Adm Ralph A. Ostie
US Navy

As Berlin tensions cooled, the Truman administration returned to the fundamental dilemma of budgets and defense: How could the government defend the nation from the Soviet menace and yet not bankrupt the country? As military leaders urged greater spending on rearmament, President Truman worried that not only would additional spending fuel devastating inflation, but increased arms might provoke war. Consequently, the president insisted on a budget cap on military expenditures, which exacerbated disputes among the armed services over proper roles and missions. The apparent triumph of airpower during World War II spurred the debate. Not only did the Air Force tout strategic airpower as a war-winning weapon, but the Navy also advanced naval airpower as an instrument of power projection. The Navy was worried about Air Force claims to its role as the nation's first line of defense and airmen's coveting of naval aviation. This led to the Navy challenging the assumptions behind strategic airpower. Navy leaders attacked Air Force capability and the strategic bombardment doctrine. Although the Air Force and strategic air war emerged from the Congressional hearings relatively unscathed, the Navy's criticism of one aspect of strategic air warfare against the Soviet Union proved apt. In hindsight, by examining the USAF Reconnaissance Program of 1949, SAC's collection capabilities, and the Air Force assessments of Soviet defenses, the shortfalls of USAF strategic reconnaissance become clear. The intelligence assumptions used by JCS war planners for the strategic air attack in Joint Emergency War Plan Offtackle appear speculative and unproven.

The rhetoric in the interservice dispute over roles and missions intensified with reduced budgets. The paring of the fiscal year (FY) 1950 budget estimates began in 1948. The bitter presidential election campaign and perilous relations with the Soviet Union influenced the budget process. President Truman stressed his commitment to a sound economy and downplayed US-Soviet hostility. He remained committed to a budget ceiling of $14.4 billion for military appropriations. With the realization that inadequate funds prevented balanced forces, the Army and Air Force challenged the Navy's requirements for aircraft carriers.[1]

To the Navy, aircraft carriers represented the future of naval warfare. The epic naval air battles against the Japanese demonstrated the vital importance of the airplane to sea power. Moreover, naval airpower expanded the Navy's role in power projection. With the advent of atomic weapons, the Navy understood the importance of gaining an air-atomic capability. The sea service was determined to preserve its traditional role as America's first line of defense. As a result, the Navy attacked the *upstart* Air Force following budget talks in October 1948. Leading the charge, Adm Louis E. Denfeld, chief of naval operations (CNO), attacked the competence of the junior service: "[The] unpleasant fact remains that the Navy has honest and sincere misgivings as to the ability of the Air Force successfully to deliver the [atomic] weapon by means of unescorted missions flown by present-day bombers, deep into enemy territory in the face of strong Soviet air defenses, and to drop it on targets whose locations are not accurately known."[2]

On the other hand, the Air Force viewed Navy criticism as a ploy to create a rival strategic air force. With the struggle for its independence fresh, Air Force leaders refuted the Navy's charges and instead questioned the rationale behind the Navy's projected new "supercarrier"—the 65,000-ton USS *United States.* Intended to operate aircraft weighing up to 100,000 pounds, the new carrier provided proof of the Navy's designs on strategic air warfare. To airmen, the Navy's carrier emphasis seemed misdirected; after all, the Soviets possessed a small surface fleet and threatened sea-lanes primarily through submarines. According to Maj Gen Hugh J. Knerr, Air Force inspector general, "To maintain a five-ocean navy to fight a no-ocean opponent . . . is a foolish waste of time, men and resources."[3]

In 1948, despite conferences at Key West, Florida, and the Naval War College at Newport, Rhode Island, the interservice dispute over roles and missions continued unabated.[4] In October 1948, James V. Forrestal, secretary of defense, attempted to resolve the impasse over strategic bombing by asking the JCS to address two questions:

1. What were the chances that U.S. strategic aircraft, operating in accordance with current war plans, could successfully deliver atomic bombs on their targets in the face of Soviet air defenses?

2. What military and psychological effects would successful delivery have on the Soviet war effort?[5]

Eventually, the answers to these questions appeared in two Top Secret reports. The May 1949 Harmon Report examined the impact of strategic bombing on the Soviet Union, while the February 1950 Weapons Systems Evaluation Group (WSEG) assessed SAC's ability to strike Soviet targets.

Before the administration had an opportunity to examine the studies of strategic air war, the interservice feud captured public attention in what became known as the Revolt of the Admirals. The revolt was spurred by the 23 April 1949 cancellation of the USS *United States* by Louis A. Johnson, the new secretary of defense. The cancellation led to Mr. Cedric R. Worth, a civilian assistant to the undersecretary of the Navy, releasing to the press an anonymous document that charged Johnson and the Air Force with fraud in the procurement of the Convair B-36 bomber. Instead of providing a state-of-the-art intercontinental bomber, the plane represented a "billion dollar blunder." The publicity generated by the allegations prompted an investigation by the House Armed Services Committee headed by Cong. Carl Vinson. A session held from 9 to 25 August 1949 examined Worth's allegations. The hearings found not "one iota, not one scintilla of evidence . . . that would support charges that collusion, fraud, corruption, influence, or favoritism played any part whatsoever in the procurement of the B-36 bomber."[6] Undeterred, the Navy still viewed the Air Force B-36 program as a challenge to its mission.

Dissatisfied with the first round of Congressional hearings, Capt John G. Crommelin, a respected, highly decorated naval officer, launched a second round of testimony when he told reporters that the Navy was being "nibbled to death." Crommelin's statement unleashed the frustrations of senior naval officers who felt their service jeopardized by Air Force doctrinal claims. The second session focused on the Navy's challenge to the theory and morality of strategic bombing. On the other hand, Gen Omar N. Bradley, commander of Joint Chiefs of Staff, (CJCS) and Gen Hoyt S. Vandenberg, Air Force chief of staff, refuted Navy claims and backed the performance of USAAF bombers during World War II. After rounds of heated testimony, the Armed Services Committee refrained from attempting to resolve professional military disagreements and proposed no interference with the B-36 program.[7] In many ways similar to the tactics of Billy Mitchell 25 years earlier, the Navy raised some valid points during the investigation. However, like Mitchell's appeals, vitriolic rhetoric overshadowed sound reasoning. Lost in the spectacle were astute Navy criticisms of the inadequate intelligence foundation of current war plans. Instead of a Congressional circus, the Navy should have insisted upon a review of Air Force strategic intelligence capabilities in the proper forum.

By 1949 Air Force electronic reconnaissance provided the bulk of "hard intelligence" on Soviet defenses. Directed by the JCS to conduct "an aggressive program to obtain the maximum amount of intelligence concerning foreign electronic developments," the Air Force drafted the USAF Electronic Reconnaissance Program on 21 July 1949.[8] At the heart of the program, SAC assumed responsibility for electronic reconnaissance. Although theater commanders still covered their respective areas with available resources, SAC coordinated efforts and asserted operational control.[9] Additionally, the USAF Electronic Reconnaissance Program outlined the aircraft and organizational plans, mission and deployment guidelines, intelligence requirements, mission reporting procedures, and applicable directives that superseded previous organizational efforts.[10] With this program, the Air Force furthered the bureaucratic reforms begun the previous year.

Although similar to the RB-29A in appearance and speed, the Boeing RB-50 featured more powerful engines, which increased payload capacity and range. At 25,000 feet, the RB-50G could fly 5,050 nautical miles.

SAC's 324th Strategic Reconnaissance Squadron (SRS), Electronic, conducted the revised electronic reconnaissance program.[11] To increase future intelligence collection, the Air Force planned to replace the unit's planes with new RB-50B Ferret aircraft by June 1950. Although the RB-50 closely resembled the RB-29 in appearance and speed, the new aircraft offered greater payloads and superior range.[12] As a result, the squadron deployed two aircraft with trained crews to each reconnaissance base in the United Kingdom, Alaska, and Japan for operational sorties while four aircraft remained in the United States for training.[13] While the reconnaissance plan continued the Ferret's mission to explore unknown areas and electronic frequencies, the program also emphasized the need to repeat coverage of existing sites. Only through repetition could analysts identify details, detect anomalies, and determine trends that provided intelligence

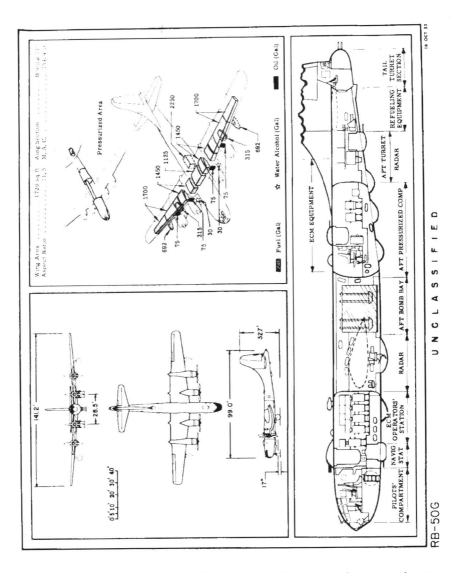

Flying first in May 1951, the RB-50G served as the electronic reconnaissance model of the B-50 bomber and was accepted into service in 1951. It proved a rugged workhorse for a crew of 16, including two pilots, a navigator, a flight engineer, five gunners, a radio operator, and six electronic warfare officers.

insight.[14] Thus, by centering electronic reconnaissance in one organization, the Air Force hoped to keep abreast of current intelligence on foreign electronic activity.

To focus Ferret efforts, the USAF Electronic Reconnaissance program established specific intelligence requirements. The first requirement resembled earlier directives that sought information on the location, characteristics, and capability of foreign radars. The Air Force also ordered a search of the electronic spectrum for evidence of Soviet research and development. Air Force Intelligence sought clues to Soviet advances in electronics, guided missiles, and pilotless aircraft. To aid efforts, the plan provided a prioritized list of frequency bands.[15] With this information, analysts could map enemy radar nets, determine radar detection capabilities, and assess Soviet electronic potential. For the immediate future, the Air Force wanted to confirm the transition of Soviet radar defenses from foreign (British and American lend-lease equipment and captured German and Japanese sets) to sets of Russian design and manufacture.

Although aware of the transfer of equipment, the staff officers who drafted the electronic reconnaissance program apparently did not understand the magnitude of US and British lend-lease assistance. According to historians Louis Brown and Steven J. Zaloga, the British provided the Soviets 302 GL Mark II fire control radars, 329 naval radars, and 1,474 other ground radars of various types, delivering some systems as early as October 1941. Beginning in 1944, US lend-lease contributed significant numbers of top line American radars to bolster Soviet antiaircraft artillery (AAA) defenses against the Germans. In total, the United States supplied 25 SCR-268 fire and searchlight control radars, 15 SCR-545 multipurpose control, search, and tracking radars, 49 SCR-585 fire control radars, three M-9 and one M-10 electronic AAA gun directors. Although some analysts considered the British GL Mark II relatively ineffective, they agree that the American equipment was first-rate and that the SCR-584 represented the finest fire control radar of World War II.[16]

In sum, the USAF Electronic Reconnaissance program completed efforts to centralize strategic intelligence within the Air Force. The plan coordinated collection efforts with the needs of higher headquarters. Nevertheless, the program focused on peacetime reconnaissance and failed to address wartime needs. No formal planning requirements existed for the number of target reconnaissance missions, bomb damage assessment (BDA) sorties, or pioneer flights for new targets.[17] Additionally, no plan matched existing capability with anticipated wartime reconnaissance sorties. Thus, the new program proved useful for streamlining peacetime reconnaissance efforts, but it failed to prepare the Air Force for strategic air war.

Following the Berlin crisis, the new SAC commander, Lt Gen Curtis E. LeMay, entirely revamped the Strategic Air Command. From his perspective as a former World War II bomb group commander and commander of USAFE, LeMay viewed SAC as an empty facade that lacked any real combat capability. As a result, he directed a change in emphasis from "providing" strategic air forces to "operating" a combat-ready strike force.[18] To dramatize his point in January 1949, LeMay ordered an operational readiness test of the entire command by conducting a simulated attack on Dayton, Ohio. Bomb units received target materials and maps based on a 1938 photograph of the target, Wright AFB, Ohio. Instead of allowing daylight attacks at medium altitudes, reflecting current SAC training, LeMay ordered the planes to strike at night, in bad weather, using radar-bombing techniques.

The photo depicts a B-50 bomber refueled by a KB-29 tanker on 24 July 1950. SAC concentrated on developing an intercontinental strike force. Aerial refueling also extended the range of RB-50 Ferret aircraft.

The results backed LeMay's assessment: "not one crew finished the mission as briefed, not one."[19]

Reflecting LeMay's influence, SAC concentrated upon developing an intercontinental strike force, capable of hitting its assigned targets. Efforts intensified to improve bombing accuracy, to develop air-to-air refueling techniques, and to transition from the B-29 to the long-range B-36 and B-50.[20] In addition, headquarters personnel struggled to define the mission for each unit, to identify the specific tasks required for mission success, and to design training plans to accomplish these tasks. For SAC reconnaissance, a series of discussions between SAC Headquarters, Air Force Intelligence, and the 311th Air Division identified six essential tasks in August 1949:

1. Radar Scope Photography

2. Bomb Damage Assessment Photography

3. Target Verification Photography

4. "Pioneer" or Target Development Photography

5. Procurement of Weather Intelligence under combat conditions and

6. Procurement, by Ferret methods, of intelligence concerning enemy electronic emissions[21]

For each task, intelligence requirements established the performance criteria. For example, target verification photography sought to attain the following standard in (priority order):

First Priority—Photography of sufficient interpretability to distinguish thirty (30) foot cubes thirty (30) feet apart within each target complex (urban area), and of sufficient coverage (60–70 square miles for the average target) to permit the production of photographic target materials.

Second Priority—Photography of sufficient interpretability covering certain installations selected . . . to determine the functions, production rates, and structural compositions of such installations.[22]

Unfortunately, existing political and technological limits prevented SAC reconnaissance from accomplishing these tasks. In an effort to overcome its shortcomings, the 311th Air Division recommended two technical innovations. In March 1949, the 311th Air Division proposed equipping RB-36 aircraft with TV-guided drones. The RB-36 would operate at 40,000 feet and fly its drone to lower altitudes. In another proposal, the RB-36 would carry one or more reconnaissance-modified fighter aircraft within fighter range of targets, launch the planes to photograph targets, and then carry the smaller jet back to home base. Although the Air Force tested the feasibility of parasite fighters for the B-36, the appearance of jet RB-45 and RB-47 prototypes shelved consideration of the drones.[23]

During this period of SAC reorientation, peripheral reconnaissance sorties continued along Soviet borders. Pointing to the intelligence benefit gained from long-range photography of northeastern Siberia in 1948, Lt Gen Nathan F. Twining, AAC commander, received permission to repeat the photographic coverage of the Chukotski Peninsula. As a result, RB-29 aircraft equipped with K-30, 100-inch focal-length cameras covered 20 targets on the Soviet coastline.[24] The photography tracked Soviet efforts to stockpile equipment and improve airfields that might indicate preparations for attack.[25] To assess the reliability of the reconnaissance, the AAC also conducted Project Stonework that photographed portions of the Alaskan coast under the same conditions for comparison.[26]

In Europe electronic reconnaissance flights marked the transition of Soviet air defenses to Russian-designed radar systems. Ferrets gathered signals of 72 Mcs, which indicated RUS-2 radar at seven additional locations on the Baltic coast.[27] In an effort to extend the range of electronic reconnaissance, Col John M. Schweitzer Jr. suggested the employment of B-29s from the 509th Bomb Group for supplemental reconnaissance missions. He reasoned that such electronic search missions would increase the appreciation of electronic warfare by bomber crews, provide realistic training for ECM operators, and further intelligence collection.[28] The Air Staff quickly silenced the proposal because the 30 (code-named Silverplate) B-29s of the 509th Bomb Group represented the only atomic-capable aircraft in SAC. The potential ramifications of a mishap or incident involving planes and crews intended for atomic delivery outweighed any intelligence or training gain.[29]

Despite the regularization of strategic reconnaissance and apparent organizational improvements, poor results threatened the electronic reconnaissance program. Throughout 1949, the intelligence information collected from Ferret missions declined. In particular, Alaskan and FEAF sorties reported "negative results" with increased frequency. Since electronic reconnaissance represented the primary source of USAF intelligence, the Air Staff conducted an immediate review of Ferret procedures. According to Maj Gen Francis L. Ankenbrandt, director of communications, the Soviets determined Air Force reconnaissance methods from the Ferret's indiscriminate use of airborne radar for navigation.[30] When USAF reconnaissance planes entered an area, the Soviets simply switched off their radar equipment; consequently, the study suggested steps to prevent the tip-off of the Ferrets. This frustrating experience reinforced the difficulty of collecting intelligence against the Soviet Union.

What types of intelligence assessment did the Air Force produce as a result of its strategic reconnaissance program? The answer to this question assumed a pivotal role in the interservice debate over budget allocations and force structure during 1949. Increased funding for the B-50 and B-36 bomber programs as well as new jet bombers (B-47s and B-52s) depended upon the viability of strategic bombing doctrine. In addition, the undisputed power of an air-atomic strategy, whether as deterrent of war or punishment for aggression, provided the justification for keeping manpower levels low, particularly for the ground services. Therefore, Air Force threat assessment contained important fiscal ramifications as well as strategic impact.

Formed largely from information gained from US electronic reconnaissance flights, the Air Force assessment of the Soviet threat depicted a powerful, unwieldy colossus featuring large numbers of technologically backward weapons. Air Intelligence worried about the Soviet development of weapons of mass destruction, the means to deliver atomic weapons, and Soviet defenses against US airpower. In 1949 the JIC produced a series of reports closely based upon Air Force Intelligence assessments of Soviet atomic status, Soviet bombers, guided missiles, radars, ECM, and antiaircraft guns.

With JCS war plans based upon an American monopoly of atomic weapons, the Soviet development of atomic bombs ranked as the greatest concern of American military leaders. According to a Joint Nuclear Energy Intelligence Committee

(JNEIC) estimate of 1 July 1949, the earliest possible date for a Soviet atomic bomb was mid-1950, and the most probable date appeared to be mid-1953. The available evidence indicated Soviet research was targeting the production of a plutonium bomb. With the amount of uranium ore as the limiting factor, the JNEIC predicted an atomic stockpile numbering 60 bombs by mid-1955 and 150 bombs by 1957 based upon a 1953 initial date. If the Soviets achieved the earliest possible date of 1950, their atomic stockpile could number as many as 130 bombs by 1955 and 150 by 1957.[31] The Soviet possession of atomic weapons would prove less concern if they lacked the means to "deliver" the bomb. As a result, Air Force reconnaissance missions searched for information related to Soviet aircraft and missile production.

The Soviets copied the B-29 to produce the Tupolev Tu-4 bomber. Fears of "Soviet B-29" bases led to photographic and electronic aerial reconnaissance of the Soviet Far East in 1948–49.

According to Air Force Intelligence, the Soviet aviation industry posed a moderate threat to the United States in 1949. Air Force analysts considered the Tupolev Tu-4 "Bull," a Soviet copy of the B-29, as the most likely means to drop atomic bombs.[32] With a 10,000-pound bombload (the approximate weight of early atomic bombs), the Air Force estimated the Soviet B-29 to have an 1,800-nautical-mile (NM) combat radius; however, the range could be extended to 2,150 NM by stripping the bomber of defensive armament and extra crew members. Therefore, from bases on the Chukotski Peninsula, two-way missions of Soviet B-29s could attack Seattle, Washington, and one-way strikes could reach Wichita, Kansas.[33] Scenarios involving Soviet air refueling of the bombers or seizing staging bases in Alaska added to the perception of threat.[34] Although strategic reconnaissance showed no long-range bombers based in northeastern Siberia, Air Force Intelligence considered airfields at Anadyr, Russkaya, and Uelen, Russia, capable of staging approximately 200 Soviet B-29s.[35] In other words, from an Air Force perspective, the Soviet bomber force presented a potential threat to the United States.

Soviet missile developments represented another great concern. By 1952 the Air Force Directorate of Intelligence had credited the Soviets with the capability for producing surface-to-surface guided missiles based on the German V-2. In addition, analysts anticipated an improved V-1-type missile capable of launching from a submarine against coastal installations.[36] For defense, the Soviets appeared to be developing the German *Wasserfall* surface-to-air missile, the *Mannheim* system for target detection, and the *Würzberg-Reise* radar for tracking.[37] Although the Soviets would not deploy an electronic missile guidance system before mid-1950, Air Material Command sought additional Ferret information in order to design countermeasures.

In comparison to information about Soviet offensive capability, knowledge of Soviet aerial defenses seemed abundant. Assessments of Soviet radar networks in 1949 benefited from two years of Ferret flights (fig. 3). Although Air Intelligence lacked basic knowledge about the capability of the Soviet electronics industry, analysts formed a better picture of the Soviet early warning system. According to electronic reconnaissance, the Soviets assembled a radar chain from Finland to Albania in Europe and from Wrangel Island, Alaska, to Korea in the Far East (fig. 4). The initial chain used captured German and Japanese equipment, along with US and British lend-lease radar sets. Reconnaissance indicated the transition to Soviet-designed RUS-2 early warning radar during the autumn of 1948 to mid-1949, evidenced by a significant drop in electronic intercepts.[38] Analysts surmised that the switch occurred for one or all of the following reasons:

a. A shortage of spare parts has forced the junking of radars of foreign manufacture.

b. A desire on the part of the Soviets to provide maximum protection for centers within the USSR has resulted in the withdrawal of foreign designed radars, which are superior in performance to Soviet radars from peripheral areas to areas inside the Soviet Union.

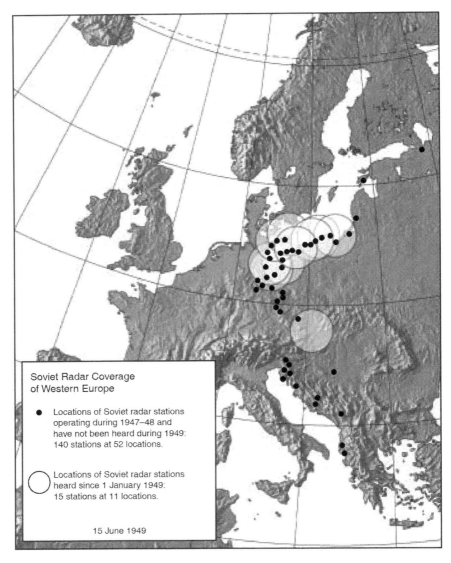

Soviet Radar Coverage of Western Europe

● Locations of Soviet radar stations operating during 1947–48 and have not been heard during 1949: 140 stations at 52 locations.

○ Locations of Soviet radar stations heard since 1 January 1949: 15 stations at 11 locations.

15 June 1949

Figure 3. Soviet Radar Coverage of Western Europe

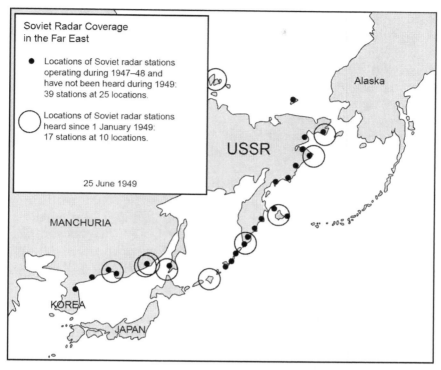

Figure 4. Soviet Radar Coverage in the Far East

c. The problem of training operators and maintenance personnel for foreign equipment has proved to be to difficult; it has therefore become necessary to substitute Soviet radars on a wholesale basis, these radars being simpler to operate and maintain.[39]

Air Force Intelligence estimated that the Soviets constructed early warning radar networks along the anticipated flight paths of US bombers and near Moscow, Leningrad, Murmansk-Arkhangelsk, and the Baku oil region, USSR, but no supporting evidence existed.[40] In qualitative terms, Air Force technicians rated the RUS-2 an elementary device with little antijamming protection, but it would provide warning of approximately 100 miles.[41]

Although Ferret aircraft provided good coverage of Soviet radar systems on the periphery of the Soviet Union, they could not provide details on Soviet defenses within the USSR. As a result, analysts for Air Force Intelligence and the JIC resorted to speculation for the remaining components of Soviet air defenses. American radar specialists believed that the Soviets possessed a limited ground controlled intercept and AI capability. They reasoned that the Soviets employed former Lend-Lease Act equipment to form a GCI network for a few critical areas. In addition, the analysts believed the Soviets continued to operate a portion of the 160 AI sets provided by the Allies during the war. The JIC considered the systems a limited threat. Unlike more modern US or British systems, the Soviet equipment lacked protection from jamming, and the GCI system possessed limited ability to position a fighter for a firing run.[42] The JIC considered it "improbable" that the Soviets could overcome production problems associated with microwave tubes. Therefore, analysts believed the Soviets possessed few AI radar capable of operating above 30,000 feet.[43] Still, the United States had no direct evidence supporting these assessments.

Along the same lines, the US intelligence community regarded Soviet antiaircraft capabilities as inferior. Based upon German assessment of Soviet AAA performance during World War II, the JIC rated the capabilities of Soviet fire control systems and AAA shell fuzes lower than comparable Western systems. Despite the shipment of US M-9 and M-10 fire control directors under lend-lease and the Soviet capture of Germany's latest system, the *Kommandogerat* 41E, available intelligence showed no Soviet modifications or use of the systems. In addition, the United States possessed no intelligence on whether the Soviets were using 80 British and American SCR-584 antiaircraft radar.[44] Despite this lack of information, Air Force Intelligence and the JIC doubted that Soviet air defenders had overcome their technological backwardness. In April 1949 the JCS directed the Joint Staff Planning Committee to prepare a joint outline emergency war plan for the first two years of a war beginning on 1 July 1949.

To comply with President Truman's directions, the plan adhered to the force structure available under the constraints of the FY 1950 budget.[45] As a result, Joint Outline Emergency War Plan Offtackle reflected the difficult decisions forced by those with limited means, trying to accomplish virtually unlimited ends.[46] Consequently, Offtackle represented the epitome of US reliance on an air-atomic strategy.[47]

In many respects, Offtackle continued the strategic thinking of the Joint Emergency War Plans Pincher and Broiler. Like its predecessors, Offtackle proposed an overall strategic concept based on the destruction of the Soviet will and capacity to resist. In order to accomplish this, the plan repeated basic undertakings seen before: the defense of the Western Hemisphere and strategic bases worldwide, a limited defense of Europe and the Far East, a strategic air campaign to destroy Soviet vital centers and provide time for US mobilization, and an eventual counterattack in "Western Eurasia."[48] In addition, Offtackle presented a revised version of US war aims based on National Security Council (NSC) NSC 20, *United States Objectives and Programs for National Security*, a policy statement approved by the president to

a. reduce the power and influence of the USSR to limits which no longer constitute a threat to the peace, national independence and stability of the world family of nations and

b. bring about a basic change in the conduct of international relations by the government in power in Russia to conform with the purposes and principles set forth in the United Nations Charter.[49]

Finally, the war plan featured a four-phase strategic air offensive that intended to knock out Soviet war capacity through atomic attacks on Soviet cities. The first phase called for the bulk of the atomic offensive launching in the first three months.[50] Depending on the success of the first phase, the remaining three phases outlined a general "policing" of target systems already attacked and the "full exploitation" of opportunities created.[51] In many ways, Offtackle confirmed the earlier doctrinal shift from precision bombardment to urban area attack with atomic weapons.

Despite its many similarities, Offtackle differed from earlier war plans in a few key areas. Although not emphasized heavily, the plan acknowledged the need for European allies and the importance of providing aid to them. Offtackle also recognized opportunities to "[e]xploit . . . the psychological weaknesses of the USSR and its satellites by informational activities and other special operations."[52] Finally, Offtackle presented calculated risks due to inadequate budgets:

a. The ground forces deployed during the first year of the war will not all have the full combat equipment specified in current tables of organization and equipment. However, deficiencies in equipment are not serious enough to invalidate the plan. . . .

b. The prospective shortage of aircraft and parts therfore [sic] is such that reduced operational rates may have to be accepted

c. In addition, certain logistic deficiencies which are not sufficiently serious to invalidate the plan will, however, limit combat effectiveness to a varying degree. . . . The deficiencies are:

    (1) insufficient technical and specialist personnel for units to enable commitment of balanced forces with full logistic support;

    (2) insufficient supply items in all Services;

    (3) insufficient construction units in all services and;

    (4) an indicated shortage of aviation fuels in the early months.[53]

Although the JCS considered these risks acceptable, a follow-on study declared Offtackle logistically unfeasible in terms of aircraft because the Air Force and Navy lacked adequate numbers of carrier-borne aircraft, medium bombers, light bombers, and fighters (table 2).[54]

Table 2

Mission Accomplishment

Type of Attack	Soviet Capability	Sorties	Bombs on Target	Percent Strike
Night	Lower	871	186	84
Night	Higher	1,039	176	80

Source: JCS 1952/11, WSEG Report No. 1, 10 February 1950, enclosure C, c-3, 163, in Steven T. Ross and David Alan Rosenberg, eds., America's Plans for War against the Soviet Union (New York: Garland Publishing, 1989), vol. 13, Evaluating the Air Offensive: The WSEG 1 Study.

Despite this problem, the report urged acceptance of Off-tackle "since an undue amount of planning time has already been spent on the current emergency plan, to the detriment of mobilization planning, intermediate range planning, and next year's emergency plan, the Joint Chiefs of Staff may elect to accept the risk of shortages in Offtackle and approve it as submitted by the Joint Strategic Plans Committee."[55] On 8 February 1950, the JCS accepted the recommendations and approved Offtackle. Thus, War Plan Offtackle served as the formal emergency war plan for FY 1950–51.

On 11 May 1949, a committee of Army, Navy, and Air Force officers headed by Lt Gen Hubert R. Harmon, USAF, issued an *Evaluation of Effect on Soviet War Effort Resulting from the Strategic Air Offensive*, better known as the *Harmon Report*. Inspired by Secretary of Defense Forrestal's questions of October 1948, the report examined the impact of the planned strategic air offensive on the Soviet war effort and included an appraisal of the psychological aspect of the campaign.[56] Based on an attack of 70 Soviet cities with all assigned targets hit, the report concluded that the SAC atomic offensive would reduce Soviet industrial capacity by 30 to 40 percent, kill 2.7 million people, inflict 4 million additional casualties, and destroy the homes of 28 million city dwellers.[57] Nevertheless, the psychological effects of the attack would *not* "bring about capitulation, destroy the roots of communism or critically weaken the power of Soviet leadership to dominate people."[58] The attack *would* create a psychological crisis within the USSR between a majority who might view the American bombing as verification of Soviet propaganda and an indeterminate minority who might use the bombing as a pretext for liberation. Focusing on the Soviet armed forces, the bombing promised to reduce air, land, and sea mobility through fuel shortages. Finally, the *Harmon Report*'s general conclusion continued the mixed assessment:

Atomic bombing will produce certain psychological and retaliatory reactions detrimental to the achievement of Allied war objectives and its destructive effects will complicate post-hostilities problems. However, the atomic bomb would be a major element of Allied military strength in any war with the U.S.S.R., and would constitute the only means of rapidly inflicting shock and serious damage to vital elements of the Soviet war-making capacity. In particular, an early atomic offensive will facilitate greatly the application of other Allied military power with prospect of greatly lowered casualties. Full exploitation of the advantages to be obtained is dependent upon the adequacy and promptness of associated military and psychological operations. From the standpoint of our national security, the advantages of its early use would be transcending. Every reasonable effort should be devoted to providing the means to be prepared for prompt and effective delivery of the maximum numbers of atomic bombs to appropriate target systems.[59]

In sum, the *Harmon Report* presented an ambiguous appraisal generally supporting strategic bombing, but raising important qualifications. By itself, the report failed to settle the interservice dispute. Defense department officials recognized the need to assess the *Harmon Report* in conjunction with the feasibility study of the WSEG. Therefore, Louis A. Johnson, secretary of defense, delayed submitting the *Harmon Report* to the president until the completion of WSEG's *Report on Evaluation of Effectiveness of Strategic Air Operations* or *Report No. 1*, which tackled the feasibility of launching a strategic air campaign with existing forces. It evaluated the odds of penetrating Soviet air defenses, the effectiveness of atomic weapons, and SAC's ability to destroy its assigned targets. Composed of a committee of 22 civilian and retired military leaders, the WSEG employed the mathematical techniques of operations analysis to back its claims.[60] During all stages the group adhered to a narrow definition of its mission, resulting in a mammoth report that refrained from discussing the impact of the air campaign or the doctrinal assumptions of strategic bombing. Instead, the researchers remained faithful to the original question: Could SAC bombers penetrate Soviet defenses and hit their assigned targets?

Because of a lack of intelligence, the WSEG drafted two sets of assumptions concerning Soviet air defenses. The lower level presumed that the Soviets maintained a poorly integrated net of radar and GCI facilities, AAA improved little over World War II performance, and smaller numbers of jet and conventional interceptor aircraft.[61] In contrast, the higher set of assumptions credited the Soviets with a radar-GCI net based on

British and German examples, improved AAA that included unguided rockets based on the German *Taifun* System, and greater numbers of jet and piston engine aircraft.[62] Although the report acknowledged that actual Soviet capability might not resemble either set of assumptions, no other options existed for the assessment.[63]

Along the same lines, the WSEG measured SAC capabilities based on statistical analysis of World War II bomber performance and SAC training records. The report considered not only statistics for the circular error probable (CEP) (the radius within which one-half of the bombs dropped may be expected to fall), but also the type of target, its distance from the aiming point, and the lethal area of the bomb against the type of structure in question. For daylight visual bombing, the WSEG estimated a CEP between 1,000 and 1,500 feet with about 10 percent of the bombs falling outside the target area. On the other hand, the group assessed the CEP for SAC's radar bombing as 3,000 feet for "easy" targets and 5,000 feet for "difficult" targets based on the anticipated quality of the target's radar return.[64] WSEG *Report No. 1* stressed the importance of bombing accuracy even with atomic weapons. The board estimated a damage assessment of 0.90 (90 percent of the target damaged beyond repair) for a CEP of 1,500 feet. When CEPs increased to 3,000 feet and 5,000 feet, the damage assessment dropped to 0.63 and 0.34 respectively.[65]

After similar assessments of fighter versus bomber engagements, the effects of ECM upon both defenses and bombing radar, and other calculations, the WSEG determined the overall success and losses of several hypothetical air-atomic campaigns based on the current War Plan Offtackle.[66] In each attack, a total force of 360 medium bombers, 30 heavy bombers, and 72 reconnaissance aircraft sought to deliver 220 atomic bombs on Soviet urban areas. Subtracting planes lost for routine maintenance and air aborts, the remaining aircraft would accomplish bombings as outlined in table 2.

On the other hand, the bombers would suffer casualties as outlined in table 3.[67]

Table 3

Projected Losses

Type of Attack	Soviet Capability	Sorties	Lost Over Enemy Territory	Damaged Beyond Repair	Percent Strike
Night	Lower	871	33	23	12
Night	Higher	1,039	123	25	32
Day	Lower	993	168	22	41
Day	Higher	1,221	222	27	55

Source: JCS 1952/11, WSEG Report No. 1, 10 February 1950, enclosure C, c-3, 191, in Steven T. Ross and David Alan Rosenberg, eds., America's Plans for War against the Soviet Union (New York: Garland Publishing, 1989), vol. 13, Evaluating the Air Offensive: The WSEG 1 Study.

According to the WSEG, SAC proved capable of conducting the atomic phase of the strategic air campaign proposed by Offtackle. Nevertheless, the hypothetical day attacks suggested that unacceptable casualties might result even against lower Soviet air defense capability. Moreover, WSEG Report No. 1 ruled the conventional aspects of Offtackle unfeasible for logistical reasons. The report cited inadequate numbers of medium bombers, overseas bases, transport aircraft, and insufficient aviation fuel stocks as reasons for making the full strategic air campaign impossible.[68] The report also identified a major problem with the war plan's reconnaissance:

> One of the difficult tasks in planning those raids was to incorporate reconnaissance missions into the raid pattern. The loss rates of unescorted reconnaissance planes appear to be too large to sustain such operations in daylight. Since 43 of the targets under the current plan may require visual reconnaissance, it appears that the required reconnaissance sorties can be obtained only by running the reconnaissance planes in with a massed day raid. A re-attack of the same region would therefore be required at a later time.[69]

In overall terms, WSEG Report No. 1 represented a comprehensive, unbiased attempt to assess whether a strategic air campaign would work. Combined with the Harmon Report, the

WSEG evaluation supported Air Force confidence in strategic bombardment, but in guarded, cautious terms. Neither the Air Force nor the Navy was pleased by the findings. The Navy disagreed with even the limited endorsement of strategic air warfare, while the Air Force disputed the assessment of high-casualties and adverse psychological effects associated with atomic bomb use. Because the reports backed neither side convincingly, President Truman found them ambiguous and inconclusive.[70] Lost amid the bureaucratic controversy, the WSEG report emphasized the grave deficiencies of existing intelligence.[71]

The inadequacy of strategic intelligence challenged the accuracy of the WSEG's reasoned, yet speculative, sets of assumptions. Although the report mentioned the consequences of a German breakthrough in night fighter radar and tactics, the WSEG assumed that the Soviets were incapable of making unexpected technological advances.[72] In addition, the report acknowledged the susceptibility of existing US bombing radar to noise jamming. It recognized that the United States knew little about Soviet ECM capability, but the report assumed that the Soviets could not exploit this US weakness.[73] Furthermore, the WSEG never considered the Soviet development of radar or jet fighters superior to US equipment. This proved somewhat ironic considering that the Soviets had already flown the advanced MiG-15 fighter nearly two years before.[74] Therefore, although the WSEG *Report No. 1* represented the best assessment possible, inadequate intelligence weakened its conclusions. Without genuine knowledge of Soviet air defense capability, an accurate evaluation of US strategic air war plans was impossible.

While government officials argued over the wisdom of American defense strategy, international events changed the political context of the debate. Since World War II, the United States based its war plans on the existence of an atomic monopoly. On 29 August 1949, the Soviets shattered this assumption by exploding an atomic bomb, which was first detected by Air Force reconnaissance aircraft flying under Project Snifden. The news of the Soviet atomic bomb startled the US military establishment.[75] Moreover, President Truman's announcement of the event rocked American public opinion. Previously,

America's sole possession of the atomic bomb inspired confidence and permitted the overall reduction of military forces. The surprise detonation of a Soviet atomic device changed the situation drastically.

The Soviet atomic explosion underscored the importance of USAF aerial reconnaissance. Ironically, the Air Force Long Range Detection Program began because of the efforts of Atomic Energy Commissioner Lewis L. Strauss over the objections of the military establishment.[76] In April 1947, Strauss observed that no system existed for monitoring Soviet atomic testing. Although the military services argued that the Soviets lacked the capability to build a bomb in the near future, Strauss eventually prevailed. In June 1947, the Long Range Detection Program directed the Air Force to determine "the time and place of all large explosions which might occur anywhere in the world and to ascertain in a manner which would leave no question, whether or not they were of nuclear origin."[77]

The Air Force developed techniques for the airborne collection of atomic samples during the Sandstone atomic tests in April and May 1948. Technicians mounted large boxlike cans on top of B-29s from the 373d Reconnaissance Squadron, Very Long Range, Weather. The cans contained filters capable of detecting radioactive particles.[78] Between 12 May 1948 and 3 September 1949, the WB-29s (as the modified aircraft were designated) registered 111 atomic-detection-system alerts that occurred when the filters showed radiation counts greater than 50 counts per minute. Nevertheless, analysts determined that all the alerts were due to natural causes. On 3 September 1949, a WB-29 on patrol between Japan and Alaska detected radiation levels greater than 85 counts per minute and additional flights produced filters with counts more than 1,000 counts per minute. Teams of experts from Los Alamos, New Mexico, and the Naval Research Laboratory concluded that the samples "are consistent with the view that the origin of the fission products was the explosion of an atomic bomb whose nuclear composition was similar to the Alamogordo bomb and that the explosion occurred between the 26th and 29th of August at some point between the east 35th meridian and 170th meridian over the Asiatic land mass."[79]

Although the detection of the Soviet atomic bomb proved the value of aerial reconnaissance, the event undermined confidence in US intelligence. As mentioned in Offtackle, most intelligence assessments viewed mid-1953 as the most probable date and mid-1950 as the earliest possible date for the Soviet development of atomic weapons. The surprise Soviet breakthrough shattered illusions of Soviet technical backwardness. If the Soviets could successfully explode an atomic bomb, considered a most difficult technical challenge, how valid were estimates of Soviet electronic and aviation capabilities? The lukewarm support of strategic bombing by WSEG *Report No.1* presumed no Soviet breakthroughs—now one had occurred. How could the United States assess the viability of its strategic air doctrine or the feasibility of its war plans? Without the technology to penetrate Soviet borders, the United States lacked the means to properly assess an evolving Soviet threat.

To make matters worse, the Communist triumph in the Chinese Civil War added to the shock of the Soviet atomic bomb. Although the Truman administration eventually realized the inept, corrupt nature of Chiang Kai-shek's Nationalist China, the president failed to prepare the American public for a Nationalist defeat. Hence, President Truman and other Democrats suffered vehement attacks from conservative Republicans for the "loss of China" and the erosion of US strength. As a result, President Truman directed a comprehensive study of US national security.

In April 1950, a select committee headed by Paul H. Nitze, director of the State Department's policy planning staff, produced NSC-68, *States Objectives and Programs for National Security*, a fundamental reassessment of the containment policy of the United States. Although retaining the term *containment,* NSC-68 shifted emphasis from long-term political and economic competition to countering an immediate military threat. A concluding paragraph summarized the rationale and recommendations of the document:

> In particular, the United States now faces the contingency that within the next four or five years the Soviet Union will possess the military capability of delivering a surprise atomic attack of such weight that the United States must have substantially increased general air, ground, and sea strength, atomic capabilities, and air and civilian defenses to

deter war and to provide reasonable assurance, in the event of war, that it could survive the initial blow and go on to the eventual attainment of its objectives. In turn, this contingency requires the intensification of our efforts in the fields of intelligence and research and development.[80]

In contrast to the previous pronouncements of the Truman administration, NSC-68 argued that the US economy could sustain increased defense spending and tolerate short-term budget deficits. In fact, Keynesian economists observed that increased defense spending would stimulate the overall domestic economy.[81] In general, NSC-68 provided the intellectual foundation for postwar American rearmament. Increased budgets diffused the Navy–Air Force feud over the merits of strategic air bombardment. In practical terms, NSC-68 played a lesser role in the buildup of US military strength. By the time President Truman approved the revised NSC-68/2 in September 1950, American "boys" were fighting and dying in Korea.

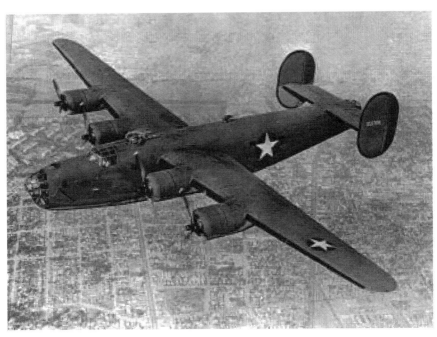

On 8 April 1950, Soviet fighters shot down a Navy PB4Y Privateer over the Baltic Sea removing the veil of secrecy from aerial reconnaissance efforts.

While the NSC deliberated NSC-68, the Soviets removed the shroud of secrecy surrounding the Ferret program. On 8 April 1950, Soviet fighters shot down an unarmed Navy PB4Y Privateer patrol plane with a crew of 10 men over the Baltic Sea. Three days later, Soviet foreign minister Andrei Y. Vishinsky handed the US ambassador, Adm Alan G. Kirk, the following note of protest:

> According to verified data, on 8 April this year at 17 hours 39 minutes, there was observed south of Libaya (Libau) a four-motored military airplane B-29 (Flying Fortress) with American identification signs which went into [the] territory of [the] Soviet Union for 21 kilometers. As [the] American airplane continued going deeper into Soviet territory, [a] flight of Soviet fighters arose from [a] nearby airdrome, demanding that [the] American airplane follow them for landing at [the] airdrome, [the] American airplane not only did not submit to this demand, but opened fire on [the] Soviet airplanes. In view [of] this, [the] leading Soviet fighter was compelled to return fire, after which [the] American airplane turned toward [the] sea and disappeared.
>
> [The] Soviet Government states [a] resolute protest to [the] Government [of the] USA against [this] gross violation of [the] Soviet border by American military airplanes which is at [the] same time [an] unheard of violation [of] elementary standards [of] international law.[82]

In his telegram to Dean Acheson, secretary of state, Ambassador Kirk observed, "Vishinsky's manner was serious but not aggressive nor antagonistic . . . recommend publicity on our side be avoided or if unavoidable, minimized. I did not have [the] impression [that] Vishinsky was preparing [to] create [a] situation of real gravity although his manner [is] definitely serious and may mask something in propaganda line."[83]

Following an investigation of the incident, Adm Forrest Sherman, CNO, reported that an unarmed Navy patrol plane, not a B-29 as the Soviets claimed, departed Wiesbaden, Germany, at 10:31 Greenwich meantime. The plane was on a "properly scheduled flight pursuant to directives of the Commander in Chief, U.S. Naval Forces, Eastern Atlantic and Mediterranean, for purposes previously approved by the Chief of Naval Operations."[84] Admiral Sherman added that standing orders required US Navy aircraft to "make no approach closer than 20 miles to any shore of the USSR, its possessions or its satellites." Verifying that the aircraft was unarmed, Admiral

Sherman concluded that "a relatively slow unarmed patrol plane could not have attacked a Russian fighter and the Soviet note is untrue in that regard. It is probably untrue also with respect to the location of the incident. It is not likely that competent personnel would overfly Soviet occupied Latvia, nor that Soviet fighters would break off action over land under such circumstances."[85] Significantly, Admiral Sherman did not mention that the aircraft was on a covert, electronic reconnaissance mission.

The attack launched a wave of frenzied rhetoric by outraged politicians and vigilant newsmen. For example, the *New York Herald Tribune* announced that "a proposal by the House Democratic leader, Rep. John W. McCormick, Massachusetts, that the United States should sever diplomatic relations with the Soviet Union, or, perhaps, recall Ambassador Kirk." Not to be outdone, Rep. Carl Vinson compared the incident to the Japanese attack on the USS *Panay* in 1937: "Here, in the same pattern, in the same manner, for the same purpose, with the same ruthlessness, with the same contempt for life, for democratic institutions, for international law, for decency—a barbaric attack is made on an unarmed defenseless American aircraft." Reminding Americans of their unpreparedness for the last war, Vinson called for increased spending for military aircraft to "maintain sufficient force to insure Russian respect."[86]

Within a few weeks, probing reporters uncovered the plane's secret mission. In a *Washington Post* article, Marquis Childs revealed that "the Russians believed that the American plane was carrying a recently developed type of reconnaissance equipment. This electronic equipment makes it possible to do reconnaissance at much greater distances than has ever more been possible."[87] Columnist Drew Pearson claimed the Navy's posted list of crew members, showing the presence of electronics specialists, broadcast the patrol plane's mission to the Russians even before its take off. "They knew the plane was equipped with high-powered radar and electronics equipment that could watch amphibian maneuvers and the flight of rockets over the Russians' most secret rocket-testing ground—the Baltic."[88]

In his *Washington Post* column, Walter Lippman speculated that the Soviets destroyed the Navy Privateer as a deliberate act of policy. He believed the Soviets set a trap for the patrol plane. "The known facts indicate that the Soviet intelligence had advance notice that the plane would fly a course over the Baltic Sea, that though it was known to be unarmed the Soviet intelligence believed it carried important electronic equipment, and that orders were given to the Soviet fighter command to intercept it, to capture it if possible, and failing that, to shoot it down."[89] The fact that no wreckage could be produced over Soviet territory disproved the Russian claim of violated territorial sovereignty. Lippman questioned the motives of the Soviets in decorating the fighter pilots credited for the kill.

> The ostentatious award of "The Order of the Red Banner" to four Soviet flying officers was plainly intended to advertise the exploit. The award is particularly significant, it seems to me, because these officers did not in fact succeed in doing what, according to M. Vishinsky, they tried to do. He says that they tried to capture the plane by making it land in Latvia. He says that they did not do that. Failing the capture of the airplane, the Soviet fighters ought to have been able to shoot it down within Soviet territory. M. Vishinsky says that they did not do that either. What then did these fighters do that entitled them to special honors and decorations?[90]

Answering his question, Lippman postulated that the incident served a twofold purpose: "One, which probably failed, was to capture a plane with valuable military secrets; the other was to demonstrate to the world that the Soviet air defenses are able to repel American strategic air power." Obviously, the second objective proved more important in the eyes of the Soviet hierarchy and resulted in the widespread publicity of the incident: "The affair lends considerable weight to the view that the Russians are intent first of all upon making their own territory invulnerable to American airpower. If they could make it invulnerable, then the Red [A]rmy would be virtually unopposed around the periphery of the Soviet Union. This Baltic incident is meant, I believe, to convince the Russian people and also the people of Europe that the Soviet Union has achieved an air defense."[91]

Regardless of whether the speculation of national columnists was correct or the tirades of politicians justified, the 1950 Baltic incident thrust aerial reconnaissance into the limelight. Largely caught unaware, President Truman called for a 30-day suspension of flights until matters could be properly assessed. The political volatility of the missions had to be weighed against the need for intelligence. As Gen Omar Bradley stated in a memorandum to the secretary of defense, "It is recognized that there is a risk of repetition of such incidents upon resumption of these flights, but it is felt that there would be more serious disadvantages occurring to the United States if the cessation of these operations were to be extended over an excessively long period."[92]

The immediate impact of the 1950 Baltic incident upon US aerial reconnaissance stemmed from the review ordered by the president. On 5 May 1950, the JCS formalized the goals and operating procedures of Ferret missions, now called the Special Electronic Airborne Search Project. In a memorandum to the secretary of defense, later briefed to the president, General Bradley outlined the program. The aim of the Special Electronic Airborne Search Project was to obtain "the maximum amount of intelligence concerning foreign electronic developments as a safeguard to national defense."[93] The JCS scheduled the missions to be flown along the borders of the Soviet Union to locate and analyze enemy air defenses. Strict operating procedures were set up for the flights that included the following:

- Flights will not be made closer than twenty miles to the USSR or USSR-or [sic] satellite-controlled territory.

- Flights will not deviate from or alter planned courses for other than reasons of safety.

- Aircraft engaged in these operations over routes normally flown by unarmed transport-type aircraft, i.e., the land masses of the Allied Occupied Zones and the Berlin and Vienna corridors, will continue to operate with or without armament. [The President scribbled "which?" on the copy forwarded to him. A later memo explained that the statement meant to "permit operation of either armed or unarmed aircraft dependent upon whether the armed or unarmed type is available at the particular time."]

- Aircraft engaged in these operations over all other routes adjacent to the USSR or to USSR-or [sic] satellite-controlled territory will be armed and instructed to shoot in self-defense. ["good sense, it seems to me. H.S.T."][94]

President Truman's approval of the Special Electronic Airborne Search Project proved to be a landmark in the history of aerial reconnaissance. No longer would military considerations alone determine Ferret operations—now potential political impact played a major role. Reconnaissance activities received scrutiny from the office of the president as well as the military services. For the most part, fears of the Soviet atomic potential and expanding military capability overpowered reservations of possible diplomatic crises. As the Baltic incident of 1950 showed, American efforts to gather intelligence risked reprisal from the Soviet Union that, in turn, captured headlines and aroused public indignation. The average American cared little about electronic intelligence or Ferret operations, but Communist forces killed 10 Americans on an unarmed plane. The death of the Navy fliers confirmed the arguments of those advocating vigilance in the Cold War. Thus, Truman's approval of the formal guidelines for aerial reconnaissance not only established a framework for operations to be conducted, but also foreshadowed a decade of aerial confrontation.

By mid-1950 international events changed the political, economic, and strategic assumptions that formed the initial US response to the Cold War. From the end of the Berlin airlift until the explosion of the Soviet atomic bomb, fiscal constraints upon military spending influenced strategy and sparked bitter interservice disputes. Although overshadowed by the spectacle of Congressional hearings and impassioned testimony during the Revolt of the Admirals, the Navy *did* identify the intelligence weakness of current US war planning. This weakness, acknowledged by the dispassionate findings of the *Harmon Report* and WSEG *Report No. 1*, pointed out that Joint Outline Emergency War Plan Offtackle and its predecessors suffered from an inability to assess Soviet targets and air defenses. Despite Air Force attempts to upgrade reconnaissance capabilities, technological limits denied war planners the information needed. Until solutions to the reconnaissance dilemma were found, US plans for strategic air war rested primarily upon unproven assumptions and speculation. With this in mind, the shock caused by the Soviet atomic bomb emphasized the danger of false assumptions.

Notes

1. Steven L. Rearden, *The Formative Years 1947–1950*, Alfred Goldberg, gen. ed. (Washington, D.C.: Historical Office of the Secretary of Defense, 1984) 343–44.

2. Ibid., 344.

3. Ibid., 389–90.

4. The Key West Agreement of 21 April 1948 assigned primary and secondary missions to each service. "In general terms, the division of service responsibilities remained the same, with the Navy assigned primacy in combat operations at sea; the Army assigned land combat and responsibility for providing antiaircraft artillery for air defense; the Marine Corps assigned amphibious warfare; and the Air Force assigned strategic air warfare, defense of the United States against air attack, and air and logistic support of ground units." In addition, the Newport Agreement of 21 August 1948 refined the Key West missions. The Air Force received control of the Armed Forces Special Weapons Project that handled and assembled atomic weapons, but the Air Force could not deny the Navy access to atomic bombs or exclude the Navy from strategic operations planning. The Newport Agreement also helped establish the Weapons Systems Evaluation Group (WSEG). Richard I. Wolf, *The United States Air Force Basic Documents on Roles and Missions*, Air Staff Historical Study (Washington, D.C.: Office of Air Force History, 1987), 151–69, 179–85; and Rearden, 393–402.

5. Rearden, 403.

6. House Committee on Armed Services, *Investigation of the B-36 Bomber Program*, 81st Cong., 1st sess., 1949, 654; Rearden, 410–20; and Robert J. Donovan, *Tumultuous Years: The Presidency of Harry S. Truman, 1949–1953* (New York: W. W. Norton, 1982), 106–13.

7. House Committee on Armed Services, *The National Defense Program: Unification and Strategy*, 81st Cong., 1st sess., 1949; Omar N. Bradley and Clay Blair, *A General's Life* (New York: Simon and Schuster, 1983), 506–13; Phillip S. Meilinger, *Hoyt S. Vandenberg* (Bloomington, Ind.: Indiana University Press, 1989), 130–37; Rearden, 410–20; and Donovan, 106–13.

8. Lt Gen Lauris Norstad, deputy chief of staff, Operations, to commanding general, SAC, letter, subject: USAF Electronic Reconnaissance Program, 21 July 1949, TS control no.: 2-8169, file no. 2-8100 to 2-8199, box 45, entry 214, Record Group (RG) 341, National Archives (NA); Lt Col Goodman G. Griffin Jr., executive, Air Intelligence Requirements Division, Directorate of Intelligence, to commanding general, SAC, Record and Routing (R&R) sheet, subject: Letter of Transmittal, 2 January 1950, Top Secret (TS) control no. 2-10681/10, file no. 2-10600 to 2-10699, box 47, entry 214, RG 341, NA. Document is now declassified.

9. Col John M. Schweitzer Jr., executive, Directorate of Intelligence, to director of Communications, letter, subject: Proposed Plan for Air Force Electronic Reconnaissance Program, 27 April 1949, TS control no. 2-7268, file no. 2-7200 to 2-7299, box 45, entry 214, RG 341, NA. Document is now declassified.

10. Norstad letter.

11. The Air Force frequently "redesignated" units during the immediate postwar period. The 324th Strategic Reconnaissance Squadron (SRS), Electronic, replaced the 324th SRS ECM on 14 March 1949. General Order 15, Headquarters, Strategic Air Command, Offutt AFB, Omaha, Nebraska, 14 March 1949, in Historian Strategic Air Command, 1949, vol. 8, General Orders 1-78, file no. 416.01, USAF Historical Research Center (hereafter US-AFHRC).

12. For a basic mission, an RB-29A was capable of 329 knots at a 25,000-foot altitude under maximum power, having a 4,075 NM range at its best endurance airspeed and a 35,000-foot-service ceiling. An RB-50G (the eventual model used for Ferret missions that included additional electronic equipment) performed only slightly better with a 338-knot speed at 31,000 feet under maximum power, having a 5,050 NM ferry range, and a 32,900-foot-service ceiling. However, the RB-50 could carry nearly 20,000 pounds of additional fuel and equipment. For photographs of the RB-50, see app. A, *Standard Aircraft Characteristics, RB-29A Superfortress, Boeing,* 19 April 1950, file no. (R) B-29A/char., US Air Force Museum (USAFM), Wright–Patterson AFB, Ohio; and *Standard Aircraft Characteristics, RB-50G Superfortress, Boeing,* 16 October 1953, file no. (R) B-50G/char., USAFM.

13. Norstad letter.

14. Ibid.; and Schweitzer, 2–3.

15. The plan called for study of the following frequency bands (in priority order): a. 40–400 mcs; b. 2,600–3,000 mcs; c. 400–600 mcs; d. 600–2,000 mcs; e. 2,000–2,600 mcs; f. 3,000–up mcs; and g. 20–40 mcs; see Norstad letter.

16. Ibid., 1; Steven J. Zaloga, "Soviet Air Defense Radar in the Second World War," *The Journal of Soviet Military Studies,* 2, no. 1 (March 1989): 103–16; and Louis Brown, *A Radar History of World War II* (Bristol and Philadelphia: Institute of Physics Publishing, 1999), 191, 265.

17. Col Von R. Shores, acting assistant chief, Operations Division, director, Plans & Operations, to Air Intelligence Requirements Division, Directorate of Intelligence, letter, subject: Intelligence Requirements for Strategic Reconnaissance, 15 July 1949, TS control no. 2-8323, file no. 2-8300 to 2-8399, box 45, entry 214, RG 341, NA. Document is now declassified.

18. Historian SAC, 1949 vol. 1, Narrative (Offutt AFB, Nebr.: 1 June 1949) 1, 10 May 1950.

19. Gen Curtis E. LeMay, United States Air Force Oral History Program, interview no. 736 by John T. Bohn, 9 March 1971, March AFB, Calif., file no. K239.0512-736, USAFHRC; and Harry R. Borowski, *A Hollow Threat: Strategic and Containment before Korea* (Westport, Conn.: Greenwood Press, 1982), 166–68.

20. Historian SAC, 1949, vol. 1, 62.

21. Ibid., 121.

22. Maj Gen Thomas S. Power, deputy commander (SAC), to commanding general, 311th Air Division, letter, subject: Photographic Reconnaissance

Requirements, 16 August 1949, tab 106, in Historian SAC, 1949, vol. 3, Supporting Documents, Operations and Training, Exhibits 59–119, file no. 416.01, vol. 3, January–December 1949.

23. Historian SAC, 1949, vol. 1, 122–24; and Robert Jackson, *High Cold War: Strategic Air Reconnaissance and the Electronic Intelligence War* (Nr Yeovil, United Kingdom: Patrick Stephens, 1998), 57–60.

24. The coastal targets ranged from Ambarchik to Petropavlovsk and included Ostrov Vrangelya, the Kommandorski Islands, and the Northern Kuriles. Brig Gen Frank A. Armstrong Jr., commander, to chief of staff, Headquarters USAF, letter, subject: Photographic Coverage of Northeastern Siberia, 7 November 1949, TS control no. 2-10097, file no. 2-10000 to 2-10099, box 46, entry 214, RG 341, NA. Document is now declassified.

25. The Air Force assumed that airfields in northeastern Siberia would serve as bases for Soviet B-29s aimed at the United States. Hence, surveillance of these airfields provided a degree of warning from surprise attack. Lt Gen Nathan F. Twining, commander in chief, AAC, to chief of staff, USAF, letter, 1st ind., n.d., TS control no. 2-10097, file no. 2-10000 to 2-10099, box 46, entry 214, RG 341, NA. Document is now declassified.

26. Col Edward Barber, deputy, Air Intelligence Requirements Division, Directorate of Intelligence, to Col J. Tison, Operations Division, deputy chief of staff (DCS)/Operations (O), R&R, 10 August 1949, TS control no. 2-8639, file no. 2-8600 to 2-8699, box 45, entry 214, RG 341, NA. Document is now declassified.

27. Ferrets discovered Soviet radars in the following areas: Rostock, Eugen Island, Swindemunde, Kolberg, Kostin, Vietzkerstrand, and the Hel Peninsula. Col Richard P. Klocko, chief, Developmental Research Branch, Air Intelligence Division, director of Intelligence, to commanding general, USAFE, letter, subject: Comments on Biograph Missions, 13 July 1949, TS control no. 2-8303, file no. 2-8300 to 2-8399, box 45, entry 214, RG 341, NA. Document is now declassified.

28. Col John M. Schweitzer Jr., executive, Directorate of Intelligence, to director of Communications, Operations Division, director of Plans and Operations (D/P&O), letter, subject: Proposed Supplemental Electronic Reconnaissance Operations, 10 June 1949, TS control no. 2-7893-A, file no. 2-7800 to 2-7899, box 45, entry 214, RG 341, NA. Document is now declassified.

29. Col Von R. Shores, acting assistant chief, Operations Division, director, Plans & Operations, letter, subject: Proposed Supplemental Electronic Reconnaissance Operations, 13 June 1949, TS control no. 2-7893-A, file no. 2-7800 to 2-7899, box 45, entry 214, RG 341, NA. Document is now declassified.

30. Maj Gen Francis L. Ankenbrandt, director of Communications, to director of Intelligence, DOS/O, R&R, subject: Ferret Missions Reporting Negative Results, 17 March 1949, TS control no. 2-6748, file no. 2-6700 to 2-6799, box 44, entry 214, RG 341, NA. Document is now declassified.

31. Notice that the estimates show a more rapid buildup of the Soviet atomic stockpile, but the same number of bombs. This is due to estimates of limited quantities of uranium ore available to the Soviets that would limit

their total capacity. Joint Nuclear Energy Intelligence Committee, memorandum for record, subject: Status of the U.S.S.R. Atomic Energy Project, 1 July 1949, TS control no. 2-8151, file no. 2-8100 to 2-8199, box 45, entry 214, RG 341, NA. Document is now declassified.

32. Contemporary documents do not identify the Tupolev Tu-4 by name. Instead, they refer to the aircraft as "the Soviet B-29." I have adopted this practice. For further information on the Tupolev Tu-4 and the Soviet program to reverse engineer the B-29, see G. Scott Gorman, "The Tu-4: The Trevails of Technology Transfer by Imitation," *Air Power History* 45, no.1 (spring 1998): 16–27; and Von Hardesty, "Made in the U.S.S.R.," *Air & Space* 15, no. 6 (February/March 2001): 68–79.

33. Col Frank P. Sturdivant, executive, Air Intelligence Division, Directorate of Intelligence, to Industrial Planning Division, Directorate of Procurement and Industrial Planning, R&R, subject: Strategic Consideration Re Boeing Aircraft Production, 12 August 1949, TS control no. 2-8670, file no. 2-8600 to 2-8699, box 45, entry 214, RG 341, NA; and Central Intelligence Agency, IM-203, "The Soviet Air Forces," 25 July 1949, folder: Russia 1949–1952, box 187, subject file: Foreign Affairs file (Russia-1), President's Secretary's file, Harry S. Truman, Presidential Library, Independence, Mo. (hereafter HSTL). Document is now declassified.

34. Jim G. Lucas to Mr. Stone, letter, subject: Alaskan trip report, 9 April 1948, 4, file: CCS 660.2 Alaska, 3-23-45, sec. 4, RG 218, NA.

35. Sturdivant, R&R.

36. Dubbed the "buzz bomb," the German V-1 bombardment rocket featured a pulse jet engine, a 1,875-pound high-explosive warhead, and a maximum range of 125 miles. The V-2 long-range bombardment rocket carried a 2,150-pound high-explosive warhead for a 200-mile maximum range. Alfred Price, "V-Weapons," in *The Oxford Companion to World War II*, gen. ed. I. C. B. Dear (Oxford: Oxford University Press, 1995): 1249–53; "Intelligence Annex for the Air Force Research and Development Plan for the Fiscal Year 1952," 12 August 1949, TS control no. 2-8184A, file no. 2-8100 to 2-8199, box 45, entry 214, RG 341, NA; and Headquarters SAC, Intelligence brief no. 67, "Soviet Long-Range Missiles," 15 September 1948, folder 13, box 4, series 3, Harry R. Borowski Papers (hereafter Borowski Papers). Document is now declassified.

37. Brig Gen D. L. Putt, director of Research & Development Office, deputy chief of staff, Materiel, to director of Intelligence, DCS/O, letter, subject: Countermeasures to Soviet Guided Missiles, 22 December 1948, TS control no. 2-7817, file no. 2-7800 to 2-7899, box 45, entry 214, RG 341, NA. Document is now declassified.

38. JCS 1952/8, *Joint Intelligence Estimate for Basing Operational Evaluation Success of the Strategic Air Offensive*, 25 August 1949, app. C, 92, RG 218, NA in Steven T. Ross and David Alan Rosenberg, eds., *America's Plans for War against the Soviet Union* (New York: Garland Publishing, 1989), vol. 12, *Budgets and Strategy: The Road to Offtackle*.

39. Ibid., 93, RG 218. Although not mentioned in the Air Intelligence assessment, CIA historian Donald E. Welzenbach explained that the highly regarded American SCR-584 suffered "mean-time-between-failure rate" of between 10 and 12 hours for a key component. Eventually, the United States developed an operational work around for the defect by not turning on the SCR-584 until an SCR-270 (or other early warning radar) had acquired a target. Perhaps the Soviets experienced similar problems with their lend-lease sets. Donald E. Welzenbach, "The Anglo-American Orgins of Overflying the Soviet Union: The Case of the 'Invisible Aircraft,'" *Proceedings*, joint meeting of the Royal Air Force Historical Society and the Air Force Historical Foundation (Washington, D.C.: Air Force History and Museums Program, 1995), 194.

40. JCS/1952/8, app. C, in Ross and Rosenberg.

41. JIC 439/13, *Joint Intelligence Committee Estimate on Basing Operational Evaluation of Prospects of Success of Strategic Air Offensive*, 22 August 1949, 4–5, 11, file no. CCS 373 (10-23-48) sec. 4, RG 218, NA, in Ross and Rosenberg.

42. Ibid., app. A, 12.

43. JCS 1952/8, app. C, 96, in Ross and Rosenberg.

44. Ibid., 99. An Air Force intelligence report on the same subject cited only 49 SCR-584 sets provided to the Soviets in lend-lease, but agreed with JCS 1952/8 in its assessment. The higher figure (80) probably includes a British-produced version of the SCR-584, designated the GL mark 3A. Both Louis Brown and Steven Zaloga concur with the SAC Intelligence Brief figure of 49 SCR-584s provided by the US Lend-Lease Plan. The report explained that the SCR-584 had an early warning range of 70,000 yards (approx. 40 miles) and a gun-laying range of 32,000 yards (approx. 18 miles). Headquarters SAC, Intelligence Brief no. 44, "Capabilities of Soviet Anti-Aircraft for Defense Against VHB Operations," file no. 416.606-44, 12 April 1948, USAFHRC; Brown, 191; and Zaloga, 111–12.

45. JCS 1844/46, 345, in Ross and Rosenberg. See also the introduction to the volume for a summary of *Offtackle*, vii.

46. On 19 May 1948, the JCS approved a short-range emergency war plan named Halfmoon that closely followed the concepts of war plan Broiler. Although Halfmoon called for the destruction of 70 Soviet cities with 133 atomic bombs, the plan differed little from the preceding series. Since Offtackle represents the plan under discussion during the bitterest interservice feuding and the most recent of the declassified war plans, it is considered more useful for analysis. For a summary of Halfmoon, see Steven T. Ross, *American War Plans 1945–1950* (New York: Garland Publishing, 1988), 89–98.

47. Ross and Rosenberg, vol. 12, vi.

48. Ibid.; JCS 1844/37, 266; and JCS 1844/46, encl., 350, in Ross and Rosenberg.

49. JCS 1844/46, encl., 348, in Ross and Rosenberg.

50. Ibid., 358, 366.

51. Ibid., 406.

52. JCS 1844/37, 267, and JCS 1844/46, encl., 350, in Ross and Rosenberg.

53. JCS 1844/46, 8 December 1949, revision, 339, in Ross and Rosenberg.

54. Note the failure to mention a shortage of reconnaissance aircraft. Air Force leaders faced so many problems that reconnaissance did not become an overriding priority. JCS 1844/46, encl., 367, in Ross and Rosenberg.

55. JCS 1844/47, encl., 436, in Ross and Rosenberg.

56. "Evaluation of Effect on Soviet War Effort Resulting from the Strategic Air Offensive," 11 May 1949 in Thomas H. Etzold and John Lewis Gaddis, eds., *Containment: Documents on American Policy and Strategy, 1949–1950* (New York: Columbia University Press, 1978), 361.

57. Ibid., 362; and Rearden, 407.

58. Etzold and Gaddis, 362.

59. Ibid., 364.

60. Dr. Robert L. Stearns, president of the University of Colorado, served as chairman of the WSEG. Other members included, Henry C. Alexander; Donald F. Carpenter; Seymour E. Harris; Dr. John Dollard; Gen Lucius D. Clay, USA, retired; Elihu Root Jr.; Rowan Gaither; Albert J. Carey; James F. Pinkney; Walter Giford; Warren Weaver; Chester Barnard; Don Marquis; Dr. Fred Stephan; Sidney K. Wolf; Adm Ben Moreell, USN, retired; Dr. Mervin J. Kelly; James A. Perkins; Thomas W. Lamont; Junius Morgan; Edward S. Mason; and Sherman Kent. Lt Gen J. E. Hull, USA, director, WSEG, to JCS, memorandum, 31 May 1950 in Ross and Rosenberg, vol. 13, *Evaluating the Air Offensive: The WSEG 1 Study*, xx–xxi.

61. For the lower set of assumptions, the group assumed that the Soviets employed 1,800 PVO fighters and 100 night fighters. JCS 1952/11, *WSEG Report No. 1*, 10 February 1950, encl. C, c-3, in Ross and Rosenberg, vol. 13. In addition, the group assumed that the Soviets had improved only 25 percent of their 10,000 World War II antiartillery guns, had no unguided rockets, and used the standard German KG 40 fire-control director, *Würzburg* radar, and time-fused shells. JCS 1952/11, 168, in Ross and Rosenberg.

62. The higher set of assumptions added 2,200 additional planes from Soviet tactical and naval air forces to the 1,800 PVO fighters and included 300 night fighters based upon the German Me-262 jet fighter. JCS 1952/11, encl. C, c-3 and c-15, in Ross and Rosenberg. Plus, the higher set of estimated Soviet antiaircraft weapons included 3,500 modernized 88-millimeter guns; 3,500 *Taifun* rocket launchers; 8,000 conventional guns; fire control radar similar to the US SCR-584; fire control directors similar to the US M-9, and contact fused shells. JCS 1952/11, 168, in Ross and Rosenberg. In contrast, the World War II German air defense system numbered 12,000 AAA guns, 800 night fighters, and 1,500 fighters to oppose the 3,000 four-engine bombers of the US Eighth Air Force alone. JCS 1952/11, 166, in Ross and Rosenberg.

63. JCS 1952/11, 158, in Ross and Rosenberg.

64. Operating an airborne radar set was (and still is) as much of an art as a science. Certain types of buildings reflect radar energy better than other buildings. In addition, large cities often appear as amorphous blobs with few distinguishing features. Thus, cities with distinct geographical features or cities that offer land-water contrast, like San Francisco, Calif., are easy targets, while those with few distinguishing features, such as Omaha, Nebr., are difficult. Author's personal observation based on 4,600 flying hours as a navigator using 1950s vintage radar technology; JCS 1952/11, 185–88, in Ross and Rosenberg.

65. Ibid., 189.

66. Ibid., 163, 184. The projected forces available to the USAF on 1 May 1950 included 570 medium bombers (B-29s and B-50s) and 54 heavy bombers (B-36s). However, much of this force was devoted to training, command support, and replacement. In addition, the WSEG used the following data to determine air abort rates.

Altitude	B-29	B-50	B-36
20,000 ft.	4.5%	5%	11%
25,000 ft.	6%	—	—
30,000 ft.	11%	6%	14%
35,000 ft.	x	11%	—
40,000 ft.	x	x	20%

67. JCS 1952/11, 191, in Ross and Rosenberg.

68. Ibid., 158–59.

69. Ibid., 193.

70. Rearden, 408–10.

71. JCS 1952/11, 153, 161, 165, in Ross and Rosenberg.

72. In the winter of 1943–1944, the Luftwaffe combined improved SN2 AI radar and innovative, air-to-air tactics to inflict devastating casualties upon the RAF night bombing campaign.

73. JCS 1952/11, 162, 188, in Ross and Rosenberg.

74. Tony Holmes, *Jane's Historic Military Aircraft* (London: HarperCollins Publishers, 1998), 364.

75. W. Stuart Symington, secretary of the Air Force, to Louis A. Johnson, secretary of defense, memorandum, 8 November 1949, file: Atomic Energy-Russia, box 201, President's Secretary's file, HSTL; and Bradley and Blair, 513–14.

76. US Atomic Energy Commission, memorandum, subject: "History of the Long-Range Detection Program," 21 July 1948, file: Atomic Bomb-Long Range Detection Program, box 199, subject file: National Security Council-Atomic, President's Secretary's file, HSTL; and Richard G. Hewlett and Francis Duncan, *A History of the Atomic Energy Commission* (University Park, Pa.: The Pennsylvania State University Press, 1969), vol. 2, *Atomic Shield 1947–1952*, 130–31;

and Jeffrey Richelson, *American Espionage and the Soviet Target* (New York: William Morrow & Co., 1987), 115.

77. Atomic Energy Commission memorandum, 2; Lewis L. Strauss, *Men and Decisions* (Garden City, N.Y.: Doubleday, 1962), 202, 204; Richelson, 116; and Hewlett and Duncan, 131.

78. Richelson, 117.

79. Doyle L. Northrup, technical director, AFOAT-1, to Major General Nelson, memorandum, subject: Atomic Detection System Alert No. 12, 19 September 1949; and Hoyt S. Vandenberg, chief of staff, US Air Force, to secretary of defense, memorandum, subject: Long Range Detection of Atomic Explosions, 21 September 1949, file: Atomic Bomb-Long Range Detection Program, box 199, subject file: National Security Council Atomic, President's Secretary's file, HSTL; Robert J. Donovan, 98–99; and Richelson, 117–18.

80. NSC-68, *United States Objectives and Programs for National Security,* 14 April 1950, in John Lewis Gaddis and Thomas H. Etzold, *Containment: Documents on American Policy and Strategy, 1945–1950* (New York: Columbia University Press, 1978), 438.

81. John Lewis Gaddis, *Strategies of Containment* (New York: Oxford University Press, 1982), 93–94.

82. Alan G. Kirk, "Telegram: Ambassador in Soviet Union to Secretary of State, Moscow, April, 1950," in Everett Gleason and Frederick Aandahl, gen. ed., *Foreign Relations of the United States 1950,* vol. 4, *Central and Eastern Europe;* and *The Soviet Union,* Rogers P. Churchill, Charles S. Sampson, and William Z. Slanney, eds. (Washington, D.C.: Government Printing Office, 1980), 1141–42.

83. Churchill, Sampson, and Slanney, 1140–41.

84. This rather cryptic phrase appears significant because apparently the early Ferret program was conducted without specific presidential authorization. As a result, official sources dodged all questions concerning the purpose of the flight. Adm Forrest Sherman, CNO, to secretary of the Navy, memorandum, subject: Attack on United States Aircraft by Soviet Aircraft, 14 April 1950, Frederick Aandahl, 1142–43.

85. Ibid.

86. "McCormick Urges Break in Relations," *New York Herald Tribune,* 22 April 1950, 1, folder: Russo-American Incident over Baltic Area, April 1950, box 154, Democratic National Committee (DNC) Library Clipping file, Foreign Affairs File, HSTL.

87. Marquis Childs, "Baltic Plane Mystery," *Washington Post,* 28 April 1950, n.p., folder: Incident of U.S. Plane Shot Down in Baltic, April 1950, box 153, DNC, Foreign Affairs file, HSTL.

88. Ibid.; and Drew Pearson, "Washington Merry Go Round," *New York Mirror,* 9 May 1950, n.p.

89. Walter Lippman, "The Baltic Affair," *Washington Post,* 24 April 1950, n.p., folder: Incident of U.S. Plane Shot Down in Baltic, April 1950, box 153, DNC, Foreign Affairs file, HSTL.

90. Ibid.

91. Ibid.

92. Gen Omar Bradley, to secretary of defense, memorandum, subject: Special Airborne Search Operations, 5 May 1950, general file: Bradley Omar N. (hereafter Bradley file), President's Secretary's file, HSTL.

93. Ibid.

94. Although established as the Special Electronic Airborne Search Project, the reconnaissance program became known as the Special Electronic Search Project. Ground sites and naval vessels augmented the effort. Bradley, Special Electronic Airborne Search Project memorandum, 5 May 1950, HSTL; Louis Johnson, secretary of defense, to president, memorandum, subject: Special Electronic Search Operations, 24 May 1950, in Bradley file.

Chapter 5

The Test: Strategic Reconnaissance in Korea, 1950–1953

An outstanding fact of the Korean War was the number of old lessons that had to be relearned. . . . It appears that these lessons were either forgotten or never were documented—or if documented, were never disseminated.

—Gen Otto P. Weyland

The sudden North Korean attack on the Republic of Korea on 25 June 1950 challenged the resolve, doctrine, and capabilities of the United States. The war's outbreak appeared to validate the conclusions of NSC-68 and posed a test to "containment." Yet, more than a threat to the intellectual basis of American foreign policy, fighting in Korea tested the capabilities of the USAF. For air planners, the skies of Korea replaced the statistical formulas of the Weapons Systems Evaluation Group. In particular, American B-29 strategic bombers and RB-29, RB-45C, and RF-80 reconnaissance aircraft faced Soviet frontline aircraft piloted by Russians, Chinese, and North Koreans.[1] The realities of combat provided a test of strategic air war and, in particular, for aerial reconnaissance. By the end of the war, aerial reconnaissance proved invaluable; however, enemy air defenses rendered existing strategic reconnaissance aircraft obsolete.

The specter of global war formed the strategic context behind events in Korea. Like the Berlin crisis, President Truman and most allied leaders worried about escalation and a general war. In July 1950, rapid North Korean gains inspired joint strategic talks between the United Sates and the United Kingdom. Headed by Gen Omar N. Bradley, CJCS, and Ambassador Philip C. Jessup on the American side and Lord Arthur Tedder and Sir Oliver Francis on the British side, allied delegations agreed to localize the Korean conflict as much as possible. They sought to limit the involvement of troops on the Asian landmass in light of the potential threat to Europe. Consequently, the American and British

133

leaders decided to increase military strength, establish joint planning staffs, and study further options in the event of Communist Chinese intervention. However, in one critical area, the two sides disagreed. The US representatives vehemently rejected a British intelligence study of Soviet military capability. The British believed that the Soviets would not be prepared to engage in general war before 1955. On the contrary, the Americans stressed their estimate that the Russians would be prepared by 1952 or earlier, and before that time, the Russians would attempt to "cause maximum difficulties short of general war."[2] Throughout the conflict, American policy makers worried that the North Korean onslaught might simply be a diversionary tactic, an attempt to draw US attention away from a full-scale Soviet invasion of Europe.[3]

The surprise achieved by North Korean troops revealed the neglect of aerial reconnaissance in the FEAF. During the turmoil of the war's early months, UN forces suffered from short-

The North American RB-45C Tornado first flew in April 1950, entering service in July 1950. With a crew of three, it could reach a top speed of 480 miles per hour and a maximum ceiling of 37,500 feet while carrying as many as 10 cameras. Although an improvement over World War II bomber air frames, the RB-45C still lacked the performance and range for deep-penetration missions.

ages of reconnaissance aircraft, intelligence personnel, and maps. At the beginning of the war, FEAF reconnaissance included only 18 RF-80As of the 8th Tactical Reconnaissance Squadron, four RB-29s and one B-29 of the 31st SRS, and two RB-17s and three RB-45s of the 6204th Photo Mapping Flight. Of the RB-29s, only two were photoreconnaissance planes, although a pair of RF-80s had been modified to include cameras and drop tanks for extended range.[4] In addition, budget limits reduced flying training, resulting in aircrews with minimal flight proficiency. Equally important, FEAF lacked trained, experienced intelligence personnel. Within a week of the war's out-

To augment reconnaissance experience at the outbreak of the Korean War, Lt Gen George Stratemeyer specifically requested the services of Col Karl L. Prolifka, a legendary World War II reconnaissance pilot. Unfortunately, Prolifka was later killed in action.

break, the number of personnel assigned to the FEAF intelligence office doubled, but these men possessed no intelligence experience. Shortages of qualified intelligence personnel, especially photo-interpreters, made continuous surveillance of enemy troop movements, concentrations, and airfields impossible.[5] For example, as late as December 1950, Lt Gen George E. Stratemeyer, FEAF commander, sent a Top Secret "Redline" cable to Vice Chief of Staff, Gen Nathan F. Twining, requesting by name the assignment of Col Karl L. Prolifka and four reserve officers who were experienced photo-interpreters. Although General Twining provided Prolifka, who had earned renown as a reconnaissance pilot in World War II, the return cable replied, "Major portion of ZI [Zone of the Interior—the continental US] PI [photo-interpreters] resources have been drained."[6] To make matters worse, FEAF air planners discovered that previous stocks of aeronautical charts for Korea had been declared obsolete and destroyed before the war. An Air

Force–wide search uncovered only 25 remaining copies that were reproduced.[7] In sum, a later evaluation reported: "It is the old story of failure, in time of peace, to maintain within the units Intelligence personnel sufficient in numbers and in training to serve the needs of those units should they be thrown suddenly into combat operations."[8]

Despite its initial flaws, FEAF aerial reconnaissance exploited the lack of enemy air opposition to provide vital tactical reconnaissance. Photographs from RF-80s and RB-29s quickly proved the most reliable source of battlefield intelligence. Photo intelligence allowed field commanders to plan operations, track their progress, and assess results.[9] In September 1950, the two weary RB-17s of the 6204th Photo Mapping Flight began mapping North Korea. Later augmented by RB-29s of the 31st SRS, the planes provided over 12,000 miles of photomapping coverage.[10] In an effort to ascertain the enemy's air order of battle, FEAF reconnaissance flights surveyed Manchurian (northeastern China) airfields using oblique photography by occasional overflights using the two camera-equipped RF-80s.[11] Nevertheless, as a general rule, President Truman's worries over the prospect of general war prevented deep-penetration overflights of Soviet or Chinese territory. In keeping with the president's wishes, JCS memorandum 2150/5 established the following rules for aerial reconnaissance:

> In order to establish the fact of support to the North Koreans by the USSR or the Chinese Communists, you are authorized to conduct aerial reconnaissance over all Korean territory, including Korean coastal waters, up to the Yalu River on the west coast and up to but short of the Korean-Soviet international boundary on the east coast. Such aerial reconnaissance operations will be conducted from as far south of the frontiers of Manchuria or the Soviet Union as practicable and in no case will these frontiers be overflown.[12]

Thus, even though a few photoreconnaissance missions flew over Manchuria in general, political considerations limited FEAF reconnaissance efforts that may have detected Chinese infiltration of units across the Yalu River.

Even without political restrictions, FEAF aerial reconnaissance lacked the ability to provide continuous coverage of the Sino-Korean border in the fall of 1950. Since the Communist Chinese armies moved primarily at night and employed excellent camouflage, FEAF's periodic daylight photo sorties showed no troop movements. Additionally, the shortage of trained and experienced photo-interpreters meant large numbers of film negatives went unstudied. The strategic surprise achieved by the Chinese Communists emphasized the danger of inadequate aerial reconnaissance. The reports of negative activity from reconnaissance aircraft reinforced the false assumptions of the FEC, and conversely, the lack of FEC concern meant the limited intelligence resources available were not looking for Communist Chinese activity.[13] At the core of the problem, both the FEC and the JCS believed that Moscow controlled Chinese actions. Convinced that the Soviets would not allow a solo Chinese effort, US military leaders focused upon the Soviet threat.[14] In other words, inaccurate information fed faulty analysis, which in turn supported flawed preconceptions. US strategic reconnaissance missed Communist China's preparations for intervention for technical as well as political reasons. Because of this technical failure, military leaders discounted diplomatic signals of impending Chinese intervention.

Outside the Korean peninsula, the USAF renewed efforts to watch the Soviets. The president granted permission for the Air Force to resume ECM flights in the Baltic area on 6 June 1950. The flights, scheduled twice a week, followed the guidelines established by the Special Electronic Search Program (SESP). George W. Perkins, assistant secretary of state, called for a two-week suspension of the ECM missions due to the outbreak of hostilities in Korea. He believed another Baltic incident might jeopardize the strong American position in the UN and threaten efforts to localize the conflict in Korea. Reluctantly, the JCS approved the suspension, recognizing the impact of aerial reconnaissance on foreign policy. Once the UN decided to intervene on the behalf of South Korea, the State Department relented. On 22 July 1950, General Bradley ordered the Air Force to resume Baltic Sea ECM flights.[15]

European activities dramatized the expansion of strategic aerial reconnaissance in 1950. The new 55th Strategic Reconnaissance Wing (SRW) supplied detachments of three RB-50 Ferrets and two KB-29 tankers for SESP and were based at RAF Lakenheath and RAF Mildenhall, United Kingdom. The

RB-50 Ferrets flew electronic surveillance along the Soviet borders.[16] In addition, by January 1951, SAC reconnaissance aircraft had begun Project Roundout, whose mission was to photograph all potential targets in Western Europe. Since US war plans assumed a rapid Soviet conquest of the continent, SAC required target folders for strikes designed to "retard" the Soviet advance. As a result, five RB-29s photographed sites in Germany, Austria, France, the Netherlands, Belgium, and Italy.[17] Due to the slow progress made by the RB-29s in mapping the Soviet border in September 1952, SAC deployed RB-36 detachments to RAF Fairford, United Kingdom. The huge RB-36 aircraft flew mapping sorties over Western Europe, but were restricted from flying within 200 miles of Soviet-controlled territory.[18]

Adding to the expanded scope of SAC operations, creation of the 55th SRW increased the size of the US aerial reconnaissance program. The manning of the "Fighting Fifty-fifth" on 1 November 1950, provided an organization solely dedicated to strategic reconnaissance.[19] Initially based at Ramey AFB, Puerto Rico, the three reconnaissance squadrons of the 55th represented a diverse assortment of aircraft and missions. The 14 RB-50Es of the 38th SRS, Photo, provided aerial photography, visual observation, radarscope photography, and weather observations.[20] The 338th SRS, Photomapping, added the ability to accomplish electronic geodetic mapping with its 15 RB-50F aircraft. Geodetic mapping utilized the short-range navigation (SHORAN) system to produce highly accurate aeronautical charts. The information from these missions provided the basis for SHORAN bombardment, permitting bombers to strike without seeing their targets.[21] Rounding out the wing, the 14 RB-50Gs of the 343d SRS, Electronics, provided "air intelligence of enemy electronic missions throughout the full range of the usable spectrum. . . . and night aerial photography."[22] In sum, the 55th SRW formed an expanded, permanent organizational structure for Air Force strategic reconnaissance.

By early November 1950, new equipment boosted the capabilities of FEAF aerial reconnaissance. On 16 November 1950, the 91st SRS replaced the 31st SRS as the primary "heavy" reconnaissance unit in the Pacific.[23] The 91st consisted of nine

A Boeing KB-29P extends the 1,910 NM-maximum range of a North American RB-45C Tornado by aerial refueling.

RB-29 aircraft, including three equipped with SHORAN and two modified for Ferret missions. In addition, SAC provided four RB-45C jet photoreconnaissance aircraft.[24] Although the RB-45 offered only moderate speed and altitude performance, it represented a major improvement over the prop-driven RB-29s. By August 1951, the 91st added "Detachment 3" consisting of three advanced RB-50G electronic reconnaissance aircraft on rotation from SAC's 343d SRS. Each aircraft employed a crew of 16, including eight Ravens featuring an array of the most sophisticated ELINT equipment available.[25]

A massive assault by Communist Chinese troops on 25 November 1950 radically altered the Korean War and fanned US fears of global war. General Bradley expressed the mood succinctly, "We viewed the possibility of Chinese intervention as we did the possibility of Soviet intervention in North Korea: a probable signal that the Russians were moving toward global war."[26] Less than two weeks after the initial Chinese onslaught, Gen Hoyt S. Vandenberg, Air Force chief of staff, sent the following Top Secret message to his commanders in the United States: "The JCS consider that the current situation in Korea has greatly increased the possibility of general war.

Take such action as is feasible to increase readiness without creating [an] atmosphere of alarm."[27] General Stratemeyer, FEAF commander, further recommended that General Vandenberg issue a warning order to SAC and deploy atomic-capable medium bombers to FEAF Bomber Command.[28] Following this line of thought, the JCS proposed a list of recommendations to the secretary of defense in the event of various Korean developments. One particularly ominous proposal stated: "If the USSR commits units of Soviet 'volunteers' sufficient to be critical to the safety of the United Nations forces, United Nations forces should be withdrawn. The United States should then mobilize for general war."[29] Therefore, the Chinese intervention in Korea created a crisis atmosphere in US strategic planning. Military leaders viewed the conflict as a prelude to a general war demanding increased strategic intelligence and prompting a review of existing war plans.

At the height of the crisis in December 1950, General Vandenberg asked Dr. Bernard Brodie, noted author on atomic strategy, to inspect and comment on the current JCS target list. The list represented the work of the Air Intelligence Production Division (later, the Air Targets Division) of the Air Force Directorate of Intelligence and formed the basis of SAC's operational plans. Dr. Brodie strongly criticized the air planners for failing to calculate the overall impact of the strategic air offensive. His review revealed significant intelligence gaps; for example, the Air Staff did not know where all the major Soviet power plants were located. Without this knowledge, the total damage inflicted upon Soviet industry could not be calculated. In other words, no rational, quantifiable strategy for destroying the Soviet ability to wage war existed. Apparently, the planners simply expected the Soviet Union to collapse following an atomic attack.[30]

Ironically, General LeMay, SAC commander, attacked the target list from another angle. At a high-level meeting on 22 January 1951, he stressed that current planning placed unrealistic demands on his aircrews. Too many targets required visual, prestrike reconnaissance and isolated, unfamiliar target complexes would be difficult to locate by radar, especially in periods of bad weather. As a result, General LeMay argued that "we should concentrate on industry itself which is located in urban areas," so that even if a bomb missed, "a bonus will be derived from the use of the bomb."[31]

As Chinese troops routed UN forces during November and December 1950, US strategic reconnaissance prepared for war against the People's Republic of China (PRC). In response to a request from Headquarters USAF, FEAF intelligence assembled existing target information. By December researchers had compiled a list of 221 targets in Indochina, Burma, Thailand, and China in addition to those already gathered for Korea and Manchuria.[32] Reconnaissance units expanded coverage of Southeast Asia as the Air Force and Navy coordinated efforts. The 91st SRS operated SESP sorties from Yokota AB, Japan, and Kadena AB, Okinawa, to explore enemy defenses north of Shanghai, China. On the other hand, the Navy flew P4M-1Q Ferret aircraft from Sangley Point, Republic of the Philippines, for targets in South China.[33]

In addition to Ferret missions, Air Force strategic reconnaissance gathered radarscope and aerial photography of Chinese and Soviet targets. During the Chinese intervention crisis of December 1950, President Truman authorized deep-penetration overflights of Soviet territory. Headquarters USAF and the JCS selected the new Boeing B-47 Stratojet bomber as the platform for the mission. The fourth production model was modified for camera installation. Unfortunately, an accidental fire destroyed the plane on 15 August 1951 before its first overflight mission. A year later the president again approved an overflight of Siberia and the Chukotski Peninsula. On 14 October 1952, two modified B-47s penetrated Soviet territory. The primary aircraft, piloted by Col Donald E. Hillman, photographed Siberian targets, including facilities at Egvekinot, Russia; Provideniya, Russia; and the Chukotski Peninsula. The backup aircraft, led by Col Patrick D. Fleming, covered Wrangel Island and established an orbit over the Chukchi Sea. Although Hillman's crew overflew 3,500 miles of Soviet territory and Fleming's team overflew another 1,000 miles, both sorties completed the missions without incident.[34]

For the same reasons, President Truman sanctioned a joint Air Force–Navy project to combine a special Navy P2V-3W Fer-

Modified Navy P2V Neptune patrol planes conducted electronic reconnaissance missions along the coast of China and the Soviet Far East during the Korean War.

ret aircraft with an Air Force RB-29 to probe the eastern coast of Siberia. From 2 April to 16 June 1952, the duo relied on the Navy aircraft's APS-20 radar and associated electronic package to identify and locate targets for the RB-29's cameras. Based primarily out of Kodiak Island, Alaska, the Ferret photo team ventured from Kamchatka, Russia, to the Bering Strait and on to Wrangel Island, flying from 15 to 20 miles inland.[35]

Even more perilous than USAF overflights, Britain's RAF flew American reconnaissance aircraft over heavily defended areas of the western USSR. Dubbed the "Special Duty Flight" under the leadership of Squadron Leader John Crampton and Flight Lieutenant Rex Sanders, the covert unit flew three North American RB-45Cs from RAF Sculthorpe, United Kingdom, deep into European Russia on the night of 17–18 April 1952. Penetrating Soviet airspace simultaneously over the

Baltic, Belorussia, and the Ukraine, the three aircraft with RAF markings and British pilots encountered numerous Soviet interceptors. Fortunately, darkness, altitude, and luck provided sufficient protection for the crews as they sought photos of Soviet long-range air force bases.[36]

Although the expanded Ferret program and covert overflights did not totally bridge the intelligence gap, USAF, RAF, and Navy strategic reconnaissance provided previously unobtainable information. In July 1951, FEAF reconnaissance reported progress in developing aids to enable a radar bombardier to identify and bomb unfamiliar targets. Target folders included two new types of charts: the target complex radar analysis chart that featured a scale line drawing of the target area showing the height and construction material of installations and the terrain features that would appear on a radarscope, as well as the radar approach chart that displayed a series of radarscope photographs prepared on selected approach headings for significant target areas.[37] In addition to the overflight sorties previously mentioned, at least three radarscope photographic missions were flown against Chinese targets in the Shantung Peninsula in June and July 1951, but declassified details are sketchy.[38]

Navy participation in SESP projects in Southeast Asia stemmed from President Truman's decision to move the Seventh Fleet to the Formosa Strait on 10 July 1950. Originally, Navy reconnaissance efforts focused upon a potential Communist Chinese invasion of the Nationalist stronghold on Formosa (Taiwan).[39] On 28 July 1950, the JCS recommended Naval photoreconnaissance of the Chinese coast from Swatow north to latitude 26° 30′ north in an effort to spot PRC amphibious preparations against Taiwan.[40] Eventually, both Navy and Air Force reconnaissance concentrated on providing data for strategic bombing targets. For example, SESP efforts focused on 12 special targets selected on the assumption that the geographical restrictions would be lifted for UN forces.[41] Significantly, the fighting in Korea quelled the Air Force–Navy feuding over roles and missions. Unlike 1949, the services proved cooperative as budget woes eased, and a shooting war demanded effective interservice cooperation.

When a North Korean pilot defected with his MiG-15 on 21 September 1953, Air Force technicians dismantled it and reassembled it at Wright–Patterson AFB, Ohio. The MiG-15's superior performance threatened aerial reconnaissance capabilities of the RB-29, RB-50, and RB-45 in the Korean War.

Coinciding with Chinese intervention in Korea, the introduction of Soviet-built MiG-15 jet fighters threatened FEAF operations. The superior speed, acceleration, climb rate, and ceiling of the Soviet fighters shocked allied air forces. In most air-to-air engagements, the greater experience and better training of American pilots prevailed; however, the MiG's 660 miles per hour (mph) top speed outperformed all US fighters, except arguably the North American F-86 Sabre. Nevertheless, the MiG-15 totally outclassed the lumbering RB-29s and RB-50s employed for strategic reconnaissance, as well as the RF-80s and RB-45s used for tactical reconnaissance and overflight missions. Initially, communist pilots hesitated to attack FEAF aircraft, but this changed during the spring of 1951.[42] For example, on 12 April 1951, North Korean air defenses mustered over 100 MiGs to attack 48 B-29s near Sinuiju, North Korea, downing three bombers. By mid-1951, the North Korean air defense system efficiently integrated early warning, GCI, gun-laying radars, AAA, and jet fighters. Perhaps the most devastating raid occurred on 23 October 1951 when a

144

swarm of over 50 MiGs mauled a force of nine B-29s. The unescorted formation lost a total of eight—three B-29s shot down and five heavily damaged. This attack resulted in the end of daylight missions for FEAF Bomber Command.[43]

The coupling of MiG-15s with effective radar severely limited the activities of FEAF strategic reconnaissance aircraft. By June 1951, FEAF Bomber Command had restricted the slow RB-29s against operating in northwestern Korea without fighter escort.[44] Eventually, enemy fighters denied "MiG Alley" to RB-29 daylight photography. Consequently, FEAF relied upon the jet reconnaissance aircraft of the 67th Tactical Fighter Wing (TFW), but even these aircraft were hard pressed. By mid-1952, a flight of two RF-80s required an escort of 40 F-86 fighters, resulting in the 91st SRS shifting to night operations.[45] In order to provide BDA, scheduled two to four hours after a strike, the RB-29s used K-37 or K-19 cameras and M-120 flash bombs to photograph from 22,000 to 26,000 feet above the ground. Unfortunately, technical problems plagued their night photography. Too often aircraft vibration blurred the photos, or flash bombs failed to illuminate the desired targets. Even when the equipment worked, the scale of photography proved too small for proper BDA and of little use for general surveillance.[46] A comparison of the missions flown in March and August 1951 illustrates the change in focus for FEAF strategic reconnaissance.

Missions 178 and 179 flown by the 91st SRS showed efforts to study the air defenses of North Korea (fig. 5). Like other Ferret missions, the RB-50 sorties identified probable locations of enemy radars. In addition, Ravens analyzed enemy radar signals by using a Warrick high-speed 35 mm camera to photograph the radar's signal pulse as it appeared on the aircraft's Dumont oscilloscope. At the same time, the radar observers attempted to record the tone of the signal on an ANQ-1 wire recorder.[47] After returning to base, analysts used the recorded tone for setting the frequency of radar jamming equipment. The remaining March sorties explored air defenses along Communist China's coast (figs. 6 and 7). American war planners sought as much information as possible in an effort to fill intelligence gaps following China's incursion.[48]

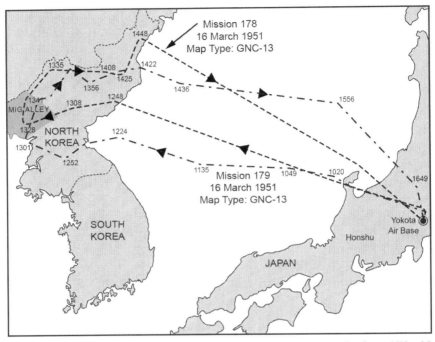

Figure 5. Location of MiG Alley and Special Photo Mission 178, 16 March 1951, and Mission 179, 16 March 1951

The missions of the 91st SRS in August 1951 demonstrated the expansion and variety of strategic reconnaissance. Adding to the ECM missions flown by RB-50Gs, the 91st SRS conducted special photoreconnaissance sorties. These flights attempted to photograph certain "hypersensitive" areas located on the borders of the Soviet Union or the PRC. For these missions, RB-29s, specially equipped with a K-30, 100-inch focal-plane camera, attempted to take long-range, oblique photographs of communist installations; occasionally RF-80s or RB-45s conducted overflights.[49] For example, special photo missions flown on 8 and 11 August 1951 concentrated on the Soviet-occupied Kurile Islands adjacent to Japan (fig. 8).

In addition, a 91st SRS RB-29 penetrated Communist Chinese airspace on a mission to photograph the city of Shanghai, China, on 25 August 1951 (fig. 9).[50] Although technical problems often marred collection efforts, these photo missions added to the American knowledge of enemy capabilities.[51]

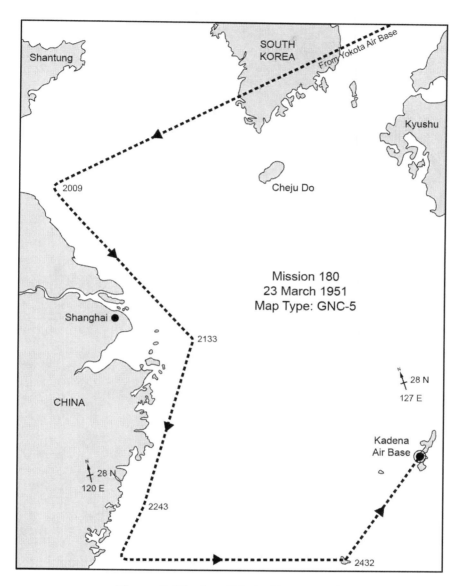

Figure 6. Mission 180, 23 March 1951

147

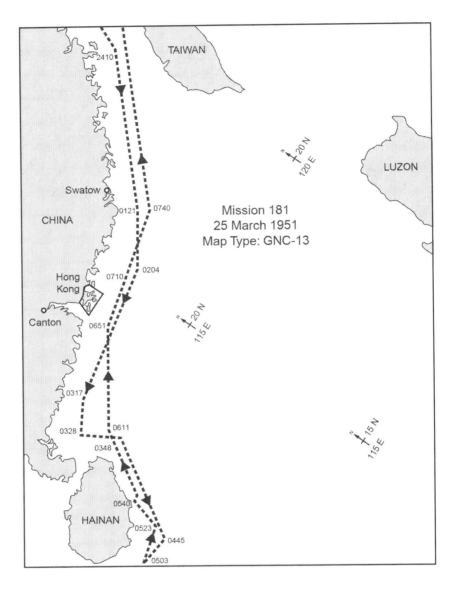

Figure 7. Mission 181, 25 March 1951

148

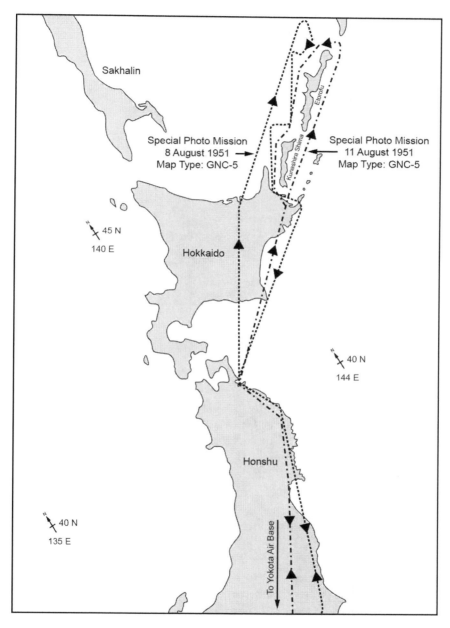

Figure 8. Special Photo Missions, 8 and 11 August 1951

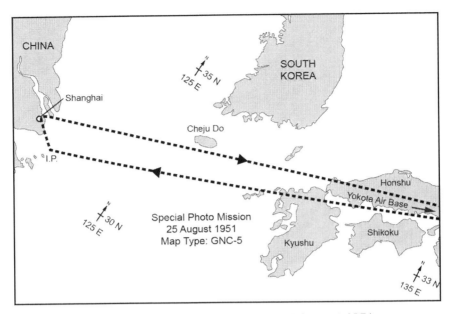

Figure 9. Special Photo Mission, 25 August 1951

A comparison of the ECM flights flown in March and August 1951 reveals a shift in emphasis from northwest Korea to the Soviet coast. Mission numbers 199 (fig. 10), 200 (fig. 11), and 204 (fig. 12) probed Soviet air defenses over the Sea of Japan and near Vladivostok. The remaining missions, numbers 201 (fig. 13) and 202 KZ (fig. 14), continued surveillance of the PRC.[52] The danger posed by the large numbers of MiG-15s was evidenced, to a large extent, by the shift away from surveillance of northwest Korea.[53] Nevertheless, the flights along the periphery of the Soviet Union represented a significant expansion in the scope of US strategic aerial reconnaissance. This expansion also reflected the need for target folders identified in previous war plans.

The Korean War demonstrated the blurring of tactical and strategic reconnaissance. For example, although intended primarily for tactical reconnaissance (BDA and targeting), RF-80s and RB-45s flew many strategic reconnaissance missions gathering information for SAC target folders.

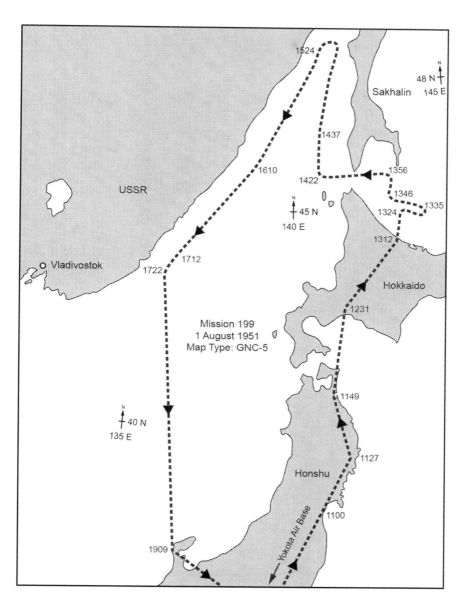

Figure 10. Mission 199, 1 August 1951

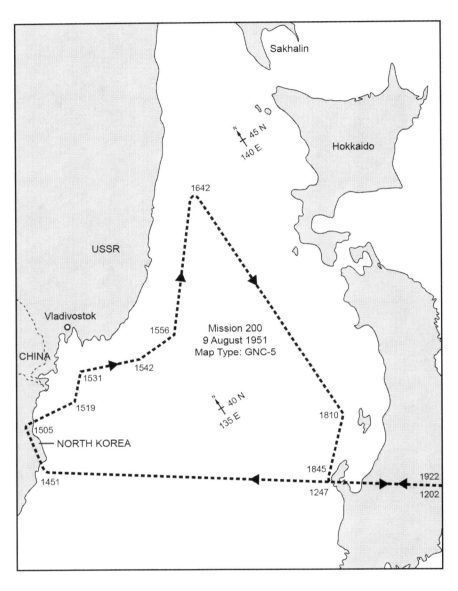

Figure 11. Mission 200, FEAF Special, 9 August 1951

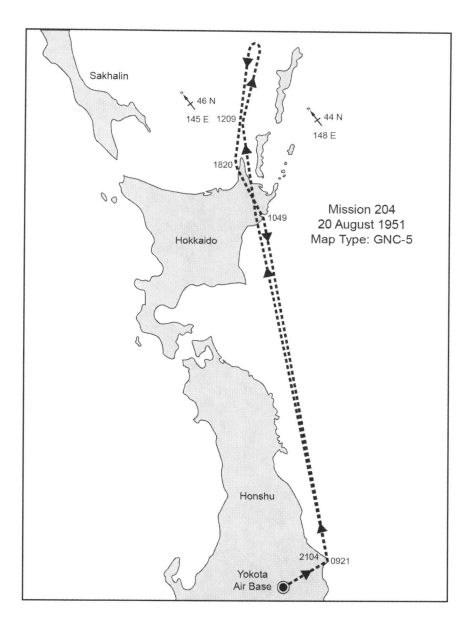

Figure 12. Mission 204, 20 August 1951

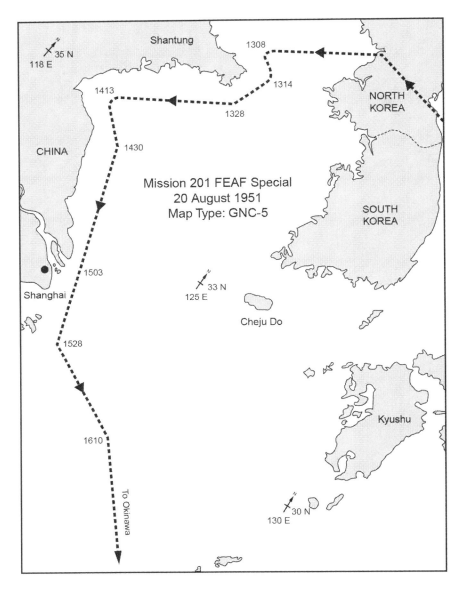

Figure 13. Mission 201, 20 August 1951

154

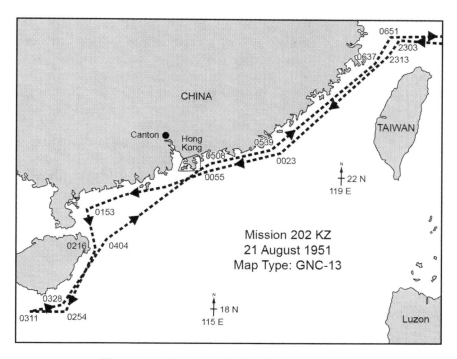

Figure 14. Mission 202 KZ, 21 August 1951

For the final 18 months of the war, growing enemy radar defenses threatened USAF strategic air operations in Korea. The total number and sophistication of the Soviet radar net increased significantly. By December 1951, 13 RUS II (or "Dumbo") radars operated in the Sinuiju to Sariwon, Korea, area alone.[54] During this period, a new type of high-frequency GCI radar, nicknamed "Token," appeared. By June 1952, Soviet radar sites guided enemy night fighters to intercept FEAF bomber formations.[55] During the latter half of 1952, the communists coordinated AAA gun-laying radar with searchlights to illuminate bombers, aiding both their night fighters and AAA. As a result, FEAF Bomber Command lost six B-29s and four crews during the month of December alone.[56] Fortunately, the enemy lacked adequate air intercept radar in their night fighters that would enable them to close for the final kill. On 30 January 1953, Brig Gen William P. Fisher, FEAF Bomber Command commander, wrote the following to Maj Gen

John B. Montgomery, SAC director of Operations: "Without wishing to appear unduly alarmed, the whole feeling here is that these guys are beginning to develop a real overall air defense team which is making our margin of security in operations slimmer all the time. If they ever crack that last link and get an all-weather capability of pressing an accurate firing attack, the B-29 business is really going to get rough."[57]

Improved enemy radar performance emphasized the equipment limits of FEAF strategic reconnaissance at a time when enhanced communist air defenses made electronic and photographic intelligence vital. FEAF strategic reconnaissance lacked the aircraft necessary to accomplish its mission. By 1953, a FEAF assessment declared the RB-29 "completely unsuited" for daytime operations where MiG-15s operated. Additionally, the RB-29 lacked an adequate long focal-length camera usable at night.[58] Problems involving the timing of the camera's shutter speed, and flash bombs that were dropped to provide illumination, plagued night photography. Even when the equipment worked, photo-interpreters found night photos difficult to analyze. Fires caused by bomb strikes distorted the shadows used by photo-interpreters to identify the height of buildings.[59] As a result of mediocre night photography, FEAF Bomber Command sought BDA from the 67th TFW jet aircraft. Unfortunately, BDA requests swamped tactical reconnaissance already overwhelmed by the needs of the Army and Fifth Air Force.[60] In theory, the jet RF-80s and RB-45s should have provided sufficient BDA coverage; however, the unarmed planes' 480 mph top speed was still too slow to survive against MiGs. In addition, the RB-45 proved particularly vulnerable to AAA. According to a FEAF report, "Even the slightest rip, tear, or battle damage affects the [RB-45's] operational characteristics."[61] As a stopgap measure, the Air Force converted six F-86 fighters to RF-86A photoreconnaissance aircraft by the spring of 1952.[62] Nevertheless, in general terms, obsolete aircraft prevented strategic reconnaissance from providing desired support for FEAF Bomber Command.

Compounding equipment problems, organizational flaws hindered reconnaissance efforts. For most of the war, SAC and FEAF acted as competing entities, with their inadequate coordination snarling reconnaissance efforts in Korea. SAC viewed preparation for a strategic air campaign against the Soviet Union as the Air Force's top priority. Under General LeMay's command, SAC recognized its shortcomings and initiated vigorous training and equipment modernization programs. This resulted in SAC considering assets sent to Korea as a diversion of scarce resources. In contrast, FEAF concentrated on the war at hand—SAC's reluctance to release aircraft and crews frustrated FEAF planners. In particular, FEAF wanted the new B-47s and RB-47s that entered the SAC inventory in 1953. Fearing compromise of the bombers' performance capabilities, General LeMay refused to release the assets.[63] Along similar lines, SAC resisted the full use of active ECM on the new aircraft.[64] Although FEAF Bomber Command (largely manned by SAC crews and staff) eventually employed jamming to counter enemy air defense radars, SAC worried that revealing too much ECM capability might jeopardize its atomic strike mission.[65] Finally, the commands failed to coordinate emergency war planning. For example, both SAC and FEAF planned to use the 91st SRS in the event of general war, and the FEAF plans duplicated targets listed in SAC Operations Plan 62-51.[66] Although General LeMay and SAC prevailed with the Air Staff, the lack of close cooperation hindered strategic reconnaissance during the Korean War.

In a similar situation, reconnaissance during the Korean War suffered due to poor communication between FEAF Bomber Command and the Fifth Air Force. Although both organizations were components of FEAF, different operational outlooks marred cooperation. FEAF Bomber Command attempted to wage a strategic air war in accordance with Air Force doctrine, while the Fifth Air Force was primarily concerned with air superiority and tactical aviation. Until a reconnaissance conference in August 1952 addressed the problem, the Fifth Air Force staff lacked access to reconnaissance photography flown by the 91st SRS.[67] Likewise, the Fifth Air Force complained of marginal ECM and ELINT capability when the 91st SRS had assembled comprehensive data on the enemy radar system. For unexplained reasons, FEAF Bomber Command failed to share information.

Gen Otto P. "Opie" Weyland assumed command of FEAF in May 1951. At the end of the Korean War, he commissioned an insightful study of aerial reconnaissance in Korea.

Following the close of hostilities in Korea, FEAF assessed the reconnaissance operations during the conflict. Commissioned by Gen Otto P. "Opie" Weyland, FEAF commander, the study scrutinized the relative effectiveness of tactical and strategic operations. The report's introduction stated, "Aerial reconnaissance proved to be of greater value than in any previous conflict and was by far the most valuable means available for obtaining intelligence on enemy activities. Aerial reconnaissance figured predominantly in every phase of the conflict."[68] The size of the reconnaissance effort alone supported this statement. Tactical reconnaissance operations in Korea surpassed the records established during World War II. For example, the 67th Tactical Reconnaissance Group (TRG) flew 2,400 sorties in May 1952, while the highest number flown by a comparable group in World War II was 1,300. Likewise, the photo group supporting the US Third Army in Europe processed 243,175 negatives a year, while the 67th TRG developed 736,684.[69]

Despite the initial statements of praise, the FEAF assessment lambasted several key aspects of reconnaissance support. The report attacked the inadequate performance of USAF reconnaissance planes in relation to enemy fighters. Inferior speed and altitude performance denied reconnaissance aircraft the freedom of movement needed to assess enemy positions. The study also listed several technical problems marring results: "Cameras failed to compensate for image motion caused by the speed of jet aircraft, night photoflash bombs lacked the necessary brightness resulting in marginal pictures, and inadequate maps reduced SHORAN bombing effectiveness."[70]

Although equipment problems handicapped reconnaissance efforts, the FEAF report cited a shortage of trained personnel as the greatest problem. Prewar budget cuts left a void in the initial number of intelligence analysts, photo-interpreters, and photographic technicians. Short tour lengths compounded the problem, causing the rotation of experienced personnel just as manning in some fields dropped below 40 percent of authorized strength.[71] Adding to the problem, many personnel assigned were of poor quality. For example, 21 percent of the airmen manning the 67th Tactical Reconnaissance Wing represented the lowest skill and aptitude scores or possessed disciplinary infractions.[72]

The Korean War demonstrated reconnaissance lagged behind other war-fighting efforts, leading the FEAF assessment to conclude by advocating for a permanent, peacetime Air Force reconnaissance program. The collection, processing, and analysis of reconnaissance suffered from equipment and personnel shortages. Additionally, the report emphasized the need for detailed, accurate mapping before hostilities began. The Korean experience taught that delay drained scarce reconnaissance resources in the critical, initial phase of conflict. In the event of atomic war, there might not be enough time to conduct prestrike mapping.[73] Therefore, the study presented the two major lessons learned in the conflict.

> One important lesson repeatedly emphasized by experience in Korea was that units which may be committed to combat should be organized with wartime personnel and equipment. Units which must absorb and train new personnel are not ready.[74]

> Secondly, there was an urgent need for an organization whose continuing responsibility would be to anticipate the needs of aerial reconnaissance, in whatever phase or field, and to devise and develop the systems, equipment, practices, and techniques necessary to fulfill these needs.[75]

The net effect of the Korean War upon aerial reconnaissance closely followed the recommendations of the FEAF study . . . one in which peacetime training and tactics could be developed. In addition, enhanced ELINT technology resulted in improved analysis of enemy defenses. Perhaps more important, the Korean War expanded the scope of reconnaissance activity in quantity, geographic area, and risk. During the fighting in Korea, the 91st SRS regularly explored the coastal waters of Communist China, North Korea, and the Soviet Far East, along with the 55th SRW detachments probing the Baltic Sea under the SESP. Of greater risk, the Korean War produced overflights of Soviet and Chinese territory of greater duration and danger than the isolated prewar sorties. Although still few in number and highly secret, these missions raised the threshold of acceptable risk for future photographic overflights.

As a test of strategic air war, the Korean War experience proved inconclusive. Advocates of strategic airpower noted that even aging B-29 bombers successfully completed assigned missions. Although the Sinuiju missions of April and October 1951 proved a setback, a shift to night missions and increased use of ECM countered enemy defenses. FEAF Bomber Command statistics showed 35 aircraft lost out of 23,572 sorties—a minuscule .0015 loss rate.[76] Furthermore, in Korea, the Air Force never employed atomic bombs—the trump card of strategic bombardment. In a November 1951 letter to Brig Gen Joe W. Kelly, commanding general, FEAF Bomber Command, General LeMay emphasized the following:

> The enemy enjoys a unique advantage in that he knows fairly accurately from the time your bombers show up in the radar screen, where they are going, what their target is, what time they will get there, how high they will be, and what track they will follow. Thus, most of his air defense problems are solved for him. Your restricted target area, coupled with the Manchurian sanctuary for enemy fighters, creates a condition which effectively denies the bomber its traditional tactical flexibility and shifts the balance of advantage in favor of the defense.[77]

On the other hand, the short-range, fighter-escorted missions over Korea shared little with the long-range sorties planned for the USSR. In a general war, SAC bombers would face first-line Soviet radar and fighter defenses. Whereas MiGs rarely pressed attacks against bomber formations over Korea, in all probability SAC aircrews would face fighters flown with suicidal tenacity in defense of Soviet targets. Finally, in the Korean War, the initial phase of the air war permitted unopposed strategic reconnaissance. This reduced the problem of identifying targets and made a "precision" air campaign possible. In a general war, strategic reconnaissance faced daunting missions, such as finding strategic bombing targets, analyzing air defenses, and assessing bomb damage. Against Soviet air defenses, obsolete strategic reconnaissance aircraft faced annihilation.[78]

Notes

1. For further information on Soviet and Communist Chinese participation in the Korean air war, please see Jon Halliday, "Air Operations in Korea: The Soviet Side of the Story," in *A Revolutionary War: Korea and the Transformation of the Postwar World*, ed. William J. Williams (Chicago: Imprint Publications, 1993); Xiaoming Zhang, "China and the Air War in Korea, 1950–1953," *Journal of Military History* 62 (April 1998): 335–70; and Idem., *Red Wings Over the Yalu: China, the Soviet Union, and the Air War in Korea* (College Station: Texas A & M University Press, 2002).

2. Summary of US/United Kingdom Discussions on Present World Situation, 20–24 July 1950, Washington, D.C., 6, general file JCS, President's Secretary's file, Harry S. Truman, Presidential Library, Independence, Mo. (hereafter HSTL).

3. John Lewis Gaddis and Thomas H. Etzold, *Strategies of Containment: A Critical Appraisal of Postwar American National Security Policy* (New York: Oxford University Press, 1982), 114.

4. History FEAF (hereafter History FEAF), 25 June–31 December 1950, 158, file no. K-720.01, vol. 1, 25 June–31 December 1950; and R. Cargill Hall, "The Truth About Overflights," *MHQ [Military History Quarterly]: The Quarterly Journal of Military History* 9, no. 3 (spring 1997): 24–39.

5. History FEAF, 25 June–31 December 1950, 157.

6. Redline messages were Top Secret, "very important messages for prompt and special handling. By then-current Air Force regulations, the secretary of the Air Force, the undersecretary, the chief of staff USAF, and certain other individuals as spelled out by regulations were the only persons authorized to send or receive redline messages." Lt Gen George E. Stratemeyer, *The Three Wars of Lt. Gen. George E. Stratemeyer: His Korean War Diary*, ed. William T. Y' Blood (Washington, D.C.: Air Force History and Museums Program, 1997), 42; Message, A4873B, General Stratemeyer to General Twining, 20 December 1950; and Message, RL-132, Headquarters USAF to Commanding General FEAF, 22 December 1950, folder 6, December 1950, box 86, Hoyt S. Vandenberg Papers (hereafter Vandenberg Papers), Library of Congress (LOC).

7. Ironically, in an effort to save time, the Air Force contracted Japanese companies to print the charts. History FEAF, 25 June–31 December 1950, 153, 158, file no. K-720.01, vol. 1, 25 June–31 December 1950.

8. Quoted in Robert F. Futrell, "A Case Study: USAF Intelligence in the Korean War," paper delivered at the Thirteenth Military History Symposium, USAF Academy (USAFA), 12–14 October 1988, 12. In 1991 the paper was published in *The Intelligence Revolution: A Historical Perspective*, Proceedings of the Thirteenth Military History Symposium, Lt Col Walter T. Hitch-

cock, ed. (Washington, D.C.: USAFA and Office of Air Force History, 1991), 282.

9. FEAF Reconnaissance in the Korea Conflict, in History FEAF, Report on Korea, 9–10, file no. K-720.04D, 25 June 1950–27 July 1953.

10. History FEAF, 25 June–31 December 1950, 176.

11. 1st Lt Bryce Poe, who later rose to the rank of four-star general, described the flights in a presentation at an Air Force History and Museums Program conference, "The USAF Remembers Korea," 24 June 2000, Senate Executive Office Building, Washington, D.C. He emphasized the range of the RF-80 as a limiting factor.

12. JCS 2150/5, 5 August 1950, quoted in JCS 2150/9, "Delimitation of Air Operations Along the North Korean Border," 6 November 1950, Records Group (RG) 218, Natinal Archives (NA), in Steven T. Ross and David Alan Rosenberg, eds., *America's Plans for War against the Soviet Union* 1945–1950 (New York: Garland Publishing, 1990), vol. 6, *Plan Frolic and American Resources*.

13. Stratemeyer, *The Three Wars*, 256–57.

14. Omar N. Bradley and Clay Blair, *A General's Life* (New York: Simon and Schuster, 1983), 557. For a masterful account of Soviet-Chinese negotiations leading to Chinese intervention in the Korean War, see Zhang, *Red Wings Over the Yalu*, 55–77.

15. Gen Omar Bradley, memorandum to the secretary of defense, subject: Special Electronic Airborne Search Operations, 22 July 1950, in Omar N. Bradley, President's Secretary's file, Harry S. Truman Library (HSTL).

16. Historical Division, Operating Instruction, 7th Air Division, "SAC Operations in the United Kingdom, 1948–1956," 27, file no: K-DIV-7-HI, 1948–1956, US Air Force Historical Research Center (hereafter USAFHRC).

17. Ibid., 26. In addition, Roundout included targets in Spain, Portugal, Sweden, Denmark, and Switzerland on a lower priority.

18. In *American Espionage and the Soviet Threat*, Jeffrey Richelson claims RB-36s flew long-range reconnaissance missions that penetrated Soviet airspace. Robert Jackson makes a similar claim in his *High Cold War*. I have found no documentary evidence for this claim. In a July 2001 interview, Maj Gen Foster L. Smith, the Air Staff officer responsible for overflight authorizations from 1949–1951, knew of no RB-36 overflights during this period. In addition, General LeMay consistently resisted efforts to permit newer models of SAC aircraft (B-50s, B-36s, and B-47s) to operate in areas where their performance characteristics might be compromised. He did not want the Soviets to learn the strengths and weaknesses of SAC aircraft. Jeffery Richelson, *American Espionage and the Soviet Threat* (New York: William Morrow & Co., 1987), 12; Robert Jackson, *High Cold War: Strategic Air Reconnaissance and the Electronic Intelligence War* (Nr Yeovil, Somerset, United Kingdom: Patrick Stephens, 1998) 56; History of the 55th SRW (hereafter History 55th SRW), Medium (M), Forbes AFB, Kansas, 1–28 February 1953, prepared by 2d Lt David Hosley and SSgt Wesley T. Lassetter, "SAC Operations in

the United Kingdom," 26; and Maj Gen Foster L. Smith, interviewed by author, 18 July 2001.

19. History 55th SRW, 6, file no. KG-WG-55-HI, February 1953, USAFHRC.

20. Ibid., September 1951, 4; and Gordon Swanborough and Peter M. Bowers, *United States Military Aircraft Since 1908* (London: Putnam, 1971), 105.

21. "In SHORAN controlled aerial photography, the cameras automatically take pictures every two, five, or 10 seconds. The system utilized electronic ground stations and a special receiver in the RB-50. . . . The ground stations are accurately positioned in relation to the area that is desired to photograph. The principle involved in this operation is a measurement of the time it takes electronic signals, simultaneously transmitted from two ground stations, to arrive at the RB-50's receiver. The time differential of arrival of these signals at the airborne receiver can be measured and recorded as the geographical position of the RB-50, at any particular instant. In this manner, spaced photo flight lines over an area of interest can be very accurately flown because the plane has a constant true position." Harry Lever, "Strat Recon + Technical Aids + Pinpoint Bombing," *Flying,* April 1952, cited in Bruce M. Bailey, *"We See All: A History of the 55th Strategic Reconnaissance Wing, 1947–1967* (Tucson, Ariz.: 55th ELINT Association Historian, 1982) 30; History 55th SRW, September 1951, 4; and Robert F. Futrell, *The United States Air Force in Korea,* revised ed. (Washington, D.C.: Office of Air Force History, 1983), 105.

22. In addition, crews from the 343d SRS augmented the Ferret flights staged by the 91st SRS in Korea. History 55th SRW, February 1951, 4.

23. Ibid., 551.

24. History Fifth Air Force, 91st Strategic Reconnaissance Squadron (M) Photo, January–July 1953, vol. 2, Supporting Documents, file no. K-713.01-38, vol. 2, January–27 July 1953, USAFHRC.

25. Ibid., and Bailey, 21.

26. Bradley and Blair, 564.

27. Message, RL-117, Personal from Vandenberg, 6 December 1950, folder 6, December 1950, box 86, Vandenberg Papers.

28. Message, Stratemeyer to Vandenberg, folder 5, November 1950, box 86, Vandenberg Papers.

29. Omar N. Bradley, memorandum to the secretary of defense, subject: Military Action in Korea, 5 April 1951, general file JCS, HSTL.

30. David Alan Rosenberg, "The Origins of Overkill: Nuclear Weapons and American Strategy, 1945–1960," in *Strategy and Nuclear Deterrence,* ed. Steven E. Miller (Princeton, N.J.: Princeton University Press, 1984), 128.

31. Ibid., "Diary of General Curtis LeMay, 23 January 1951," 128.

32. History FEAF, 25 June–31 December 1950, 213.

33. L. D. McCormick, acting CNO to commander in chief, US Pacific Fleet, letter, subject: Assignment of P4M-1Q aircraft to Special Electronic Search Project (SESP) in the Pacific, 26 June 1951, folder, Command File Post, 1 January 1946, Naval Historical Center (NHC).

34. Currently the historian for the National Reconnaissance Office, Dr. R. Cargill Hall, has done more than any one else to bring to light the classified history of Cold War aerial overflight missions. In addition to the ground-breaking article cited, he coordinated a historic symposium, "Early Cold War Overflights," held at the Defense Intelligence Agency, Washington, D.C., 22–23 February 2001, where he arranged a forum for many of the surviving participants. R. Cargill Hall, "The Truth About Overflights," *MHQ: The Quarterly Journal of Military History* 9, no. 3 (spring 1997): 26, 28, 31–32; and Robert Smith Hopkins, "U.S. Strategic Aerial Reconnaissance and the Cold War, 1945–1961" (PhD diss., University of Va., 1998), 78–79.

35. Hall, 30–31.

36. Ibid., 29–30. Following this flight, the RAF disbanded the Special Duty Flight until the spring of 1953. It would fly additional overflight missions in 1954; Hopkins, 75–76.

37. History FEAF, 1 June 1951–31 December 1951, file no. K-720.01, vol. 1, 1 July–31 December 1951.

38. In April 1951 General LeMay created a position, "Deputy Commanding General, SAC XRAY," to streamline the chain of command in the Far East in the event an atomic war broke out. Initially, LeMay's deputy, General Power, filled the position, but by June 1951 the commanding general of FEAF Bomber Command Provisional, Brig Gen Robert H. Terrill, assumed the role. Thus, for conventional operations, General Terrill responded to FEAF direction and in the event of atomic war, he would follow orders from LeMay's SAC.

A series of telegrams in the LeMay Papers describe FEAF Bomber Command efforts to obtain radarscope photography. The RB-45Cs were tasked to fly over targets on the same axis as called for in SAC Operations Order 61-51. Two targets were photographed on 5 June 1951 and two more on 8 July 1951. Seven others were photographed on unspecified dates. Although the telegrams are declassified, the code names for the targets do not accompany the telegrams. Col Winton R. Close to Maj Gen Thomas S. Power, Headquarters SAC, letter, subject: SAC XRAY, folder, B-11651, box-198, 6 June 1951, Curtis E. LeMay Papers (hereafter LeMay Papers), LOC; Message, CG FEAF BMR COMD JAPAN to CG SAC OFFUTT AFB OMAHA NEB, 8 July 1951, file no. 11931, box B-198, LeMay Papers; Telegram, CG SAC/XRAY/ TOKYO JAPAN to CG SAC OFFUTT AFB OMAHA NEB, 9 June 1951, file no. B-11929, box B-198, LeMay Papers.

General Terrill, commanding general, FEAF Bomber Command Provisional, to General Power, deputy commander, Headquarters SAC, subject: SAC XRAY, 16 August 1951, folder B-12789/1, box B-198, LeMay Papers; Conrad C. Crane, *American Airpower Strategy in Korea, 1950–1953* (Lawrence, Kans., University Press of Kansas, 2000), 70–72.

39. Commander in Chief, U.S. Pacific Fleet, Korean War, U.S. Pacific Fleet Operations, Third Evaluation Report, 1 May–31 December 1951, 7-5, 7–6, NHC, Washington Navy Yard, Washington, D.C.

40. The proposal recommended daily RB-29 photo flights over the target area, but FEAF records show only an average of 12 sorties per month for this

period, including missions over North Korea, Manchuria, and the Soviet Far East. JCS 2150/2, "Photo Reconnaissance of the China Coast from Swatow to Latitude 26° 30' N," folder, CCS 062 Far East (7-4-50), sec. 1, box 17, geographic file 1948–1950, RG 218, NA, in Ross and Rosenberg.

41. Unfortunately, the specific target list did not accompany the source document. This reveals a research problem where many command histories were written at the "Secret" level and did not include "Top Secret" material. Although many Top Secret annexes and other documents dated before 1950 have been declassified, other Top Secret documents related to intelligence remain classified. History FEAF, 25 June–31 December 1950, 213.

42. History Fifth Air Force, 1 January–30 June 1952, 151, file no. K730.01, vol. 1, 30 January–June 1952.

43. Lt Col Daniel T. Kuehl, "Electronic Warfare and USAF B-29 Operations," paper delivered to 23d Annual Northern Great Plains History Conference, Eveleth, Minn., 23 September 1988, 3. For the communist perspective of the event, see Zhang, 131.

44. Futrell, *The United States Air Force in Korea*, 548.

45. History FEAF, file no. K-720.04D, 25 June 1950–27 July 1953.

46. Ibid., January–July 1953, vol. 1, 47–48, file no. K713.01, January–July 1953, vol. 1.

47. 1st Lt John Hammerer, History 91st Strategic Reconnaissance Squadron (hereafter History 91st SRS), (M), Photo, Yokota AFB, Japan, 1–30 April 1953, vol. 2, March 1951, 4, file no. K-SQ-RCN-91-HI, April 1953.

48. Ibid.

49. Ibid., May 1951, 5.

50. Ibid., August 1951.

51. Ibid., May 1951, 5. The K-30 camera was mounted on the left side of the RB-29 at a 15.5° angle. This caused a major problem for both the crew and the photo-interpreters. For optimum results, the aircraft had to be flown with the wing raised, or lowered, three to six degrees. Unfortunately, the plane could not maintain a constant heading with this attitude. This constant turn caused the operators to stop and realign the camera every eight to 10 miles. In addition, when flying at 25,000 feet, the bottom of a picture would show a target 12 miles away, while the top depicted a target 25 miles away.

52. Ibid., August 1951.

53. Futrell, *The United States Air Force in Korea*, 548.

54. History 91st SRS, 1 January–30 June 1952, 151.

55. The Token radar operated in the "S-band" frequency around 3,000 megacycles. First detected in Moscow in 1951, the new GCI radar could direct several fighters simultaneously at ranges up to 70 miles away. Kuehl, 7; Col R. C. Lewis, adjutant general, Fifth Air Force, to CG FEAF, letter, subject: Request for priority increase on ECM Aircraft Project, 7 July 1952, in History FEAF, 1 January–30 June 1952, file no. K-730.01, vol. 2, 1 January–30 June 1952.

56. Brig Gen W. P. Fisher, commanding FEAF Bomber Command, to Maj Gen John B. Montgomery, director of Operations, SAC, letter, no subject, 30

January 1953, in History Fifth Air Force, January–July 1953, vol. 2; supporting documents, file no. K-713.01-38, January–27 July 1953.

57. Ibid.

58. History Fifth Air Force, 91st SRS (M) Photo, January–July 1952, vol. 2, supporting documents.

59. Report on Reconnaissance Conference, Joint Army–Air Force Reconnaissance Conference, 12–13 August 1952, in History Fifth Air Force, 1 July–31 December 1952, vol. 2, app. 1, file no. K-730.01, 1 July–31 December 1952, vol. 2.

60. Lt Col James F. Brady, deputy for Intelligence FEAF Bomber Command, "Reconnaissance Plan for the RB-45," n.d., in History FEAF Bomber Command, vol. 2, supporting documents, file no. K713.01-32, July–December 1952, vol. 2; and History FEAF, January–July 1953, vol. 1, 48, file no. K713.01-36, January–July 1953, vol. 1.

61. Brady.

62. Brig Gen John K. Gerhart to General Vandenberg, memorandum, subject: USAF Utilization in FEAF, 18 April 1952, 6, folder, annex 2 memorandum, "Impact of the Korean War," box 87, Vandenberg Papers.

63. Instead, SAC offered additional RB-45s. Telegram, Gen Nathan F. Twining from Gen Curtis E. LeMay, CG 0277, 1 January 1953, file no. B-23446, box B-203, LeMay Papers; Gen Nathan F. Twining to Gen Curtis E. LeMay and Gen Otto P. Weyland, message, 18 February 1953, file no. B-24065, box B-203, LeMay Papers.

64. "Active" countermeasures involve electronic jamming, while the use of chaff or WINDOW comprise "passive" ECM. FEAF Bomber Command first authorized limited active ECM on 24 November 1950. On 17 April 1951 following the Sinuiju, Korea, bomber raid, FEAF Bomber Command allowed greater use of electronic jamming but still required prior headquarters approval. Capt Eugene Freeman, FEAF Bomber Command ECM Summary, September 1951, annex 4, History FEAF, History of ECM during the Korean Conflict, file no. K-720.04C, June 1950–July 1953.

65. Kuehl, 14.

66. Maj Gen Thomas S. Power, deputy commander, SAC to Col William F. Coleman, office (chief of staff, general headquarters, Far East Command) C/S, GHQ, FEC, letter, 14 March 1952, file no. B-16973, box B-200, LeMay Papers.

67. History Fifth Air Force, Report on Joint Army–Air Force Reconnaissance Conference, 12–13 August 1952, 1 July–31 December 1952, vol. 2, app. 1, file no. K-730.01-32.

68. Gen Otto P. Weyland served as Lt Gen George E. Stratemeyer's deputy during the first half of the Korean War and then assumed command of FEAF following Stratemeyer's heart attack on 20 May 1951. Historical Report, November 1953, Development of FEAF's Intelligence Collection Plan, 34, file no. K-720.02, box 4, November 1953, in History FEAF. An expanded version is found in History FEAF, FEAF Reconnaissance in the Korean Conflict, 1, in FEAF Report on Korea, file no. K-720.04D, 25 June 1950–27 July 1953.

69. Futrell, *The United States Air Force in Korea*, 556.

70. History FEAF, November 1953, 35, 40.

71. Ibid., FEAF Reconnaissance in Korea, 1–2.

72. Ibid., 67. "Of the airmen assigned, 261 had a Court-Martial conviction or Article 15 on their records, 123 were at the 10 skill level, 136 had a below four average aptitude index. This was a total of 520, or 21 percent of total manning. Ideally, there should be no more than five to eight percent of such personnel for maximum efficiency."

73. Ibid., November 1953, 43.

74. Ibid., Personnel Problems, Report on Korea, 58.

75. Ibid., November 1953, 35–36.

76. Ibid., annex 16, History of ECM during the Korean Conflict, 3 May 1954, file no. K-720.04C, June 1950–July 1953.

77. Gen Curtis E. LeMay, commanding, Headquarters SAC, to Gen Joe W. Kelly, commanding general, FEAF Bomber Command, Provisional, letter, no subject, 28 November 1951, file B-14698, box B198, in LeMay Papers.

78. The 91st SRS lost eight aircraft (seven RB-29s and one RB-45) during the Korean War. Considering that the squadron never numbered more than 12 RB-29s and four RB-45s, this substantiates a rather pessimistic view in History FEAF, annex 15.

Chapter 6

Conclusion

The JCS and everyone else committed one cardinal sin. We seriously misjudged Chinese communist reaction to our plans to cross the 38th parallel. It is the duty and responsibility of military advisers to gauge a potential enemy's capabilities rather than his intentions. In this case we Joint Chiefs allowed ourselves to be overly influenced by various estimates of Chinese communist intentions. As historians have now shown, those who drew those estimates ignored too many obvious warning flags and miscalculated badly.

—Omar N. Bradley

Photo reconnaissance. . . . It is the one positive means by which we are able to study the enemy's back yard. Its relative importance cannot be over-rated—we must have it.

—Unidentified Army Representative
to FEAF Reconnaissance
Conference, August 1952

From the first balloon ascent in 1783, aerial reconnaissance provided an unmatched tool for commanders. Aerial observation offered a means to surprise the foe or, equally important, prevent enemy surprise. World War I experiences introduced photoreconnaissance as a valuable source of tactical intelligence. The Great War also inspired a generation of theorists who viewed airpower as a new, decisive means of warfare. Emphasizing the airplane's ability to circumvent traditional armies and navies, theories of strategic air war called for aircraft to strike directly the enemy's vital industrial and military centers. Unfortunately, as pioneers developed aviation technology, aerial reconnaissance lagged. In the US Army Air Corps, Capt George Goddard's innovative aerial cameras proved a rare exception; otherwise, reconnaissance methods remained shackled to First World War practices.

During World War II, aerial reconnaissance played a key role in the success of Allied strategic bombing campaigns. Using techniques fostered by Britain's Royal Air Force, Allied photographic reconnaissance aircraft provided the information necessary to identify targets, to plan strikes, and to assess bomb damage. With the introduction of effective, radar-guided air defense systems, electronic warfare emerged as a new aspect of aerial combat. Although Britain and Germany played leading roles in the overall development of electronic warfare tactics and equipment, the United States advanced the specialized field of airborne electronic reconnaissance. Dr. Frederick E. Terman's Radio Research Laboratory pioneered ELINT and ECM technology, and the USAAF's specialized Ferret aircraft adapted the new equipment to the strategic air war. Despite electronic warfare's vital contribution, eventual Allied air superiority reduced the need for electronic reconnaissance. In addition, the atomic bomb's impact overshadowed the role of electronic warfare. Thus, strategic aerial reconnaissance emerged from World War II with a mixed legacy: commanders appreciated photographic reconnaissance, but paid little attention to electronic warfare or ELINT collection.

With no apparent military threat and public pressure to demobilize, US military capability declined rapidly following World War II. Faced with limited budget appropriations, air leaders cut all nonessential programs. Viewed as *nice to have*, electronic reconnaissance did not survive, and cuts reduced photographic reconnaissance to limited photomapping duties. Instead, senior airmen battled to retain a strategic bombardment force that supported their claim for organizational independence. In September 1947, airmen realized their dream with the creation of the US Air Force, while an emerging Soviet threat dramatized the weakness of the new Air Force.

As Cold War tensions mounted, "need to know" tactical and strategic intelligence dominated war planning. Limited by fiscal constraints and inadequate ground forces, American leaders struggled to form an appropriate military response to the Soviet military potential. With no apparent alternatives, the JCS adopted Joint Basic Outline War Plan Pincher based upon the precepts of strategic air war. Recognizing the limited US atomic arsenal, Pincher called for a precision bombing campaign against vital Soviet industrial targets; however, the plan revealed a lack of strategic intelligence that jeopardized strategic bombing doctrine. Without adequate target information, maps, weather data, and knowledge of enemy air defenses, a strategic air campaign risked defeat.

The intelligence shortfalls of Pincher prompted postwar strategic aerial reconnaissance. The first reconnaissance sorties of August 1946 explored the Arctic to assess polar routes for strategic bombers. Photographic reconnaissance mapped little-known polar regions and improvised Ferret aircraft searched for Soviet radars. Later efforts would probe Soviet air defenses in Western Europe. Unfortunately, these uncoordinated, ad hoc measures paled in comparison to the need for target information.

With President Truman's declaration of containment, the Air Force advanced organizational steps to improve strategic aerial reconnaissance. Aware of intelligence gaps, the Air Staff established formal procedures for peacetime strategic reconnaissance in 1948, eventually placing it under SAC control. Beginning in 1947 improved B-29 Ferret aircraft collected valuable information about Soviet radar defenses along communist borders and photoreconnaissance planes attempted both oblique photography of the Chukotski Peninsula and a few (less than a dozen) special overflight missions of Soviet territory that barely scratched the surface.[1] Nevertheless, technological limitations blocked efforts to gather target information from the Soviet heartland. Existing jet aircraft lacked sufficient range, and modified bombers lacked the speed and altitude needed for survival. This technological hurdle confronted aerial reconnaissance throughout the early years of the Cold War.

Operational constraints affected Air Force doctrine. For nearly 30 years, airpower advocates stressed strategic bombing as the epitome of warfare. In the United States, airmen advanced a doctrine of precision bombardment of carefully selected industries to destroy the enemy's capacity for war. Despite heavy losses over Europe in the opening phase of the Combined Bomber Offensive and RAF arguments for night area bombing, Air Force leaders believed World War II experiences vindicated their doctrinal assertions. Although airmen acknowledged the importance of the atomic bomb, postwar studies by the *United States Strategic Bombing Survey* and the Spaatz board reinforced their belief in precision bombing. Nevertheless, faced with a lack of strategic target intelligence, the Air Force abandoned the doctrine. With JCS approval of War Plan Broiler in February 1948, the planned strategic air campaign shifted to atomic-urban-area bombing, which required less precise intelligence. Influenced by the fear surrounding the Berlin crisis and the Soviet detonation of an atomic bomb in August 1949, the Air Force considered war a distinct possibility. In response, the JCS approved War Plan Offtackle in November 1949. Offtackle's reliance on a massive atomic attack on Soviet cities completed a doctrinal transformation by the Air Force. Instead of selecting key industrial targets within enemy cities for destruction by precision bombing, air planners now targeted entire cities with atomic bombs. Therefore, between 1945 and 1953, strategic aerial reconnaissance proved to be more than a tool for war planning; the limits of aerial reconnaissance shaped strategic doctrine.

The sudden outbreak of the Korean War represented a test of postwar Air Force reconnaissance. Viewed as a potential prelude to a general war, the Korean conflict demonstrated the value of aerial reconnaissance in providing both tactical and strategic intelligence. Expanded to near-global coverage, strategic aerial reconnaissance played a key role in assessing communist military capabilities. Electronic and photographic intelligence proved their worth; however, the unexpected Chinese intervention in Korea showed the perils of inadequate intelligence. The Chinese invasion spurred direct Ferret overflights of communist territory. Although relatively limited in number, range, and capability, the periodic risky penetrations of Soviet and Chinese air space evidenced the worry and desperate boldness for intelligence not seen previously. These early penetration overflights established the precedent for later Cold War reconnaissance efforts.

The close of hostilities brought home the lessons learned from the Korean War experience, implying a threat to current US war plans. Obsolescent equipment and inadequate attention to the entire intelligence cycle raised doubts over plans for strategic air war. Intelligence shortfalls showed that planning, direction, production, and dissemination of intelligence material were equally important as collection. Without well-trained analysts, photo-interpreters, electronic specialists, and other intelligence personnel, even good aerial photographs or clear Ferret recordings would go to waste. Therefore, the FEAF assessment of reconnaissance during Korea stressed the need for a fully manned, adequately funded, reconnaissance organization to exploit the intelligence potential in peacetime.

The close of the Korean War ended a phase of US strategic aerial reconnaissance marked by inadequate capability. Before this time, meager funding and technological limitations had handicapped US strategic intelligence collection even though policy makers desperately required information. Greatly expanded wartime appropriations benefited the Air Force with the introduction of the new Boeing B-47 jet bomber in 1953, a reconnaissance version designated the RB-47 a year later, and the Lockheed Martin RB-57, adapted from the British Canberra bomber. Of greater importance, Clarence Kelly Johnson's revolutionary Lockheed U-2 represented a technological breakthrough. From 1956 to 1960, deep penetration overflights of the Soviet Union using the high-flying, long-range aircraft provided photographic intelligence previously impossible. For the first time, American policy makers acquired substantive intelligence regarding Soviet military capabilities, giving the JCS vital target information for war planning. Although Soviet surface-to-air missiles ended the U-2's immunity in May 1960 and caused an unprecedented international scandal, the launch of *Discoverer 13* three months later opened a new era of satellite reconnaissance.

This study of aerial reconnaissance in the early years of the Cold War contributes to military history by emphasizing the importance of intelligence in strategic planning. By concentrating on the operational aspects of strategic intelligence and war planning, this book does not challenge the body of literature focused on the theoretical, political, and moral aspects of nuclear strategy. Instead, this book of strategic aerial reconnaissance complements earlier works by focusing on the means to assess the enemy threat. In the context of the Cold War, military and political leaders feared Soviet potential but knew little of actual enemy capabilities. With the memory of Pearl Harbor fresh, this fear demanded vigilance. Hence, strategic aerial reconnaissance represented a vital tool for policy makers. Moreover, the limits of reconnaissance capability in the first eight years of the Cold War emphasize the influence of technology upon intelligence collection. Understanding the limits of reconnaissance technology in the early Cold War explains the uncertainty and fear that underscored JCS plans.[2] Aware of US military weakness, the JCS proved well aware of the wisdom behind Sun Tzu's famous line, "Therefore I say: Know the enemy and know yourself; in a hundred battles you will never be in peril."[3]

Aerial reconnaissance provided the best means to *know the enemy* during the early years of the Cold War. As the Cold War fades, the diminished overt military threat has resulted in significant reductions of US armed forces. Hopefully, American military leaders will not repeat the errors that followed World War II. Well-trained, well-equipped reconnaissance units and intelligence organizations provide the means to assess future threats and shape strategic alternatives. Furthermore, adequate collection capability alone is not sufficient—constant attention to the entire intelligence cycle is necessary to assure national security in a world of change. Otherwise, the less well-known verses of Sun Tzu may again prove true: "When you are ignorant of the enemy but know yourself, your chances of winning or losing are equal. If ignorant both of your enemy and of yourself, you are certain in every battle to be in peril."[4]

Notes

1. Maj Gen Foster L. Smith, interviewed by author, 18 July 2001, Arlington, Va.

2. The anxiety surrounding the "search for Scuds" in the 1991 Persian Gulf War and NATO's frustrations in finding and striking Serbian fielded forces in 1999 illustrates the limits of even today's technology and its impact on strategy.

3. Sun Tzu, *The Art of War*, trans. and intro. by Samuel B. Griffith (London: Oxford University Press, 1971), 84.

4. Ibid.

Appendix A

Radar Principles

For those who are not technologically inclined, the discussion of radar characteristics, Ferret operations, and jamming techniques can be confusing. Fortunately, the principles behind radar (originally used as an acronym, RAdio Detection And Ranging) are relatively simple. The following appendix summarizes a US Navy publication, *Radar Bulletin No. 12 (RAD TWELVE): Airborne Radar Countermeasures Operator's Manual,* published in 1946.

Radar works on the principle of echoes. Just as it takes a certain amount of time for a voice echo to return after shouting, it takes a short amount of time for radio waves to return after they bounce off an object. Radar measures this time and determines the distance of the object. In other words, a radar station is a two-way radio system that includes a transmitter and a receiver. The transmitter sends out short pulses of high-frequency radio waves, and the receiver detects the echoes of the waves after they have bounced off a target. The time between transmitted pulse and received echo is converted into the distance of the object. Since the echo returns with far less energy than originally transmitted, an amplifier works with the receiver, and the results are projected upon an oscilloscope. Because the whole process occurs in fractions of a second, the oscilloscope, or radar screen, presents a continuous picture.

The primary purpose of electronic reconnaissance or Ferret aircraft centers on locating enemy radar stations and analyzing the performance characteristics of the set. The Ferret uses radar intercept receivers to detect enemy radar transmissions and a pulse analyzer to display the radio waves received upon an oscilloscope for analysis. The Ferret operator (called radar observer, RCM officer, electronic warfare officer [EWO], Raven, or Crow at various times) seeks the following performance characteristics:

Frequency: The usual way of recognizing a radar is on the basis of the carrier frequency of the radio waves it sends out. This frequency is usually expressed in terms of megacycles or millions of cycles per second. Thus, the radar frequency is like the radio channel of a conventional radio set.

Pulse Repetition Frequency: A measure of the rate at which radio pulses are transmitted. Radars do not transmit continuously. They must pause briefly in order to receive the returning echo. The rate of pulses (pulse repetition frequency), or PRF, produces an audible humming sound or whine. Proficient Ravens recognize individual radar types by their sound.

Pulse Length: The duration of the pulse of transmitted radio energy. The pulse lengths are usually so brief that they are expressed in millionths of a second or microseconds.

Beam Width: A radar sends out a beam of radio-frequency energy much as a searchlight sends out a beam of light. The beam width is expressed in degrees. The radar beam is not as sharp as a beam of light and usually measures 10 or 15 degrees wide. Although a sharper beam is more accurate, it is also more likely to miss an elusive target.

Lobe Switching: A means of determining the bearing of a target. The radar looks to one side and then to the other of a particular target. When the radar is looking at equal angles to each side of the target, it is said to be "on target" or "locked on." Lobe switching occurs rapidly, roughly 50 times per second in certain radars and indicates the relative accuracy of the radar.

Ferrets determined the function of the radar from these performance characteristics. For example, early warning radars featured high-power, low frequency, low PRF, long-pulse length, and wide-beam widths to achieve high rates of detection at great distances. Ground controlled intercept (GCI) sets on the other hand, displayed higher frequencies and PRFs, shorter pulse lengths, and narrower beam widths resulting in greater accuracy, but shorter ranges. Additionally, Ferrets recorded new signals that allowed analysts to track enemy technical progress.

Appendix B

Definitions and Terms

The following information is extracted from Joint Chiefs of Staff (JCS) Publication 1, *Department of Defense Dictionary of Military and Associated Terms*, 1984.

air photographic reconnaissance—The obtaining of information by air photography. Air photographic reconnaissance is divided into three types: (a) strategic photographic reconnaissance; (b) tactical photographic reconnaissance; and (c) survey or cartographic photography-air photography taken for survey or cartographic purposes and to survey or cartographic standards for accuracy. It may be strategic or tactical. (JCS Pub 1, 19)

air reconnaissance—The acquisition of intelligence information by employing visual observation and/or sensors in air vehicles. (JCS Pub 1, 20)

communications intelligence (COMINT)—Technical and intelligence information derived from foreign communications by other than the intended recipients. (JCS Pub 1, 80)

electronic reconnaissance—The detection, identification, evaluation, and location of foreign electromagnetic radiations emanating from other than nuclear detonations or radioactive sources. (JCS Pub 1, 128)

electronics intelligence (ELINT)—Technical and intelligence information derived from foreign noncommunications electromagnetic radiations emanating from other than nuclear detonations or radioactive sources. (JCS Pub 1, 128)

electronic warfare (EW)—Military action involving the use of electromagnetic energy to determine, exploit, reduce, or prevent hostile use of the electromagnetic spectrum and action that retains friendly use of electromagnetic spectrum. There are three divisions of electronic warfare—(a) *Electronic countermeasures (ECM)*—That division of electronic warfare involving actions taken to prevent or reduce an enemy's effective use of the electromagnetic spectrum. Electronic countermeasures include—(1) *Electronic jamming*—The deliberate radiation, reradiation, or reflection of electromagnetic energy for the purpose of disrupting enemy use of electronic devices, equipment, or systems and (2) *Electronic deception*—The deliberate radiation, reradiation, alteration, suppression, absorption, denial, enhancement, or reflection of electromagnetic information and to deny valid information to an enemy. (b) *Electronic countercountermeasures (ECCM)*—The division of electronic warfare involving actions taken to ensure friendly effective use of the electromagnetic spectrum despite the enemy's use of electronic warfare. (c) *Electronic warfare support measures (ESM)*— The division of electronic warfare involving actions taken under direct control of an operational commander to search for, intercept, identify, and locate sources of radiated electromagnetic energy for the purpose of immediate threat recognition. Thus, ESM measures provide a source of information required for immediate decisions involving ECM, ECCM, avoidance, targeting, and other tactical employment of forces. ESM data can be used to produce signals intelligence (SIGINT), both COMINT and ELINT. (JCS Pub 1, 129)

Ferret—An aircraft, ship, or vehicle especially equipped for the detection, location, and analyzing of electromagnetic radiation. (JCS Pub 1, 143) In 1949 the term was defined as "aircraft specifically modified to perform electronic reconnaissance only."[1]

intelligence—the product resulting from the collection, processing, integration, analysis, evaluation, and interpretation of available information concerning foreign countries or areas. (JCS Pub 1, 188)

intelligence cycle—The five-step process by which information is converted into intelligence and made available to users follows:

    a. *planning and direction*—Determination of intelligence requirements, preparation of a collection plan, issuance of orders and requests to information collection agencies, and a continuous check on the productivity of collection agencies.

    b. *collection*—Acquisition of information and the provision of this information to processing and/or production elements.

c. *processing*—Conversion of collected information into a form suitable to the production of intelligence.

d. *production*—Conversion of information into intelligence through the integration, analysis, evaluation, and interpretation of all source data and the preparation of intelligence products in support of known or anticipated user requirements.

e. *dissemination*—The conveyance of intelligence to users in a suitable form. (JCS Pub 1, 189)

intercept receiver—A receiver designed to detect and provide visual and/or aural indication of electromagnetic emissions occurring within the particular portion of the electromagnetic spectrum to which it is tuned. (JCS Pub 1, 190–91)

need to know—Criterion used in security procedures that requires the custodians of classified information to establish, before disclosure, that the intended recipient must have access to the information to perform his official duties. (JCS Pub 1, 248)

proximity fuze—A fuze wherein primary initiation occurs by remotely sensing the presence, distance, and/or direction of a target or its associated environment by means of a signal generated by the fuze or emitted by the target, or by detecting a disturbance of a natural field surrounding the target. (JCS Pub 1, 292)

oblique air photograph—An air photograph taken with the camera axis directed between the horizontal and vertical planes. Commonly referred to as an oblique. (a) *high oblique*—One in which the apparent horizon appears; and (b) *low oblique*—One in which the apparent horizon does not appear. (JCS Pub 1, 259)

pulse repetition frequency (PRF)—In radar, the number of pulses that occur each second. Not to be confused with transmission frequency which is determined by the rate at which cycles are repeated within the transmitted pulse. (JCS Pub 1, 294)

reconnaissance (recce)—A mission undertaken to obtain, by visual observation or other detection methods, information about the activities and resources of an enemy or potential enemy; or to secure data concerning the meteorological, hydrographic, or geographic characteristics of a particular area. (JCS Pub 1, 304) *security classification*—A category to which national security information and material is assigned to denote the degree of damage that unauthorized disclosure would cause to national defense or foreign relations of the United States and to denote the degree of protection required. There are three such categories:

a. *top secret*—National security information or material that requires the highest degree of protection and the unauthorized disclosure of which could reasonably be expected to cause exceptionally grave damage to the national security. Examples of exceptionally grave damage include armed hostilities against the United States or its allies; disruption of foreign relations vitally affecting the national security; the compromise of vital national defense plans or complex cryptologic and communications intelligence systems; the revelation of sensitive intelligence operations; and the disclosure of scientific or technological developments vital to national security.

b. *secret*—National security information or material that requires a substantial degree of protection and the unauthorized disclosure of which would reasonably be expected to cause serious damage to the national security. Examples of serious damage include disruption of foreign relations significantly affecting the national security; significant impairment of a program or policy directly related to the national security; revelation of significant military plans or intelligence operations; and compromise of significant scientific or technological developments relating to national security.

c. *confidential*—National security information or material that requires protection and the unauthorized disclosure of which could reasonably be expected to cause damage to the national security. (JCS Pub 1, 327–28)

signals intelligence (SIGINT)—A category of intelligence information comprising all communications intelligence, electronics intelligence, and telemetry intelligence. (JCS Pub 1, 334)

strategic aerial reconnaissance—The use of aircraft to gather information necessary to conduct strategic air war; the use of aircraft to collect strategic intelligence using photographic or electronic means.

strategic air warfare—Air combat and supporting operations designed to effect, through the systematic application of force to a selected series of vital targets, the progressive destruction and disintegration of the enemy's war-making capacity to a point where the enemy no longer retains the ability or the will to wage war. Vital targets may include key manufacturing systems, sources of raw material, critical material, stockpiles, power systems, transportation systems, communication facilities, concentration of uncommitted elements of enemy armed forces, key agricultural areas, and other such target systems. (JCS Pub 1, 349) [Note: The current definition is the same as the 1949 definition of the term.][2]

strategic intelligence—Intelligence that is required for the formation of policy and military plans at national and international levels. Strategic intelligence and tactical intelligence differ primarily in level of application but may also vary in terms of scope and detail. (JCS Pub 1, 350)

tactical air reconnaissance—The use of air vehicles to obtain information concerning terrain, weather, and the disposition, composition, movement, installations, lines of communications, electronic, and communication emissions of enemy forces. Also included are artillery and naval gunfire adjustment, and systematic and random observation of ground battle area. (JCS Pub 1, 361)

Notes

1. Gen Lauris Norstad, to commanding general SAC, letter, subject: USAF Electronic Reconnaissance Program, tab A, 21 July 1949, file no. 2-8100 to 2-8199, box 45, entry 214, Records Group (RG) 341, National Archives (NA).

2. Brig Gen E. Moore, chief, Air Intelligence division, to Lt Gen Hubert R. Harmon, memorandum, 21 April 1949, file no. 2-7200 to 2-7299, box 45, RG 341, NA.

Bibliography

Primary Sources

Air Force Studies, Manuals, and Government Reports

Air Corps Advanced Flying School, *Observation Manual*, 20 February 1935.

Air Force Manual 51-40. *Air Navigation*, 15 March 1983.

Assistant Chief of Staff, A-2, Headquarters USAFE. *The Contribution of Air Power to the Defeat of Germany*, Appendix M: Miscellaneous Aspects of Air Power, n.d. box 274. Carl A. Spaatz Papers.

Commander in Chief, US Pacific Fleet. Korean War, U.S. Pacific Fleet Operations. Third Evaluation Report, 1 May–31 December 1951.

Department of Ground Instruction. Air Corps Primary Flying School. *Reconnaissance*. 2d ed., 8 November 1928.

"Evaluation of Effect on Soviet War Effort Resulting from the Strategic Air Offensive," 11 May 1949.

History. Development of FEAF's Intelligence Collection Plan, November 1953.

------. FEAF Reconnaissance in the Korean Conflict, 25 June 1950–27 July 1953.

------. Japanese-American Friction over Wringer Program, November 1953.

Historical Tables Budget of the US Government, Fiscal Year 1989.

Navy Department. Office of the Chief of Naval Operations. *Radar Bulletin, no. 12 (RAD TWELVE): Airborne Radar Countermeasures Operator's Manual*, 8 April 1946.

Schwandt, Harold A. "Camera Equipment for Reconnaissance over Unmapped Areas." Air Command and Staff School Research Paper, May 1949.

SAC Technical Manual 122-1. *Command Summary*, December 1948.

Spaatz, Gen Carl A. "Spaatz Board Report." 23 October 1945.

Standard Aircraft Characteristics, RB-29A Superfortress, Boeing, 19 April 1950.

Standard Aircraft Characteristics, RB-50G Superfortress, Boeing, 16 October 1953.

Statistical Control Office, SAC. *Strategic Air Command Statistical Summary.* Vol. 4, 21 March 1946–31 December 1946, USAFHRC.

―――. Vol. 1, no. 1, 1 June 1946, USAFHRC.

―――. Vol. 1, no. 2, 1 September 1946, USAFHRC.

―――. Vol. 1, no. 3, 1 October 1946, USAFHRC.

―――. Vol. 1, no. 4, 1 November 1946, USAFHRC.

―――. Vol. 1, no. 5, 1 December 1946, USAFHRC.

―――. Vol. 1, no. 6, 1 January 1947, USAFHRC.

―――. Vol. 1, no. 8, 1 March 1947, USAFHRC.

――――. Headquarters SAC, 1 October 1947.

United States Strategic Bombing Survey, Over-all Report (European War), 30 September 1945.

――――. Summary Report (Pacific War), 1 July 1946.

――――. *(European War) (Pacific War).* Reprinted, 1987.

Unit and Command Histories

Historian, SAC. Strategic Air Command–1946: Organization, Mission, Training and Personnel. Vol. 1, Text. April 1948.

――――. SAC–1946: Organization, Mission, Training and Personnel. Vol. 2.

――――. Strategic Air Command-1948. Vol. 1, Narrative.

Historical Division, Fifth Air Force. History of the Fifth Air Force, 1 January 1952–30 June 1952.

―――. History of the Fifth Air Force, January–July 1953, vol. 1.

Historical Division, OI. Seventh Air Force. *SAC Operations in the United Kingdom, 1948–1956.*

Historical Office, FEAF. History of the Far East Air Forces, 25 June–31 December 1950.

―――. History of FEAF, 1 June–31 December 1951.

―――. FEAF History of ECM during the Korean Conflict, June 1950–July 1953.

Historical Office, FEAF Bomber Command. History of the Far East Air Forces Bomber Command, January–July 1953.

Historical Section, SAC. The Strategic Air Command 1947, vol. 1.

———. History Strategic Air Command 1949, vol. 1, 19 May 1950.

Headquarters, 55th Strategic Reconnaissance Wing. History of the 55th Strategic Reconnaissance Wing (M), November 1952–March 1953.

Headquarters, 91st Strategic Reconnaissance Squadron. History of the 91st Strategic Reconnaissance Squadron (M), Photo, March 1951–30 April 1953.

Terman, F. E. *Administrative History of the Radio Research Laboratory.* Office of Scientific Research and Development, National Defense Research Committee, Division of Radio Coordination (15), 26 March 1946.

Joint Chiefs of Staff (JCS) Documents

JCS Publication 1. *Department of Defense Dictionary of Military and Associated Terms,* 1984.

JCS 1844/37. *Preparation of a Joint Outline Emergency War Plan,* 27 April 1949.

JCS 1844/46. *Joint Emergency Outline War Plan "Offtackle,"* 8 November 1949.

JCS 1844/47. *Report by the Joint Logistics Plans Committee to the Joint Chief of Staff on Logistics Implications of "Offtackle,"* 15 November 1949.

JCS 1952/8. *Joint Intelligence Estimate for Basing Operational Evaluation Success of the Strategic Air Offensive,* 25 August 1949.

JCS 1952/11. *Weapons Systems Evaluation Group Report no. 1,* 10 February 1950.

JCS 2150/2. *Photo Reconnaissance of the China Coast from Swatow to Latitude 26° 30'N.*

JCS 2150/9. *Delimitation of Air Operations Along the North Korean Border,* 5 August 1950.

Joint Intelligence Committee (JIC) 250/6. *Soviet Capabilities,* 29 November 1945.

JIC 439/13. *Joint Intelligence Committee Estimate on Basing Operational Evaluation of Prospects of Success of Strategic Air Offensive*, 22 August 1949.

Joint Staff Planners (JPS) 789. *Concept of Operations for "Pincher,"* 2 March 1946.

JPS 789/1. *Staff Studies of Certain Military Problems Deriving from "Concept of Operations for 'Pincher,'"* 13 April 1946–1950.

Joint Strategic Plans Group (JSPG) 496/4. *Broiler,* 11 February 1948.

Joint Strategic Survey Committee. "Over-All Effect of Atomic Bomb on Warfare and Military Organization," 26 October 1945.

Joint War Plans Committee (JWPC) 432/3. "Design for Global War: The Pincher Plans," 1945–1950.

Lectures/Speeches

Lowe, Dr. James. "Intelligence Basis for Selecting Strategic Target Systems." Address to Air War College, 13 December 1946.

Letters

Agee, Brig Gen Walter R., chief, Air Intel. Req. Div., directorate of Intelligence. To Commander in Chief, Alaskan Command. Letter. 15 December 1948.

AFOIR-CM. To Commander in Chief, Alaska. Letter. Subject: Violations of Soviet Frontier, n.d.

Anderson, Maj Gen F. L., deputy commander, Operations. To Maj Gen Barney M. Giles, chief of Air Staff. Letter. 8 November 1944.

Armstrong, Brig Gen Frank A., Jr. To chief of staff, Headquarters U. S. Air Force. Letter. Subject: Photographic Coverage of Northeastern Siberia, 7 November 1949.

Bergquist, Col Kenneth R., deputy assistant chief of Air Staff. To commanding general, SAC. Letter. Subject: Operation Eardrum, 3 March 1947.

Cabell, Maj Gen C. P., director of Intelligence, Office of Deputy Chief of Staff, Operations. To commanding general,

Alaskan Air Command. Letter. Subject: RCM Ferret Program—Alaskan Air Command, 26 July 1948.

Cleland, 1st Lt Enos L., Flight "B" commander. To commanding officer, 46th Recon Sq (VLR) Photographic. Letter. Subject: Progress Report for Flight "B," 30 July 1947.

Close, Col Winton R. To Maj Gen T. S. Power, Headquarters SAC. Letter, 6 June 1951.

Commanding general, SAC. To commanding general, AAF, Letter. Subject: Operational and Administrative Control of the 311th Reconnaissance Wing and its Assigned Units, 15 August 1946.

Cullen, Brig Gen P. T., commanding, Headquarters, 311th Air Division, Reconnaissance. To commanding general, SAC. Letter. Subject: Proposal for Study of Reconnaissance, 4 June 1948.

———. To Maj Gen Clements McMullen, Headquarters, SAC. Letter. No subject. 8 September 1948.

Edwards, Maj Gen I. H., US Army, Headquarters, USAFE, office of the commanding general. To the commanding general, AAF. Letter. Subject: British Cooperation on Post Hostilities Mapping Program, 25 April 1946.

Fisher, Brig Gen W. P., commanding (FEAF Bomber Command). To Maj Gen John B. Montgomery, director of Operations, SAC. Letter. 30 January 1952.

Klocko, Col Richard P., chief, Developmental Research Branch, Air Intelligence Division, director of Intelligence. To commanding general, USAFE. Letter. Subject: Comments on Biograph Missions, 13 July 1949.

LeMay, Gen Curtis E., commanding general, Headquarters SAC. To Brig Gen Joe W. Kelly, commanding general, FEAF Bomber Command, Provisional. Letter. 28 November 1951.

Lewis, Col R. C., Adjutant General, Fifth Air Force. To commanding general, FEAF. Letter. Subject: Request for priority increase on ECM Aircraft Project, 7 July 1952.

McCormick, L. D., acting chief of Naval Operations. To CNC, US Pacific Fleet. Letter. Subject: Assignment of P4M-1Q aircraft to Special Electronic Search Project (SESP) in the Pacific, 26 June 1951.

McDonald, Maj Gen George C., director of Intelligence, office of deputy chief of staff, Operations. To Air Communications Group, DCS/O. Letter. Subject: Electronic Reconnaissance Project, 24 February 1948.

―――. To director of Training and Requirements. Letter. Subject: Transmittal of Intelligence Requirements, 28 January 1948.

―――. To director of Training & Requirements. Letter, 19 February 1948.

―――. To Military Attaché, US Embassy, Stockholm, Sweden. Letter. Subject: Loan of Aerial Cameras, 20 November 1947.

Monjar, Lt Col H. C. To Frank Voltaggio. Letter, 10 June 1982.

Monroe, Col H. M., chief of staff, Headquarters Alaskan Command. To chief of staff, USAF. Letter. Subject: Importance of Long-range Photography to Alaskan Theater, n.d.

Norstad, Lt Gen Lauris, deputy chief of staff, Operations. To commanding general, SAC. Letter. Subject: USAF Electronic Reconnaissance Program, 21 July 1949.

Partridge, Maj Gen E. E., assistant chief of Air Staff-3. To AC/AS-5, AC/AS-2 in turn. Letter. Subject: Northern European Ferret Flights, 20 August 1947.

Perry, Col Robert R. To Alfred Price. Letter. 2 June 1982.

Power, Maj Gen Thomas S., deputy commander, SAC. To Col William F. Coleman, Office C/S, GHQ, FEC. Letter. 14 March 1952.

―――. To commanding general, 311th Air Division. Letter. Subject: Photographic Reconnaissance Requirements, 16 August 1949.

Putt, Brig Gen D. L., director of Research & Development, Office, deputy chief of staff, Materiel. To directorate of Intelligence, DCS/O. Letter. Subject: Countermeasures to Soviet Missiles, 22 December 1948.

Schweizer, Col John M., Jr., executive officer, Directorate of Intelligence. To director of Communications. Letter. Subject: Proposed Plan for Air Force Electronic Reconnaissance Program, 27 April 1949.

———. To Director of Communications, Operations Division, D/P & O. Letter. Subject: Proposed Supplemental Electronic Reconnaissance Operations, 10 June 1949.

Shores, Col Von R., Act. Assistant chief, Operations Division, Director, Plans & Operations. To Air Intelligence Requirements Division, D/I. Letter. Subject: Intelligence Requirements for Strategic Reconnaissance, 15 July 1949.

———. Letter. Subject: Proposed Supplemental Electronic Reconnaissance Operations, 13 June 1949.

Twining, Lt Gen Nathan F., commander in chief, AAC. To chief of staff, USAF. Letter. n.d.

Villard, O. G., O.S.R.D.-London Mission. To A. Earl Cullum Jr., R.R.L. Letter. n.d.

Intelligence Reports

Central Intelligence Agency. IM-203. "The Soviet Air Forces," 25 July 1949.

Headquarters AAF Air Intelligence Report no. 100-146/4-34. "Operational Capabilities of U.S.S.R. in Certain Areas." Headquarters, Army Air Forces. Assistant Chief of Staff-2 (Intelligence Division). Study no. 146/4, 5 June 1947.

Headquarters SAC. Intelligence Brief no. 26. "Indications of Atomic Energy Facilities in U.S.S.R.," 25 November 1947.

———. Intelligence Brief no. 44. "Capabilities of Soviet Anti-Aircraft for Defense Against VHB Operations," 12 April 1948.

———. Intelligence Brief no. 67. "Soviet Long-Range Missiles," 15 September 1948.

"Intelligence Annex for the Air Force Research and Development Plan for the Fiscal Year 1952," 12 August 1949.

Memoranda, Routing and Record Sheets, and Staff Summary Sheets

AC/AS-2. Staff Summary Sheet. To deputy chief of staff for Research and Development. Subject: Project Abstract, 29 July 1947.

Air Intelligence Requirements Division (AFOIR-RC). R & R sheet. Subject: Photographic Coverage—Chukotski Peninsula, n.d.

Ankenbrandt, Maj Gen (Francis L.), director of Communications. R & R sheet. To director of Intelligence, DCS/O.

Barber, Col Edward, deputy, Air Intelligence Requirements Division, Directorate of Intelligence. R & R sheet. To Col J. Tison, operations Division, DCS/O, 10 August 1949.

Bradley, Gen Omar. Memorandum. To the secretary of defense. Subject: Military Action in Korea, 5 April 1951.

———. Memorandum. To the secretary of defense. Subject: Special Electronic Airborne Search Operations (SESP), 5 May 1950.

———. Memorandum. To the secretary of defense. Subject: Special Electronic Airborne Search Operations, 22 July 1950.

Cabell, Maj Gen C. P., acting director of Intelligence. Memorandum for record. To secretary, Joint Intelligence Committee. 12 March 1948.

Director of Intelligence. R & R sheet. To director of Plans and Operations. Subject: Photographic Coverage—Chukotski Peninsula Airfields, 7 May 1948.

Gerhart, Brig Gen John K. Memorandum. To General Vandenberg. Subject: USAF Utilization in FEAF, 18 April 1952.

Green, Maj Carl M., Reconnaissance Branch, Air Intelligence Requirements Division, Directorate of Intelligence. Memorandum. To chief, Air Intelligence Requirements Division. Subject: Coordination of Photo and Photo Intelligence Activities, 11 December 1947.

Griffin, Lt Col Goodman, G., executive, Air Intelligence Requirements Division, Directorate of Intelligence. R & R sheet. To commanding general, SAC. Subject: Letter of Transmittal, 2 January 1950.

Headquarters USAFE, office of the commanding general. Memorandum. Subject: Electronics Intelligence sub-section, directorate of Intelligence, Headquarters, US Strategic Air Forces in Europe, 3 September 1944.

Headquarters USAF-AFOIR-RC. R & R sheet. To CSGID. Subject: Photography of Floodlight (Project No. 5), 18 November 1948.

Holden, Maj Raymond B. (for J. B. Montgomery, Brig Gen, USAF, director of Operations). R & R sheet. To Historical Section, Headquarters SAC, 18 August 1949.

Johnson, Louis, secretary of defense. Memorandum. To the president. Subject: Special Electronic Search Operations (SESP), 24 May 1950.

Langbehn, Maj. Memorandum for record. Subject: To prepare cable to Headquarters USAFE requesting information as to Photo material and whether photos were being taken of Targets of Opportunity during Ferret operations, n.d.

McDonald, Maj Gen George C., deputy assistant chief of Air Staff-2. Memorandum. To assistant chief of Air Staff. Subject: Ferret Operations, 23 July 1947.

———. Memorandum. To Lt Gen Lewis H. Brereton, chairman, Military Liaison Committee, Atomic Energy Commission. Subject: Denial of Clearances by the Atomic Energy Commission of AAF Key Personnel, 23 July 1947.

Memorandum. Subject: "Conference held in the Office of Deputy Commander, Operations, USSTAF," 9 October 1944.

———. Subject: "Functions of the Office of the Director of Intelligence," n.d.

———. Subject: "Project for Procuring Special Information Pertaining to USSR," 29 September 1947.

———. To Col L. P. Weicker, deputy director of Intelligence. Subject: Principal U.S. Agencies in the United Kingdom Concerned with Electronic Intelligence, n.d.

Memorandum for record. Subject: Coordination and Dissemination of Aerial and Radar Scope Photography by the Alaskan Air Command with Headquarters AAF, Air Intelligence Division, n.d.

———. Subject: To advise COMGENUSAFE, Wiesbaden (sic) regarding further flights in the Baltic Area, n.d.

———. Subject: To provide recently established Photo Intelligence to supplement the information contained in the article "Chukotsky Peninsula" appearing in the March issue of the Air Intelligence Digest, n.d.

———. Subject: To provide the Alaskan Air Command with a directive to cover the electronic reconnaissance activities of the ferret aircraft under the control of that command, n.d.

————. Subject: Status of the U.S.S.R. Atomic Energy Project—1 July 1949 (Joint Nuclear Energy Intelligence Committee).

————. Subject: Photographic Coverage—Chukotski Peninsula, n.d.

————. Subject: "To brief background facts on establishment of 40-mile limit for reconnaissance flights in Pacific Area," n.d.

————. Subject: To request that director of Supply and Services, DCS/M direct Base Accountable Officer, Bolling, AFB, issue property for urgent use, 4 February 1948.

————. Subject: "To present an electronic intelligence requirement," n.d.

Musset, Col E. R., chief, Plans & Policy Branch, Executive Division, AC/AS-2. Memorandum for record. Subject: Daily Activity Report, n.d.

Northrup, Doyle L., technical director, AFOAT-1. Memorandum. To Major General Nelson. Subject: Atomic Detection System Alert no. 12, 19 September 1949.

Partridge, Maj Gen E. E., director of Training and Requirements. Memorandum. To General McDonald. Subject: Strategic Reconnaissance, 31 January 1948.

Routing and Record sheet. Sturdivant, Colonel, executive, Air Intelligence Division, directorate of Intelligence. To Industrial Planning Division, directorate of Procurement and Industrial Planning. Subject: Strategic Consideration Re Boeing Aircraft Production, 12 August 1949.

Spaatz, Gen Carl, chief of staff, USAF. Memorandum. To the secretary of the Air Force. Subject: Some Reports of Soviet Activities in Alaska and Adjacent Thereto, 25 March 1948.

Sherman, Adm Forrest, CNO. Memorandum. To secretary of the Navy. Subject: Attack on United States Aircraft by Soviet Aircraft, 14 April 1950.

Staff Summary Sheet. To deputy AC/AS-2. Subject: Re issuance of instructions regarding two 46th Recon A/C now being fitted w/RCM ferret equipment, 20 August 1947.

Sturdivant, Colonel, executive, Air Intelligence Division, directorate of Intelligence. R & R sheet. To Industrial Planning Division, directorate of Procurement and Industrial Planning. Subject: Strategic Consideration Re Boeing Aircraft Production, 12 August 1949.

Symington, W. Stuart. Memorandum. To (Louis A.) Johnson, 8 November 1948.

———. Memorandum. To General Spaatz, 5 April 1948.

Taylor, Col Robert, chief, Collection Branch, Air Intelligence Requirements Division. Memorandum. To Col Hugh D. Wallace. Subject: Distribution of Studies, 8 March 1948.

U. S. Atomic Energy Commission. Memorandum. Subject: History of the Long-Range Detection Program, 21 July 1948.

Vandenberg, Gen Hoyt S., chief of staff, USAF. Memorandum. To secretary of defense. Subject: Long Range Detection of Atomic Explosions, 21 September 1949.

Telegrams, Messages, and Cables

Message. July 1951. CG FEAF BMR COMD JAPAN. To CG SAC OFFUTT AFB OMAHA NEB, 8 July 1951.

———. June 1951. CG SAC/XRAY/TOKYO JAPAN. To CG SAC OFFUTT AFB OMAHA NEB, 9 June 1951.

———. 24 July 1947. AFACE signed Spaatz. To COMGEN USAFE, Wiesbaden, Germany.

———. 0277 1 Jan 53. LeMay, commanding general. To General Twining.

———. A4873B 20 Dec 1950. Lt General Stratemeyer. To General Twining, December 1950.

———. RL-132 22 Dec 1950. HQ USAF. To commanding general FEAF, December 1950.

Telegram. Kirk, Alan G., Ambassador in Soviet Union. To secretary of state, April 1950.

Other Official Sources

National Security Council (NSC)-68. United States Objectives and Programs for National Security, 14 April 1950.

Personnel Distribution Weekly Lists (Radio Research Laboratory).

Report on Reconnaissance Conference (Joint Army-Air Force Reconnaissance Conference, 12–13 August 1952). In History of the Fifth Air Force, 1 July–31 December 1952.

Soviet Note no. 261. Embassy of the Union of Soviet Socialist Republics, 5 January 1948.

Summary of U.S./U.K. Discussions on Present World Situation, 20–24 July 1950.

US House Committee on Armed Services. *Investigation of the B-36 Bomber Program*, 81st Cong., 1st sess., 1949.

———. *The National Defense Program—Unification and Strategy*, 81st Cong., 1st sess., 1949.

Wolf, Richard I. *The United States Air Force Basic Documents on Roles and Missions*. Air Staff Historical Study.

Secondary Sources

Books

Acheson, Dean. *Present at the Creation: My Years at the State Department*. New York: W. W. Norton & Co., 1969.

Bailey, Bruce M. *"We See All": A History of the 55th Strategic Reconnaissance Wing, 1947–1967*. Tucson, Ariz.: 55th ELINT Association Historian, 1982.

Bamford, James. *The Puzzle Palace: A Report on NSA, America's Most Secret Agency*. Boston: Houghton Mifflin, 1982.

Borowski, Harry R. *A Hollow Threat: Strategic Air Power and Containment Before Korea*. Westport, Conn.: Greenwood Press, 1982.

Bradley, Omar N., and Clay Blair. *A General's Life*. New York: Simon and Schuster, 1983.

Burrows, William E. *Deep Black: Space Espionage and National Security*. New York: Random House, 1986.

Clausewitz, Carl von. *On War*. Edited and translated by Michael Howard and Peter Paret. Princeton, N.J.: Princeton University Press, 1976.

Craven, Wesley F., and James L. Cate, eds. *The Army Air Forces in World War II,*. 7 vols. 1948–1958. Chicago: University of Chicago Press.

Dear, I. C. B., gen. ed. *The Oxford Companion to World War II*. Oxford: Oxford University Press, 1995.

Donovan, Robert J. *Tumultuous Years: The Presidency of Harry S. Truman, 1949–1953*. New York: W. W. Norton, 1982.

Douhet, Giulio. *The Command of the Air*. Translated by Dino Ferrari. New York: Coward-McCann, 1942.

Freedman, Lawrence. *The Evolution of Nuclear Strategy*. 2d ed. New York: St. Martin's Press, 1989.

Futrell, Robert Frank. *Ideas, Concepts, Doctrine: Basic Thinking in the United States Air Force*. 2 vols. Maxwell AFB, Ala.: Air University Press, 1989. Vol. 1, 1907–1960.

Futrell, Robert F. *The United States Air Force in Korea*. Revised ed. Washington, D.C.: Office of Air Force History, 1983.

Gaddis, John Lewis. *Strategies of Containment: A Critical Appraisal of Postwar American National Security Policy*. New York: Oxford University Press, 1982.

———. *We Now Know*. Oxford: Clarendon Press, 1997.

Goddard, Brig Gen George W., with DeWitt S. Copp. *Overview: A Life-Long Adventure in Aerial Photography*. Garden City, N.Y.: Doubleday, 1969.

Hansell, Haywood S., Jr. *The Strategic Air War Against Germany and Japan*. Washington, D.C.: Office of Air Force History, 1986.

Herken, Gregg. *The Winning Weapon: The Atomic Bomb in the Cold War 1945–1950*. New York: Alfred A. Knopf, 1980.

Hewlett, Richard G., and Francis Duncan. *A History of the Atomic Energy Commission*. University Park, Pa.: Pennsylvania State University Press, 1969.

Hinsley, Francis H. *British Intelligence in the Second World War*. 4 vols. 1979–1988. London: Her Majesty's Stationery Office.

Hitchcock, Lt Col Walter T., ed. *The Intelligence Revolution: A Historical Perspective*. Proceedings of the Thirteenth Military History Proceedings. Washington: US Air Force Academy and Office of Air Force History, 1991.

Hurley, Alfred F. *Billy Mitchell: Crusader for Air Power*. Bloomington: Indiana University Press, 1964, 1975.

Infield, Glenn B. *Unarmed and Unafraid*. New York: Macmillan, 1970.

Jackson, Robert. *High Cold War: Strategic Air Reconnaissance and the Electronic Intelligence War*. Nr Yeovil, Somerset, United Kingdom: Patrick Stephens, 1998.

Jeffreys-Jones, Rhodri. *The CIA and American Democracy*. New Haven, Conn.: Yale University Press, 1989.

Jones, R. V. *Most Secret War*. London: Hamish Hamilton, 1978.

Kahn, David. *The Codebreakers*. New York: Macmillan, 1974.

Kennan, George F. *Memoirs 1925–1950*. Boston: Little, Brown and Co., 1967.

Kennett, Lee. *The First Air War 1914–1918*. New York: Free Press, 1991.

Lashmar, Paul. *Spy Flights of the Cold War*. Phoenix Mill, United Kingdom: Sutton Publishing, 1996.

LeMay, Gen Curtis E., with MacKinlay Kantor. *Mission with LeMay: My Story*. Garden City, N.Y.: Doubleday, 1965.

Lewin, Ronald. *Ultra Goes to War*. New York: McGraw-Hill, 1978.

MacIsaac, David. *Strategic Bombing in World War Two: The Story of the United States Strategic Bombing Survey*. New York: Garland Publishing, 1976.

Mauer, Mauer, ed. *The United States Air Service in World War I*. 2 vols. 1978. Maxwell AFB, Ala.: Albert F. Simpson Historical Research Center.

Mead, Peter. *The Eye in the Air: History of Air Observation and Reconnaissance for the Army*. London: Her Majesty's Stationery Office, 1983.

Meilinger, Phillip S. *Hoyt S. Vandenberg: The Life of a General*. Bloomington: Indiana University Press, 1989.

Mets, David R. *Master of Airpower: General Carl A. Spaatz*. Novato, Calif.: Presidio Press, 1988.

Millett, Allan R., and Peter Maslowski. *For the Common Defense: A Military History of the United States of America*. New York: Free Press, 1984.

———. *For the Common Defense: A Military History of the United States of American*. Revised. New York: Free Press, 1994.

Mitchell, William. *Winged Defense: The Development and Possibilities of Modern Air Power—Economic and Military*. Reprint ed. Port Washington, N.Y.: Kennikat Press, 1971.

Morrow, John H., Jr. *The Great War in the Air: Military Aviation from 1909 to 1921*. Washington: Smithsonian Institution Press, 1993.

Murray, Williamson. *Luftwaffe*. Baltimore: Nautical & Aviation Publishing Co., 1985.

Nesbit, Roy Conyers. *Eyes of the RAF: A History of Photo-Reconnaissance.* Phoenix Mill, United Kingdom: Alan Sutton Publishing, 1996.

Overy, R. J. *The Air War 1939–1945.* Paperback ed. New York: Stein and Day, 1985.

Price, Alfred. *The History of US Electronic Warfare.* 2 vols. 1989. Alexandria, Va.: Association of Old Crows.

Raleigh, Walter. *The War in the Air: Being the Story of The part played in the Great War by the Royal Air Force.* Vol. 1. Oxford: Clarendon Press, 1922.

Rearden, Steven L. *The Formative Years 1947–1950.* History of the Office of the Secretary of Defense. Alfred Goldberg, gen. ed. Washington, D.C.: Historical Office, Office of the Secretary of Defense, 1984.

Richelson, Jeffrey. *American Espionage and the Soviet Target.* New York: William Morrow & Co., 1987.

Ross, Steven T. *American War Plans, 1945–1950.* New York: Garland Publishing, 1988.

Ross, Steven T. and Rosenberg, David Alan eds., *America's Plans for War against the Soviet Union.* New York: Garland Publishing, 1989.

Sherry, Michael S. *The Rise of American Air Power: The Creation of Armageddon.* New Haven, Conn.: Yale University Press, 1987.

Smith, Bradley F. *The Shadow Warriors: O. S. S. and the Origins of the C. I. A.* New York: Basic Books, 1983.

Smith, Constance Babbington. *Evidence in Camera: The Story of Photographic Intelligence in World War II.* London: Chatto and Windus, 1958.

Strauss, Lewis L. *Men and Decisions.* Garden City, N.Y.: Doubleday, 1962.

Stratemeyer, Lt Gen George E. *The Three Wars of Lt. Gen. George E. Stratemeyer: His Korean War Diary.* William T. Y'Blood, ed. Washington, D.C.: Air Force History and Museums Program, 1997.

Sun Tzu. *The Art of War.* Translated and introduction by Samuel B. Griffith. Paperback edition. London: Oxford University Press, 1971.

Swanborough, Gordon, and Peter M. Bowers. *United States Military Aircraft Since 1908*. London: Putam, 1971.

Truman, Harry S. *Memoirs by Harry S. Truman*. Garden City, N.Y.: Doubleday & Co., 1956. Vol. 2, *Years of Trial and Hope*.

Wagner, Ray. *American Combat Planes*. Revised edition. Garden City, N.Y.: Doubleday & Co., 1968.

Webster, Sir Charles and Noble Frankland. *The Strategic Air Offensive against Germany 1939–1945*. 3 vols. 1961. London: Her Majesty's Stationery Office.

Winterbotham, F. W., *The Ultra Secret*. New York: Harper & Row, 1974.

Articles

Eaton, Maj Charles. "The Ferrets," 1947. File no. Africa Ferrets. Association of Old Crows.

Gorman, G. Scott. "The Tu-4: The Travails of Technology Transfer by Imitation." *Air Power History* 45, no. 1 (spring 1998): 16–27.

Greenwood, John T. "The Atomic Bomb—Early Air Force Thinking and the Strategic Air Force, August 1945–March 1946." *Aerospace Historian* 34 (fall/September 1987): 158–66.

Hall, R. Cargill. "The Truth About Overflights." *Military History Quarterly: The Quarterly Journal of Military History* 9, no. 3 (spring 1997): 24–39.

Halliday, Jon. "Air Operations in Korea: The Soviet Side of the Story," in *A Revolutionary War: Korea and the Transformation of the Postwar World*. William J. Williams, ed. Chicago: Imprint Publications, 1993.

Hardesty, Von. "Made in the U.S.S.R." *Air & Space* 15, no. 6 (February/March 2001): 68–79.

Horne, Alistair. "The Balloons of Paris." *Military History Quarterly: The Quarterly Journal of Military History* 13, no. 4 (summer 2001): 80–87.

Kennan, George F. "X," "The Sources of Soviet Conduct," *Foreign Affairs* 25 (July 1947): 566–82.

Kuehl, Daniel T. "Refighting the Last War: Electronic Warfare and U.S. Air Force Operations in the Korean War." *Journal of Military History* 56 (January 1992): 87–112.

Launias, Roger D. "The Berlin Airlift: Constructive Air Power." *Airpower History* 36 (spring 1989): 8–22.

McCarthy, Michael J. "Uncertain Enemies: Soviet Pilots in the Korean War." *Air Power History* 44, no. 1 (spring 1997): 32–45.

Miller, Roger G. "Freedom's Eagles: The Berlin Airlift, 1948–1949." *Air Power History* 45, no. 3 (fall 1998): 4–39.

Rosenberg, David Alan. "The Origins of Overkill: Nuclear Weapons and American Strategy, 1945–1960," in *Strategy and Nuclear Deterrence.* Steven E. Miller, ed. Princeton, N.J.: Princeton University Press, 1984.

———. "American Atomic Strategy and the Hydrogen Bomb Decision." *Journal of American History* 66 (June 1979): 62–87.

Voltaggio, Frank. "Out in the Cold . . . : Early ELINT Activities of the Strategic Air Command." File: Voltaggio. Association of Old Crows.

Academic Papers and Theses

Futrell, Robert F. "A Case Study: USAF Intelligence in the Korean War." Paper delivered to the Thirteenth Military History Symposium, USAFA, 12–14 October 1988.

Hopkins, Robert Smith. "U.S. Strategic Aerial Reconnaissance and the Cold War, 1945–1961." PhD diss., University of Virginia, 1998.

Kuehl, Lt Col Daniel T., USAF. "Electronic Warfare and USAF B-29 Operations in the Korean War." Paper delivered to the 23d Annual Northern Great Plains History Conference, Eveleth, Minn., 23 September 1988.

Marsh, Edwin L. "The History of Tactical Reconnaissance: 1793 to 7 December 1941." Air Command and Staff College thesis. Maxwell AFB, Ala.: Air University, 1967.

Index

209

trench warfare, 3–5
Trenchard, Hugh, 6
Trimetrogon, 8, 60
Truman Doctrine, 49
Truman, Harry, 25–27, 41, 49–50, 71, 76, 80, 93–94, 108, 115, 117–18, 121, 123, 133, 136, 141, 143, 169
Turkey, 33–34, 49, 70–71
Twining, Nathan F., 102, 135
Tzu, Sun, 1, 172

ULTRA and wireless intercept (Y-service), 30
ultraviolet, 52
Union of Soviet Socialist Republics (USSR), 56, 64, 69–70, 74, 79, 106, 109, 111, 119, 122, 136, 140, 142, 160
United Kingdom, 30, 71, 75, 97, 133, 137–38, 142
United Nations (UN), 26, 32, 134, 137, 141, 143
United Nations forces, 140
United States Air Force (USAF), 50, 53, 56, 61, 64, 68–70, 75, 93–94, 96, 99, 103, 111, 116, 137, 144–43, 150, 158
United States Air Forces in Europe (USAFE), 38
United States Army Air Force (USAAF), 10–11, 13–16, 18, 26–33, 37–39, 41, 51, 56, 62–63
United States Strategic Bombing Survey (USSBS), 28, 36–37, 68–69
urban area attack, 109
US Army Air Service, 5
US Department of State, 61
US Strategic Air Forces in Europe, 18

USAF Electronic Reconnaissance Program, 96, 99

V-1-type missile, 105
V-2 missile, 70
Vandenberg, Hoyt S., 28, 96, 139
vertical and oblique aerial photographs, 5
Villette, André-Giroud de, 2
Vinson, Carl, 95, 120
Vishinsky, Andrei Y., 119
visual reconnaissance missions, 3
vital centers, 6, 33, 35, 71, 109
Vladivostok, Russia, 150

War Department, 30, 33, 57, 72
Warrick high-speed 35 mm camera, 145
Weapons Systems Evaluation Group (WSEG), 95, 110, 112–15, 117, 123
Weyland, Otto P. "Opie," 91, 157
WINDOWS, 13
Winterbotham, Fred W., 9
World War I, 5, 7, 9, 167
World War II, 7, 9, 12, 17, 19, 25–26, 28–29, 32–35, 37, 39–40, 52–54, 56–57, 66–70, 72, 74, 93, 96, 99–100, 107, 112–13, 115, 134–35, 158, 168–69, 172
Worth, Cedric R., 95
Wright, 17, 40, 63, 100

Yalu River, 136
Yokota AB, Japan, 141
Y-service, 30
Yugoslavia, 40, 65

Zaloga, Steven J., 99